D0430933

Please
return
materials
on time

DEMCO

ARTHUR WALEY

The Opium War
Through
Chinese Eyes

STANFORD UNIVERSITY PRESS
STANFORD, CALIFORNIA

Stanford University Press
Stanford, California
© *George Allen & Unwin Ltd 1958*
Printed in the United States of America
First published in 1958 by George Allen & Unwin Ltd
Paperback edition first published in 1968 by Stanford University Press
ISBN 0-8047-0611-5
Last figure below indicates year of this printing:

01   00   99   98

I HAVE bothered Miss Margery Fry about English prison conditions in the early nineteenth century, the Record Office of
the Admiralty about the Battle of Kowloon, Mr Mackworth-
Young (Deputy Librarian at Windsor Castle) about Commissioner Lin's letter to Queen Victoria, Commander H. P. Mead,
R.N., of Lloyd's about the voyages of the *Thomas Coutts*, Mr
James Marjoribanks about his ancestor Charles Marjoribanks,
Mr. J. W. Catney of Madame Tussaud's about the wax-work
of Commissioner Lin—and received helpful information from
them all, for which I here express my deep thanks. I am also
particularly grateful to Dr Liu Tsun-yan, of Hongkong, who
called my attention to the photolithograph of Lin's will at
the British Museum, to Professor C. R. Boxer who lent me
Shuck's *Portfolio Sinensis*, and to Edward le Fevour who called
my attention to an article about Gutzlaff in *Hogg's Instructor*.

In this book nothing is invented. On the rare occasions when
I have suggested what was going on in people's minds I have made
it clear that I am merely speculating.

I write chiefly for the general reader. But specialists seem
sometimes to read my books as a recreation, and for their
benefit I have given references to the Chinese texts used, in the
hope that they will check up on some of my translations and
tell me of my mistakes.

I have made no attempt to give a complete consecutive story
of the war, either from the military or the diplomatic point of
view. What I have done is to translate and put into their setting
a number of intimate documents, such as diaries, auto-
biographies and confessions which tell us (in a way that
memorials and decrees fail to do) what the war felt like on the
Chinese side. Naturally, in order to explain what was going on,
I have also quoted from State documents. But these tend to use

fixed formulae, and we learn relatively little from them about what anyone was really thinking or feeling.

I have made no attempt to divide the book into parts of equal length. If Commissioner Lin gets the lion's share it is because he is far and away the most important figure of the period and, in consequence, a vast quantity of material concerning him has been preserved.

February, 1958.

CONTENTS

REFERENCES (such as IV. 471) not preceded by the name of a book are to the six-volume corpus of texts about the Opium War published at Shanghai in 1955 under the title *Ya-p'ien Chan-cheng Tzu-liao Ts'ung-k'an*, 'Corpus of Material about the Opium War'. References are often omitted in the case of Lin's two main collections of papers (II. 131 seq. and II. 229 seq.), as these are arranged chronologically and I give the dates in my text. Where it seemed necessary I have also consulted some of the collections upon which the corpus draws; for example, the *Ch'ou-pan I-wu Shih-mo* and the *Shih Lu* ('Veritable Records') of Tao-kuang's reign. A few other Chinese sources are indicated when they are quoted. There are no doubt many other sources that I might have used. But those I have named turned out to be sufficient for the sort of book I intended to write.

I do not append a bibliography of Western sources, as numerous such bibliographies already exist; for example in Fairbank's *Trade and Diplomacy on the China Coast.*

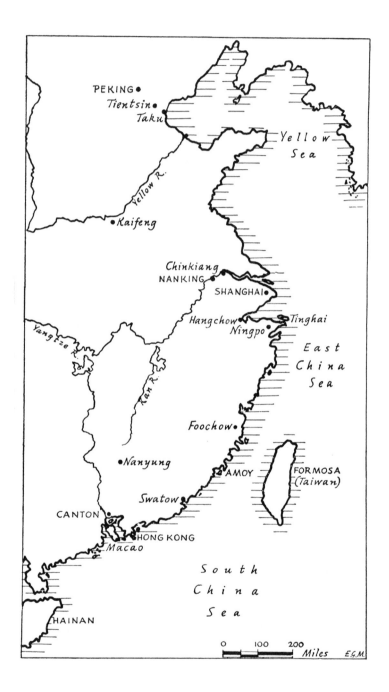

PEKING•

Tientsin•

Taku•

Yellow Sea

Yellow R.

Kaifeng•

Chinkiang

NANKING•

SHANGHAI•

Hangchow•

Ningpo•

Tinghai

East China Sea

Yangtze R.

Kan R.

Foochow•

Nanyung•

AMOY•

FORMOSA
(Taiwan)

Swatow•

CANTON•

HONG KONG
Macao•

HAINAN

South China Sea

0   100   200
Miles   E.G.M.

PART ONE

Commissioner Lin at Canton

THE following is an extract from the 1845 edition of Madame Tussaud's catalogue: 'COMMISSIONER LIN AND HIS FAVOURITE CONSORT. Modelled expressly for this Exhibition by the celebrated Lamqua,[1] from life, through the instrumentality of a gentleman resident of Canton nineteen years . . . dressed in magnificent Chinese costumes, lately imported . . . Madame Tussaud and Sons have great pleasure in introducing the above figures to their Patrons, which has been done at a great expense.'

Some ten or more books on the Opium War have been written in a number of different European languages, yet in none of them does Commissioner Lin, the leading figure on the Chinese side, ever come to life as a human being. He remains in fact an automaton, a wax-work in magnificent Chinese trappings, awe-inspiring but completely incomprehensible. In these books, most of which rely solely on European sources, he figures almost exclusively as a writer of formal documents—reports to the Manchu Emperor, stern replies to the evasive communications of the British Trade Superintendent, scathing rebukes to the Chinese guild-merchants. More recent works, chiefly by American scholars, have added a great deal to our knowledge of the formal diplomatic interchanges and official correspondence in which Lin was concerned, but there has been no attempt

[1] Lamqua was a Chinese painter who took lessons in the European style of painting from George Chinnery.

to fit his official life (which after all did not occupy his whole existence) into the framework of his other occupations and interests.

My aim here is not to rewrite the history, diplomatic or military, of the first Opium War, nor yet to attempt a complete biography of Commissioner Lin. What I want to do is to show the sort of things that were occupying his mind from the time when he came to Canton to suppress the opium traffic at the beginning of 1839 down to May 3, 1841, when under sentence of exile to Turkestan he left Canton for ever. If it is possible to bring to life this portion of his career, it is due largely to the publication in 1955 of his diary covering the period February 14, 1839, to July 16, 1841.

Lin Tse-hsü was born in 1785, at Foochow, capital of the south-eastern coastal province of Fuhkien. His father was a needy scholar, who never attained to any official position. The boy Lin, who was the second of three sons, showed an immense capacity for acquiring knowledge. After distinguishing himself in various local examinations he came out seventh out of 237 successful candidates in the final examination at Peking in 1811. He became a student in the Han-lin Academy, where he was ordered to take a course in Manchu, the language of China's conquerors. He rose rapidly, holding a succession of high provincial posts. He was still in his forties when he obtained the most coveted of such posts— the Governor-Generalship of Kiangnan and Kiangsi.

On December 31, 1838, he was ordered to go to Canton as High Commissioner, with Plenipotentiary Powers and supreme command of Canton's naval forces, 'to investigate port affairs', which in practice meant to discover a method of suppressing the opium trade. His past career in many ways qualified him for such a post. Already in 1832, as Governor of Kiangsu, he had learnt something about the complications of European mentality. In February of that year the Canton branch of the East India Company sent their ship, the *Lord*

Amherst, on a cruise up the Chinese coast to discover fresh openings for British trade. This could, of course, only be smuggling trade, as the Chinese Government did not allow the British to trade elsewhere than at Canton. When obliged by bad weather to put into a harbour on the Fuhkien coast, the British explained through an interpreter that they were on their way from Calcutta to Japan, but had been driven by a storm on to the Chinese coast. This story was quite inconsistent with a printed leaflet which they circulated. The leaflet[1] explained quite frankly that they were looking for fresh outlets for trade on the Chinese coast. It was, moreover, in Chinese (of sorts), not in Japanese, and completely gave the lie to the first story. Nor was the correct name of the ship given, so that the British authorities at Canton, when a protest was lodged, were able to say that no such ship as the one named was recorded in their lists. It is not surprising that during his Canton days Lin worked on the hypothesis that nothing the English said could be relied upon. At about the same time he managed to deal successfully with salt-smuggling (salt being a Government monopoly). In the early summer of 1838, when a number of statesmen were asked to memorialize the Throne concerning the opium question, Lin's report[2] on the subject was one of the fullest and most painstaking. The problem was a complicated one, involving the import of opium into China, its purchase by wholesale brokers, its retail sale to opium dens and individuals, and finally the actual offence of opium smoking. Accessory offenders were the different kinds of craftsmen who made the opium pipes, the porcelain bowls, the wooden or bamboo stems, the often costly and elaborate metal fittings. Into this last aspect of the matter Lin enters with an almost pedantic fullness, explaining, for example, that at Canton bowls made of foreign porcelain were generally used while in the interior brown I-hsing teapot ware was

[1] See below, p. 225.
[2] II. 133. For references of this kind, see below, p. 248.

preferred. In addition to all this, practical man that he was, he enclosed a six-page treatise, compiled from the best medical works, explaining the use of several drugs likely to help those who were trying to cure themselves of the opium habit. Some of the ingredients were *Atractylis ovata*, *Angelica polymorpha*, *Lignum aloes*, *Gastrodia elata* (a kind of orchid) and *Astible* (a kind of saxifrage).

In a secret enclosure[1] he made the suggestion that instead of selling tea, silk, rhubarb, etc., to foreigners at the same price they charged in the home market, Chinese merchants ought to be ordered to charge the foreigner 'double or even five times' the home price. In this way the disastrous outflow of Chinese silver would soon be made good. Some Chinese merchants, he admitted, would probably evade the regulation, but even so they would be certain to sell at a higher price than in the home market.

It would seem, however (and this is my comment, not Lin's), that this would have led the English to make even greater efforts to increase their sales of opium and so maintain their trade balance. But further speculation upon the effect of such a measure would not be worth while, for it is certain the Chinese administration, as it then existed, would have been incapable of enforcing it.

Finally, as Governor-General of Hupeh and Hunan, the post he held at the time he was sent to Canton, he had played a vigorous part in the new crusade to suppress opium smoking in the interior of China.

He set out from Peking, travelling by land till he reached the Yangtze, on January 8, 1839. We possess his travelling-pass, which specifies that the bearer is not accompanied by any subordinate officials, clerks or secretaries. His personal staff consists of one outrider and six men-at-arms, a chief cook and two kitchen-men. These are all travelling with him and no member of his staff is being left behind at the last place of halt or sent on ahead. Anyone falsely repre-

[1] III. 463.

senting himself as a member of his staff will at once be apprehended and tried. The twenty bearers carrying the big litter in which he travels are hired at his own expense. For the conveyance of his luggage he has himself hired two large waggons and one stretcher. The drivers and carriers are paid by him on a scale that enables them to purchase provisions for themselves and they are not allowed to requisition anything at the relay-stations through which they pass. . . . Where land travel is not practicable he will hire a boat and the necessary crew at his own expense. The bearer of this pass, being a Governor-General seconded to this special mission, is not in the same position as a high local official travelling in his own province. He is to realize that his journey imposes a burden upon the cities, towns and relay-stations through which he passes, and he must show them every possible consideration. At Government rest-houses he is only to take the ordinary, daily fare. On no account is he to be served with an elaborate repast or a menu containing costly items such as fried swallows' nests, which might seem to give a sanction to extravagance. Such luxuries are unsuitable in the case of an official passing through on a journey, and he must on no account infringe this rule.

His escort, bearers and so on are not allowed to accept gratuities of the kind known as post-fees or door-purses. Any case of such gratuities being demanded will lead to immediate arrest and anyone found guilty of secretly offering them must without fail be made the subject of a special inquiry. This pass holds good from Liang-hsiang[1] onwards to the city wall of Canton, where it is to be surrendered intact.

It might have been expected that the object of a pass issued to a Special Commissioner would have been to secure for him special privileges and facilities during the journey. But not at all! The aim of this document is to assert the rights

---

[1] The southern borough of Peking.

not of the august traveller himself, but those of the officials, rest-houses and relay-stations whose duty it would be to receive him. In the eighteenth century it had been the practice of high officials, who in those days were nearly always Manchus, to travel with hundreds of armed retainers whose exactions terrorized the whole countryside. As part of the general clean-up which followed upon the death of the Emperor Ch'ien Lung in 1799 steps were taken to put an end to this abuse and, on paper at any rate, the regulations were heavily weighted in favour of the local officials and population as against the travelling grandee.

The diary begins at Nan-k'ang (about fifty miles south of the Yangtze) on the first day of the nineteenth year of Tao-kuang, corresponding to February 14, 1839. 'Today at dawn, it being the first of the New Year, I reverently set out an incense-altar on board ship, kowtowed in the direction of the Palace at Peking and wished the Emperor a Happy New Year. Then I bowed to the shades of my ancestors and made offerings. In the early morning there was a violent north wind, but by the Hour of the Snake [9 a.m.][1] it calmed down a little and we were able to start.' When they had sailed for about forty miles, rain came on and they halted. 'This part of the river', the diary says, 'winds about a great deal and we constantly met with shallows. The wind was in our favour, but we were only able to hoist half sail. When night came on it was raining heavily.' Next day (February 15th) they reached Nan-ch'ang, the capital of Kiangsi province. They were met by a vast concourse of officials and outstanding local inhabitants. Among the latter the most interesting was a certain Pao Shih-ch'en (1775–1855) who, though during most of his life he held no official post, was regarded as a great authority on current affairs. Statesmen often consulted him and through his dealings with them he got to know a good deal of what went on behind the scenes.

[1] In translated passages, words enclosed in brackets are explanations or comments by me.

Writing three years later Pao Shih-ch'en says that on this occasion Lin devoted a whole day to questioning him about how the situation at Canton should be handled. As an example of Pao's sagacity it has been pointed out that as early as 1828 he realized that the seizure of Singapore by the British constituted a danger to China. He does not, however, stress the strategic importance of Singapore as a naval base on the route between India and China. What he feared was that the English would get into touch with Chinese settlers at Singapore and bring them to China to act as secret agents.

He was held up at Nan-ch'ang for four days by violent snow-storms. On February 19th it cleared a little. 'On the banks', he writes, 'there was more than a foot of snow. At the Hour of the Hare [5 a.m] I urged the boatman to start. The gunwales and sails were coated with ice; but they soon scraped it off, and we set out. There was a head-wind from the south-west, but it was not strong. Our chief trouble was that there were grain-transport ships anchored along both shores, and it was difficult to get past.' They reached the town of Feng-ch'eng at the Hour of the Snake (9 a.m.) on February 20th. 'There was no one about. I at once sent one of my men to the town office to hire haulers; but it was the Hour of the Tiger [3 a.m.] before they arrived.'

On February 22nd he was met by couriers, bringing letters from the high officials in Canton, welcoming him and placing themselves at his disposal. A communication from the Governor-General of the two provinces Kwangtung and Kwangsi and the Governor of Kwangtung informed him of instructions recently received from Peking regarding his mission. The appointment of a Special Commissioner had become necessary, it was said, because it had now become clear that the suppression of the opium traffic was a full-time job and could not be effectually undertaken by the Governor-General, who already had on his hands the normal administrative business of two vast provinces. Various questions, such as where the Commissioner was to live and have his office, what staff should be allotted to him, what ships should be at his disposal for tours of inspection and so on, were under discussion, and further reports would follow shortly.

Two days later, on February 24th, he drafted secret instructions to the judicial authorities at Canton to arrest a number of notorious opium offenders, whose activities had become known at Peking. He had brought with him an annotated list of about sixty names. Most of the culprits were or had formerly been small employees in Government offices at Canton. Here is one case-history, merely to serve as a specimen: 'The cashiered Captain Wang Chen-kao. Has two addresses; one at Market Bridge and one outside the Yung-ch'ing City gate. . . . Was previously found guilty, along with his associate Hsü Kuang, of a coining offence. Later he was employed by the Kuang-hsien regiment, and rose to the position of dispatch-carrier, but proved unsatisfactory and lost his higher position. He then, with the help of his previous associate Hsü Kuang, set up an opium depository which he stocked by a service of fast smuggling skiffs. By the sale of this opium he became very rich, dealing with a number of naval men, soldiers and minor employees in Government offices. In the fourteenth year of Tao-kuang [1834] he was dismissed from the army, but obtained a post on a patrol boat, and was able to use his position to protect smugglers. For every hundred catties[1] of opium that he let pass he received a "consideration" of forty dollars foreign money.'

A difficulty will be, says Lin, that most of the persons named are employees in Government offices or soldiers, whose superiors are likely to shield them in every way they can, flatly denying that such things have taken place, or declaring that the names concerned do not figure on their establishment; or alternatively, that the persons named died long ago.

Lin, then, already knew, when he set out from Peking armed with this list, that his task would consist not only in

[1] A Catty = $1\frac{3}{4}$ lb.

bringing the foreigners to heel, but also in fighting a vast network of native vested interests. Above all he was aware that some part at any rate of the naval forces over which he had been put in supreme control were likely to prove of very dubious loyalty.

On February 25th he reached Wan-an, a considerable town. Up to this point he had been able to travel both day and night, being towed, punted or sailing, according to the state of the wind. But above Wan-an were the famous Eighteen Rapids, which could only be negotiated by daylight. At this point the diary contains a long disquisition on the history of the rapids of the Kan River, showing that in early times their number had been far greater, but that later on conservancy work had increased the volume of water and submerged hundreds of large rocks. On February 27th he acquired a congenial travelling companion, the scholar Chang Pang-t'ai, who had been appointed head of the Academy of Hua-chou, near the southern frontier of the province of Kwangtung. Commissioner Lin had heard that this learned man was going south and had sent a message offering him a lift as far as Kan-chou, where Chang's route branched off. Lin notes that living in this part of China was extremely cheap. The people at Kan-chou were preparing to celebrate the Dragon Boat Festival and seemed to be in high spirits.

From a little way above Kan-chou the river was very shallow and winding, and though large stakes had been set up to give the haulers purchase, progress was slow and laborious. Soon the large boat had to be abandoned and the journey continued in a number of small boats. At Nan-an, reached on March 3rd, he was met as usual by a large number of local officials and also by numerous emissaries from Canton. After Nan-an the Kan River is no longer navigable. The next twenty-four miles of the journey have to be performed by land and include the crossing of the Mei-ling Pass, about 1,000 feet high. More than 160 bearers had to be collected to carry Lin and his luggage, which weighed over 5,000 pounds. After they had crossed the Pass and descended on the southern side a flat road led to Nan-hsiung. Here they were already in the province of Kwangtung, of which Canton is the capital. They were now able to embark again, but only in small boats, the upper waters of the North River being very shallow. But at Shao-chou, four days' journey north of Canton, they were again able to use a large vessel. About seventy miles below Shao-chou there is a rock-formation resembling an image of the Goddess Kuan-yin. Lin went ashore, and prostrated himself before the image. Like the English opium dealers, and indeed everyone whom we come across in this story, he was much given to pious observances. He reached Canton on March 10, 1839, and was of course welcomed by all the high local officials, from the Governor-General downward. After assuring them of the Emperor's good health, he paid a series of official calls at each Government department, and finally at the hour of the Second Drum (9 p.m.) retired to the Yüeh-hua Academy, which was to be his headquarters while he was at Canton. The fact that he lodged in a learned institution was not, as one might at first sight suppose, a tribute to his scholastic eminence. This Academy had in recent years been constantly requisitioned for official purposes, and it had been selected on the present occasion because it was at a conveniently short distance from the premises of the Chinese guild-merchants and the adjacent factories of the foreign traders.

Next day, March 11th, he posted two notices on the gate of his residence. The first was addressed to his staff. He announced that he would shortly be visiting the various inlets of the estuary and would expect all his staff to be in constant attendance. The secretaries employed at his bureau were to feed on the premises and would not be allowed on any pretext to wander in and out of the office. Officials, civil and military, wishing for an interview would always be received immediately. But the deputies and sentries were on no account to hand in schemes drawn up by private theoreticians, unconnected with the mission. Anyone coming to the door with an exaggerated account of his own importance and trying in this way to gain admittance will at once be arrested by the local authorities at hand, examined and severely dealt with. All meals taken at the office must be provided by the person who eats them; on no account must they allow local officials to stand them a meal. Whatever is bought must be paid for in ready money at current prices and no rebate whatever must be demanded. . . .

The second notice made clear that he was only concerned with cases involving import and export, and not at all with any other kinds of current business, such as legal disputes. Relevant petitions and so on could not be dealt with till he had been at Canton for several days. A permit authorizing the submission of a petition at a fixed time would then be given. It must be in the proper form, similar to that used in addressing the Governor-General or Governor, and must be duly stamped and authenticated. No informal petitions 'on red or white paper' were to be handed to his attendants by persons stationing themselves in the way of his carrying-chair, under circumstances in which their provenance could not be investigated. Above all no one must climb up on to the step of his carriage and throw a petition into it; not only will such petitions not be accepted, but the petitioner will be handed over to the local authorities to deal with rigorously. March 12th: 'From the Hour of the Dragon [7 a.m.] to that of the Horse [11 a.m.] I received visitors. The heat was intense and, though I was thinly clad, my sweat poured. After lunch I wrote the draft of my report. At nightfall a strong north wind rose, and it suddenly turned very cold. At the Hour of the Rat [11 p.m.] I bowed to my report and dispatched it to Peking by relay-post.' In this report he informs the Emperor that he left Peking on January 8th and that though he was held up in Kiangsi for several days by heavy snow he was able subsequently to make up for lost time.

Arriving at Canton on March 10th he had already had interviews with the Governor-General and other officials. The vigorous measures they had been taking against the opium trade had already acted as a salutary warning, and the news that a Special Commissioner was to be sent had dismayed not only Chinese culprits but also guilty foreigners. 'For example, the foreign merchant Jardine, who had been at Canton for many years, on January 26th asked for his pass, to go to Macao, and has now left for home on board an English ship.'

After an account of English ship-movements and the difficulty of keeping them under continual surveyance, Lin announces that in about ten days he hopes to go to the Bogue (the entrance to Canton River), as also to Macao and other places. He would use one of Admiral[1] Kuan T'ien-p'ei's boats and under the Admiral's guidance make a general tour of inspection. In a postscript he gives further information about William Jardine. Though he is the ringleader in the opium-smuggling trade, he has no official position, but is merely a particularly unscrupulous foreign merchant. Being of a sly and crafty disposition he has known how to take a mean advantage of our dynasty's traditional policy: 'Deal gently with those from afar.' The fact that he has become immensely wealthy through opium-dealing is known to everyone. In the winter of the sixteenth year of Tao Kuang [1836] the Governor-General Teng was ordered by Your Majesty to look into the case and expel him. But on the pretext of having to make up his accounts before he went, Jardine lingered on for two years. . . . 'Before I set out from Peking I sent a confidential agent post-haste to Canton to inquire about this Jardine's movements. He heard that it was generally rumoured in Canton that the new Commissioner's first act would be to arrest Jardine. That was why he got a pass to Macao and at once took ship to England.'

[1] The English knew him as 'The Admiral'. His Chinese title was 'Commander-in-Chief of Naval Forces'.

Actually Jardine's departure for England was not so good an omen for the future success of Lin's stern policy as Lin himself supposed. It is doubtful whether fear of what the Commissioner might do to him played any part in his decision to leave. His main motive was no doubt to get into touch with Lord Palmerston and persuade him to make war on China. Apart from that, he had made his pile, and no doubt felt that the time had come to buy himself a porticoed house in the English countryside, and get a seat in Parliament.

A few days later Lin addressed a series of four notices[1] to different classes of the Cantonese population, calling upon them to co-operate with him in the suppression of opium-smoking. The first is addressed to school-teachers. It will in future be their duty to report to the authorities any student who smokes opium or sells it. The teachers were to form the students into groups of five—the famous *pao-chia* (security group) system, the head of the group guaranteeing the good behaviour of the rest and being held responsible for any member's misdeeds. This system, which Chinese Governments have constantly employed as a means of upholding law and order, has always shocked Europeans; and it has indeed the disadvantage that it may lead to perfectly innocent people being imprisoned, banished or even executed merely because they reposed a mistaken confidence in some apparently impeccable companion. Naturally any student whom no one would guarantee fell under suspicion, and was to be reported to the authorities and examined. But there were bound to be some individuals, Lin humanely continues, who jogged along through life without picking up any acquaintances. No one would guarantee them, merely because no one knew anything about them. These were not to be forcibly enlisted into a group; their names would be entered in a separate dossier and kept on the files for reference.

[1] Parts of these notices, along with similar matter, were published by Lin as a printed pamphlet. See J. L. Shuck's *Portfolio Sinensis*, Macao, 1840.

The second note was addressed to the 'gentlemen, merchants, soldiers and peasants of Canton' at large. Unfortunately, says Lin, no province has so bad a reputation for opium offences as Kwangtung (the province of which Canton is the capital). In any province if you look into the history of an opium-dealer he almost always turns out to be a Kwangtung man. Failing that, the odds are it will turn out to be a Kwangtung man who supplied him. An opium smoker will turn out either to have brought the vice with him from Kwangtung or to have learnt it from a Kwangtung man. No one can say that the present stringent regulations are not necessary here. Most of the arrests that have been made have turned out to be fully justified. But people anxious to pick a hole in the new regulations have been alleging that all the Government employees sent out to search for opium do, is to knock people about and seize their possessions; or else, if heavily enough bribed, go away leaving the opium untouched. 'I cannot guarantee', says Lin, 'that such things have not sometimes happened. But employees found guilty of such offences are punished with the utmost severity of the law, and any official who condones such behaviour is immediately made the subject of strict inquiry.' Let no one think that it is impossible to give up opium smoking. 'Last year, when I was Governor-General of Hupeh and Hunan, there was a man who had been an addict for thirty years and smoked an ounce a day. But he managed to give it up, and immediately his cheeks began to fill out and the strength came back to his limbs. I saw the same thing happen in case after case. How can anyone suppose that a habit which can be given up in other provinces, cannot be given up in Kwangtung?' Let no one think, he continues, that this is only a temporary drive on the part of the Government. In the past there have been such drives, but 'this time we are going on until the job is finished'.

As, strictly speaking, Lin's mission related to trade with foreigners and was not specifically concerned with putting down opium smoking, one might be inclined to ask why he did not leave the suppression of this abuse to the local officials, and confine his attention to dealing with the importation of opium. The answer, of course, is that the two problems were intimately connected. If there were no more opium smokers in China, foreign import of the drug would automatically cease, and at the same time there would be an end to the outflow of Chinese silver, which was regarded by Lin and all the foremost statesmen of the time as disastrous to China's finances. For some time past there had been a constant decline in the value of copper cash. An ounce of silver was normally worth about 1,000 cash. But now, in some parts of China, as much as 1,600 cash were being given for one ounce of silver. As many taxes and dues of various kinds were collected in cash, but had to be paid at Peking in silver (partly owing to the difficulty of transporting large quantities of copper cash), an alteration in the value of cash upset the whole fiscal system. One bold economic thinker[1] even suggested in 1842 that as Khotan, the great source of jade, was now a Chinese possession, it would be a good thing to go back to the jade-standard of ancient times! No one seems to have taken up the suggestion, perhaps because of the difficulty of defining what was to be accepted as true jade, there being many substances, such as nephrite, jadite and so on which only an expert eye can distinguish from jade.

The Chinese were convinced that the decline in the value of copper cash was due to the large amount of silver that was being paid to opium smugglers. The question is a complicated one, and I will not go into it in detail. But it is worth noting that throughout a large part of Chinese history there had been continual fluctuations in the parity between silver and copper cash, and it would be hard, I think, to prove that these had any connection with foreign trade.

[1] Wei Yüan. I. 555.

A second question that arises is, why does Lin almost always take the term 'opium' as being synonymous with 'foreign opium' and to a large extent ignore the fact that a great deal of opium was made from poppy-fields in China? The answer, I think, is that the real opium addict did not find that Chinese opium satisfied his craving. The Chinese theory was that China's pure soil could not in the nature of things produce anything so deadly as less happy lands produced. However this may be, in practice Chinese opium was chiefly used to adulterate foreign opium, thus producing a cheap, second-rate brand. Foreigners often accused the Chinese of hypocrisy in making so much fuss about the importation of opium and at the same time doing so little to stop home production. But as a matter of fact a great deal had been done in this direction. Round about 1830 there were extensive poppy-fields even in so accessible and thickly populated a province as Chekiang, on the south-eastern coast; but in 1831 there was a great drive to suppress poppy growing, and it seems ultimately to have been confined chiefly to remote districts in the outer provinces.

The third in this series of remonstrances is addressed to the marines employed on patrol ships. 'Usually when such ships are in harbour', Lin writes, 'the men remain on board with nothing to do. One or two fill in the time by having a pipe of opium, and soon the rest follow suit. . . . It happens, too, that when in the course of their duties they capture a cargo of opium, they do not hand the whole of it over to the authorities, but abuse their official capacity by keeping some of it for themselves, either for their own use or to sell. Their comrades naturally do not betray them, and their officers, on condition of receiving a share of the spoil, make no attempt to stop these practices.' The result is that the supposed tough marines have become, through constant opium smoking, a pack of degraded weaklings.

The fourth note once more concerns guarantee-groups. Too often the folders containing their names are simply filed in Government offices, and never again looked at. No one troubles to find out whether the guarantors are honourable and dependable people. Lin brings forward a new plan by which the ultimate responsibility for the selection of guarantors falls upon village elders, selected as men of high character by the local gentry.

The Chinese found it hard to believe that the opium trade was carried on with the knowledge and assent of the sovereign of England. As far back as 1830 the then Governor-General of Kwangtung and Kwangsi had said in a memorial[1] to the Throne that the natural way to get the opium trouble put straight would be to send an official protest to the king of the country whose merchants were importing it. If for example it were Annam (or Siam) that were involved, a command would at once be sent to the king of the country ordering him to put a stop to the traffic. But in the case of 'outer foreigners' living tens of thousands of leagues across the sea it was doubtful if such a communication would ever arrive.

A few years later, in 1835, another memorialist suggested[2] that as well as taking energetic measures on the spot, at Canton, it would be a good thing to send a letter to the King of England telling him that in future foreign ships were not going to be allowed to carry opium and that those who infringed this rule would be dealt with in exactly the same way as Chinese who infringed the opium laws. In 1836 yet another memorialist[3] said that a letter ought to be sent to the King of England saying that opium was doing great harm in China. The Chinese Government had made its own subjects liable to heavy penalties if found guilty of opium dealing. No retrospective measures, the king was to be told, would be taken against foreign merchants who mended their ways. But any foreign merchant who went on smuggling opium would be dealt with as though he were Chinese, according to Chinese law.

[1] I. 80.   [2] I. 484.   [3] I. 475.

On about March 16, 1839, at a meeting at which Lin, the Governor-General, the Governor and also Liang T'ing-nan, the head of the Academy whose premises Lin was occupying, were present, the question of a letter to Queen Victoria was discussed:[1] Liang pointed out that both on the occasion of the Macartney mission in 1793 and of the Amherst mission in 1816 the Emperor of China had sent a letter to the King of England; so that there was a precedent for such a step. Commissioner Lin, however, recalled that no difficulty arose about sending these letters as they were entrusted to the English envoys who were then in China. Now the question was more difficult, and he for his part thought that a letter not from the Emperor but from a high official would be more appropriate. If he himself were to write one, he said, he doubted whether Elliot (the English Trade Superintendent) would be willing to send it, as it would inevitably exhibit his own conduct in an unfavourable light. Liang T'ing-nan (to whom we owe this account) recalled that during the reign of K'ang Hsi, when there was a difficulty about conveying a letter to the Czar, a Dutchman had undertaken to deliver it. Might not a Portuguese ship at Macao be used in the same way? It might be a good plan to make twenty or thirty copies of the letter, giving them to some English ships at Canton or to ships of other countries that were bound for London, one copy to each ship, to deliver when they got there. In this way it was certain that a copy would arrive. The letter written at this time was apparently never sent. Next year, as we shall see, a more discursive version was sent, though probably never received. But I am going now to translate the first version[2] which is a fine piece of moral exhortation; whereas the version sent in 1840 is more like an ordinary governmental communication.

'The Way of Heaven is fairness to all; it does not suffer us to harm others in order to benefit ourselves. Men are alike in this all the world over: that they cherish life and hate what endangers life. Your country lies twenty thousand leagues away; but for all that the Way of Heaven holds good for you as for us, and your instincts are not different from ours; for nowhere are there men so blind as not to distinguish between what brings life and what brings death, between what brings profit and what does harm.[1] Our Heavenly Court treats all within the Four Seas as one great family; the goodness of our great Emperor is like Heaven, that covers all things. There is no region so wild or so remote that he does not cherish and tend it. Ever since the port of Canton was first opened, trade has flourished. For some hundred and twenty or thirty years the natives of the place have enjoyed peaceful and profitable relations with the ships that come from abroad. Rhubarb, tea, silk are all valuable products of ours, without which foreigners could not live. The Heavenly Court, extending its benevolence to all alike, allows these things to be sold and carried away across the sea, not grudging them even to remote domains, its bounty matching the bounty of Heaven and Earth.

'But there is a class of evil foreigner that makes opium and brings it for sale, tempting fools to destroy themselves, merely in order to reap profit. Formerly the number of opium smokers was small; but now the vice has spread far and wide and the poison penetrated deeper and deeper. If there are some foolish people who yield to this craving to their own detriment, it is they who have brought upon themselves their own ruin, and in a country so populous and flourishing, we can well do without them. But our great, unified Manchu Empire regards itself as responsible for the habits and morals of its subjects and cannot rest content to see any of them become victims to a deadly poison. For this reason we have decided to inflict very severe penalties on opium dealers and opium smokers, in order to put a stop for ever to the propagation of this vice. It appears that this

[1] Blake said, 'Man is not improved by the hurt of another. States are not improved at the expense of foreigners.'

poisonous article is manufactured by certain devilish persons in places subject to your rule. It is not, of course, either made or sold at your bidding, nor do all the countries you rule produce it, but only certain of them. I am told that in your own country opium smoking is forbidden under severe penalties. This means that you are aware of how harmful it is. But better than to forbid the smoking of it would be to forbid the sale of it and, better still, to forbid the production of it, which is the only way of cleansing the contamination at its source. So long as you do not take it yourselves, but continue to make it and tempt the people of China to buy it, you will be showing yourselves careful of your own lives, but careless of the lives of other people, indifferent in your greed for gain to the harm you do to others; such conduct is repugnant to human feeling and at variance with the Way of Heaven. Our Heavenly Court's resounding might, redoubtable to its own subjects and foreigners alike, could at any moment control their fate;[1] but in its compassion and generosity it makes a practice of giving due warning before it strikes. Your Majesty has not before been thus officially notified, and you may plead ignorance of the severity of our laws. But I now give my assurance that we mean to cut off this harmful drug for ever. What it is here forbidden to consume, your dependencies must be forbidden to manufacture, and what has already been manufactured Your Majesty must immediately search out and throw it to the bottom of the sea, and never again allow such a poison to exist in Heaven or on earth. When that is done, not only will the Chinese be rid of this evil, but your people too will be safe. For so long as your subjects make opium, who knows but they will not sooner or later take to smoking it; so that an embargo on the making of it may very well be a safeguard for them, too. Both nations will enjoy the blessing of a peaceful existence, yours on its side having made clear

---

[1] Cf. *Lieh Tzu*, VII. N. The meaning is 'Their lives are in the Emperor's hands'.

its sincerity by respectful obedience to our commands. You will be showing that you understand the principles of Heaven, and calamities will be not sent down on you from above; you will be acting in accordance with decent feeling, which may also well influence the course of nature in your favour.[1]

'The laws against the consumption of opium are now so strict in China that if you continue to make it, you will find that no one buys it and no more fortunes will be made. Rather than waste your efforts on a hopeless endeavour, would it not be better to devise some other form of trade? All opium discovered in China is being cast into burning oil and destroyed. Any foreign ships that in the future arrive with opium on board, will be set fire to, and any other goods that they are carrying will inevitably be burnt along with the opium. You will then not only fail to make any profit out of us, but ruin yourselves into the bargain. Intending to harm others, you will be the first to be harmed. Our Heavenly Court would not have won the allegiance of innumerable lands did it not wield superhuman power. Do not say you have not been warned in time. On receiving this, Your Majesty will be so good as to report to me immediately on the steps that have been taken at each of your ports.'[2]

That this is a noble letter no one will deny. Had the inexperienced young Queen received it she might well at first have doubted whether we ought to persist in what Gladstone called 'this most infamous and atrocious trade'. But Palmerston would soon have damped her qualms by the accepted sophistry that it rested with the Chinese to stop the opium traffic by suppressing the consumption of opium; he would have explained that only by importing opium could the balance of trade be maintained; and that the cessation of this traffic would be disastrous to the finances of India.

[1] Text uncertain.

[2] Translated from VI. 14, with use of a few variants from *Kuo Ch'ao Ch'i-hsien. . .* , 203. 53.

On March 18th Lin sent to the Chinese guild-merchants two famous communications, one addressed to the guild-merchants themselves; the other to be transmitted by them to the foreign merchants. The main gist of the note comes at the end—he has called upon the foreigners to surrender all the opium that they have on their ships, and the Chinese guild-merchants are to see to it that the foreigners obey. If the guild-merchants fail to do this it will be taken as final proof that they are acting in collusion with the opium smugglers and they will be dealt with as traitors. He leads up to this by showing the guild-merchants that there is already plenty of evidence of their duplicity. They have for a long time past been certifying foreign ships as free from contraband on the flimsy excuse that at the time of entering the mouth of the Canton River they have no opium on board, having (as the Chinese guild-merchants are perfectly well aware) already sold their opium before entering the river. It must also be well known to the guild-merchants that despite the ban on export of silver, silver is regularly being paid in at the foreign factories and smuggled on to foreign ships at night. Lin appeals to the pride of the Chinese merchants by reminding them that in old days a foreign merchant arriving at Canton used at once to dress up in his best and wait upon the guild-merchants, who often would not see him till he had called several times. Nowadays the guild-merchants demean themselves by going all the way to Macao to meet newly-arrived foreigners. 'These foreigners, through Chinese secret agents whom they have in their pay, know all our official secrets; but if one tries to get information about the affairs of the foreigners from guild-merchants, all one gets is evasions and pretences; you are evidently determined not to give them away.' Lin ends with a threat; if the guild-merchants fail to do what is now required of them, he will obtain permission from Peking to pick out one or two of the worst of them and confiscate all their possessions, as a warning to the rest.

In the communication to foreigners, before coming to his main demand—the surrender of all opium in their possession—Lin reminds them that it is only as a favour that foreigners are allowed to trade at all. China is completely self-supporting, whereas foreigners cannot live without the tea and rhubarb that they get from China.

The belief that foreigners, and particularly the English, would die of constipation if deprived of rhubarb was widely held at this time in China. It had its origin, I think, in the practice, so widely spread in early nineteenth-century Europe, of a grand purge every spring, rhubarb-root being often an ingredient in the purgatives used. The seasonal purge was thought to be particularly necessary in the case of children, who without it would be sure to develop worms. However, about ten months later, Lin modified[1] his views about rhubarb, and said that only tea could be considered an absolute necessity. The export of rhubarb, he had discovered, was confined to very small quantities, classed at the Customs as medicine. Tea (and this, of course, is my comment, not Lin's) was another matter. Apart from the fact that it had become in England a national drink, the import tax on tea was an important item in the English budget; but there was no immediate prospect of the Englishman being altogether deprived of his cup of tea; a possible interruption in the trade had long been foreseen, and large stocks were held in reserve.

It is wrong, Lin continues, to make profit out of what is harmful to others, to bring opium (which you do not smoke in your own land) to our country, swindle people out of their money and endanger their lives. You have been doing this for twenty or thirty years, accumulating an untold amount of wrongful gain, incurring the universal resentment of man and the certain retribution of Heaven. However the days when opium was saleable in China are now over. The death penalty for opium offences has been

[1] II. 121.

approved and will shortly come into force. The new regulations will apply just as much to you as to the Chinese themselves. 'I now call upon you to hand over for destruction all the opium you have on your ships and sign an undertaking that you will never bring opium here again, and that you are aware that if you are found to have done so your goods will be confiscated and you yourselves dealt with according to the law.' There is a great future, he goes on, for good foreigners who fulfil these conditions and are content to enrich themselves by legitimate trade. He will even go so far as to suggest to the Emperor that by a special act of favour their past offences should be overlooked and that he should be allowed to bestow some kind of largesse upon them as a reward for their change of heart. He winds up by assuring them that he has made a vow not to leave Canton till the import of opium has been absolutely stopped. They must realize, he says, that their conduct has aroused tremendous popular feeling against them and that, quite apart from China's army and navy, bands of patriots could in a moment be enrolled who could easily exterminate them.

Commissioner Lin's demand for the surrender of all opium has often been described in Western books as though it were the result of some kind of brain-storm, a sudden outburst of tyrannical frenzy. This is utterly untrue. At the time he made the demand he was also arranging for the surrender of opium held by Chinese, and he was simply applying to the foreigners the standard regulations that he had applied, as Governor-General in Hupeh and Hunan, the year before. The English, of course, had theories about extra-territoriality and rejected the notion that, if they came to a country, they must obey its laws. But in the code of the Manchu dynasty there was a special clause making clear that foreigners in China were subject to the same laws as the Chinese.

Four days passed, and he still had no definite answer from the foreigners. They had only signified to the guild-merchants that the demand was under consideration. Lin had heard that the Americans, at any rate, were in favour of surrendering their opium, but had been talked out of it by Lancelot Dent. Now that Jardine was gone Dent, the head of the other great opium-smuggling firm, was the oldest China hand, and in Lin's view the arch-villain of the piece. Chiefly, I think, in order to get Dent away from the factories and prevent his influencing the other foreigners, Lin now notified the Prefects of the two boroughs of Canton that they were to summon Dent to the municipal office, get a deposition from him, have it translated, and report on what should be done with him. The long and complicated story of the attempts made next day to get Dent to go to the Governor's office has been told in many Western books. These attempts were unsuccessful, and the matter was allowed to drop, because Lin soon reached the conclusion[1] that the person who was preventing the foreigners from agreeing to surrender their opium was not Dent, but Captain Elliot, the British Superintendent of Trade. This office had been created after the dissolution of the East India Company's Canton branch in 1834. The holder of it was responsible to the Foreign Office and was, in fact, a kind of consul. I am here concerned with what the Chinese thought of Elliot rather than with what one learns of him from Western sources. To the Chinese he seemed a complete anomaly—not in the ordinary sense an official, nor yet a merchant, despite his intimate relations with the principal traders. It was never alleged that he made his living by smuggling; but his principal job seemed to the Chinese to be the protection of smugglers.

At the time when the demand for the surrender of opium was made Elliot was at Macao. He returned to Canton on the evening of March 24th, and henceforward the struggle was no longer one between Lin and the foreigners as a whole, but between Lin and Captain Elliot.

[1] II. 248.

The entry in Lin's diary for March 24th is: 'Fine weather. From early morning till midday I received visitors. In the afternoon I wrote letters to friends at Peking; it was very hot. Today I stationed armed patrol-ships at all the approaches to the quays, to prevent foreigners from embarking or disembarking.' Nearly a week had passed since he gave the foreign merchants three days in which to accept his demand for the surrender of all opium. No definite reply had been received, and Lin felt it was time to apply pressure. On the same day he gave orders that all loading and unloading were to stop, all craftsmen employed by foreigners were to leave their service, and anyone seeking service with them in future was to be dealt with according to the clause of the Code forbidding 'secret relations with foreign countries'. The small boats belonging to foreigners must not go alongside their large ships and get into touch with them. The compradors and so on employed by the foreign factories were all withdrawn. 'If there is any attempt to evade these restrictions', Lin wrote, 'I, the Governor-General, and the Governor will obtain permission from Peking to close the harbour to them and put a stop to their trade for ever.'[1] On March 26th he complained that, though in response to a request from Elliot he had sent representatives to the Chinese Guild-merchants' Hall to discuss matters, the guild-merchants had waited from early morning till late in the afternoon without Elliot turning up. Before Elliot's return from Macao the foreigners, Lin had heard, were among themselves all in favour of surrendering the opium. It was obviously Elliot who was stirring them up to resist and so put an end to the trade that had gone on for some two hundred years. 'The Sovereign of your country will take strong measures against you on hearing of this', Lin said. 'There have been many instances of British officials getting into serious trouble at home for disobeying Chinese regulations, as you must surely be aware.' Lin then lists four considerations which

[1] II. 245.

should prompt Elliot to surrender the opium immediately. In the first place, the foreigners must surely dread the anger of Heaven, which cannot fail to punish them if they continue to ruin so many Chinese homes, and cause the death of so many opium smokers and dealers; for it has now been decided that the death penalty is to be inflicted for opium offences. Again, seafarers are in particular danger from thunderstorms and gales, dragons, crocodiles and the giant salamander; and Heaven, if offended, may well use these as instruments of punishment. A number of Englishmen who have incurred Heaven's displeasure by breaking the laws of our Heavenly Court have come to a bad end; for example, the President of the Select Committee of Supercargoes, J. W. Roberts, who in 1808 plotted an English occupation of Macao and died there immediately.[1] Then there was Lord Napier who in 1834 landed at Canton without a passport and soon afterwards suddenly expired; while the missionary Robert Morrison, 'who was secretly implicated in the affair, died the same year'. Here I must say in parenthesis that Morrison's only 'implication' in Lord Napier's misdemeanours was that, when already very ill, he acted once or twice as interpreter to Napier.[2]

Secondly[3], continues Lin, there is the legal aspect of the matter. There is a clause in our Code which says that people from countries outside our sphere of influence are subject to the same penalties as the Chinese themselves. Strictly speaking, foreigners who have sold opium are now liable to suffer the death penalty. By a special act of grace you are only being asked to hand over your opium and sign our undertaking never to bring opium again and to accept that if you are caught doing so you will be dealt with according to the law and the whole of your cargo will be confiscated.

[1] Roberts died five years later.

[2] Another instance given by Lin is 'the confirmed opium smuggler Magniac, who cut his own throat'. I do not know which member of this well-known merchant family is meant. Perhaps Daniel?

[3] I only use quotation marks when I am translating word for word. Their absence means that I am summarizing.

Thirdly, there is the common-sense point of view. I ask you, where in the whole world is there a better port than Canton? Here you can buy rhubarb and tea, without which you could not exist; various kinds of silk, without which you could not make your textiles; sugar, cassia, vermilion, gamboge, alum, camphor. Are you going to let the port be closed and sacrifice all these things merely on account of opium? Fourthly, there is the nature of your situation. Your heartlessness in continuing to sell opium has made you the object of widely spread popular indignation, and it is dangerous to incur the resentment of the masses. What reason have you to cling to something which you are not allowed to sell and which no one is allowed to buy? Do you want to take it home with you? But as you know, in your country there is as little market for it as here.

On March 27th there is the entry: 'At the Hour of the Snake [9 a.m.] I received through the guild-merchants a note from the English Consul Elliot asking in obedience to my instructions to hand over the opium. I shall have to discuss my reply with the Governor-General and Governor. One must know what quantity they are surrendering. At midday ate at the Governor's place. Today it has been very hot, and many of the people were working naked. Got back to my lodging at dusk.'

The statement that Elliot had 'asked' to hand over the opium may have been a mere slip. Turning to Elliot's note of this date we see that the word 'ask' does occur, but in a different context; he 'asks' for further instructions about the disposal of the opium. The point may seem a small one; but two years later, when Lin was accused of having provoked the Opium War by seizing foreign opium, his rather disingenuous defence was that Elliot had 'asked' to surrender it. His accusers then pointed out that so far from having been voluntarily surrendered, the opium had only been given up, many days after Lin's original demand for it, as the result of a pressure that stopped short of nothing save actual shooting.[1]

March 28th: 'At the Hour of the Snake [9 a.m.] the guild-merchants brought a note from Elliot saying that the English would surrender 20,283 chests of opium and were awaiting instructions about the checking of it on reception. So I went to the Governor-General's office . . . to arrange about the day and hour for reception, and circulated urgent dispatches giving the necessary orders. I also sent to the foreigners a present of beef, mutton and other food.'

March 29th: 'Elliot is now inventing reasons for delaying the surrender of opium, insisting that liberty of movement must first be restored to the foreigners in the factories.' Elliot had ingeniously pleaded that so long as the English were virtually prisoners in their factory any order he gave to the ships about the surrender of opium would be regarded as given under duress, and would according to English law carry no weight. To this Lin replied[2] that Elliot's talk about the foreigners being held like prisoners was ridiculous. Do high authorities send presents of food to prisoners in gaol? The restrictions placed upon them were solely in order to prevent the escape of the arch-smuggler Dent. The withdrawal of their compradors and other Chinese servants was a precaution taken because it was known that these were in collusion with the English and were likely to be used in helping Dent to escape.

On March 30th Lin received a present of roebuck flesh, the name of which, *pao-lu*, means 'promotion assured', from the Emperor, accompanied by a scroll with the two words 'Good-luck' and 'long-life' written out calligraphically. 'I respectfully burnt incense and kowtowed nine times upon receiving these things.'

On March 31st a note came from Elliot asking for permission to send his assistant Mr Johnston to give instructions to the English ships about surrendering their opium. But

[1] See below, p. 129.   [2] II. 252.

this did not go down at all well. Lin pointed out that he had already ordered all ships to make a detailed declaration of their cargo. All that was now necessary was for Elliot to compel them to make this declaration and surrender opium to the amounts specified.

In addition to this preoccupation with foreigners, Lin had on his hands the task of suppressing opium smoking at home. On April 1st he interviewed a number of prominent Canton gentry who were setting up a reception-point for opium and pipes surrendered by local people.

An immense amount of organization was required to arrange for the safe delivery of the opium from the English ships to small boats, and from the small boats to the point near Chuenpi[1] where it was to be accumulated. On the afternoon of April 10th Lin left Canton and set out for the Bogue—the mouth of Canton river—at the east side of which the opium was to be deposited, a distance of some fifty miles, writing dispatches as he went. Arriving at the Bogue on April 11th, he was able to record in his diary 'Today fifty chests of opium were received'. The pace, of course, increased. Next day it was six hundred chests, on April 13th, 1,150.

At dawn on April 14th he went to the temple of the Queen of Heaven, protectress of sailors, and the shrine of Kuan Ti, God of War, and burnt incense,[2] preparatory to a visit to the Chinese fleet, anchored in the harbour, being received by Admiral Kuan, popularly supposed to be a descendant of the God of War, and a number of high officers. At about this time, as the delivery of opium was proceeding smoothly, he gave leave to the English to resume the use of their sampans (small boats), at the same time enclosing a list

[1] Island on the east side of the Bogue.

[2] This was the first day of the Chinese third month. Religious observances of this kind were generally carried out on the first and fifteenth day. In her earthly existence the goddess was a Miss Lin, living on the Fuhkien coast; so Commissioner Lin, who was a Fuhkien man, had a double reason for devotion to her.

of fifteen notorious opium dealers who were forbidden to leave the factories. The list includes the names of Dent, Young Jardine, Young Matheson, Sam Matheson and Joseph Henry.

Things were going well so that Commissioner Lin began to be able to relax a little and think, momentarily at any rate, about things other than foreigners and opium. On April 26th he received the newly arrived *Peking Gazette* and read that in the Palace Examinations the theme for an essay had been 'The gentleman must make his thoughts sincere', and the passage from the Classics to be enlarged upon: 'Through punishments there come at last to be no punishments, the people cease to transgress', from the *Book of History*. But after recording these themes, he at once adds, 'Today we collected 1,250 chests of opium'. April 29th was the Admiral's sixtieth birthday. Lin, famous as a calligrapher, inscribed a pair of fans for him as a birthday present, 'The Admiral called, bringing food, and we ate together in the Governor-General's boat'. The Governor-General, Teng T'ing-chen, was about ten years older than Lin. He had occupied this post since 1835, and was consequently better up in local affairs than Lin, who constantly sought his advice. The two became devoted to one another, and are often quoted as a classic instance of friendship between high statesmen. More news came in about the recent Literary Examinations at Peking. Numerous changes in the placing of the successful candidates had been made when the lists were revised. The first name in the Fourth Class had been erased by the Vermilion (i.e. the Emperor's) pencil. The second had made a mistake in the elevation of characters referring to the Emperor, and the third and fourth had both failed to rhyme according to the official rhyme-tables, which insisted on the pronunciation of over a thousand years ago.

On May 2nd he notified the English that passes to go to Macao would now be issued, except in the case of the notorious fifteen. On May 3rd he heard more details about the Literary Examinations. For example, the poem to be written was on the theme: 'Heart pure as an icy pool', sixteen lines of five-syllable verse, the rhyme to be used being *hsin*, 'heart'. 'I am told', says Lin, 'that the theme is a line by the Sung poet Hsü Yin.' He was not, however, told quite right. Hsü Yin was born about 870 and it is unlikely that he lived on into the Sung dynasty. On May 6th, in giving instructions about the building of a strong fence between the waterside and the factories, Lin points out that it was only when 'Elliot and the rest' found themselves shut off from all communication with the outside world that he at last caved in and agreed to surrender the opium. It was clear that he was greatly dependent on Chinese traitors who lived in the tangle of alleys and lanes behind the factories. Here, disguised as harmless shops, but sometimes betraying their criminal connection with the foreigners by sporting shop-signs in foreign writing, opium stocks and the hiring-offices of opium-running skiffs were hidden away in back-courtyards. All these must be routed out, and only genuine provision shops and so on allowed to remain.

In the next few days there was an interchange of notes about the expulsion of Dent,[1] Inglis, Young Jardine and others, all of whom had to leave, and a command to the Chinese guild-merchants to make a complete list of guilty foreigners other than the sixteen whose names Lin already had. We do not know what the response was; but as only seventeen merchants surrendered opium, the guild-merchants were probably not able to add many names.

On May 13th, after offering incense at dawn to the Queen of Heaven, 'I took the opportunity of inspecting the trenches that are being made to drain off the opium when it is destroyed'. He was thus well ahead in his plans, for over a thousand chests still remained to be delivered. On May 16th, a rainy day, he writes: 'The Governor-General sent me some

[1] Dent was still at Canton in 1841; see *Chinese Repository*, 1841, p. 58.

lychees that were still green. To the orderly who brought them I recited the following impromptu verse:

The mists and rains of foreign seas darken Lintin.[1]
Suddenly I was handed on a carven platter "a sky of populous stars",
Eighteen young damsels, each with the same smile.
Your kindness indeed is ever fresh as the green of the lychees.'

Not an easy poem to translate, with its allusions and plays on words, which it would be tedious to explain; but showing again that with the complete surrender of the opium now well in sight, Lin was beginning to feel that he could allow himself a literary distraction. 'At noon', he goes on, 'it cleared up and I went to inspect the wooden barricades and iron chains that I have had put at the mouth of the river, and the newly erected battery at Ching-yüan. A strong south wind got up and in the outer waters the waves were very high and our boat heeled over sharply. Late in the afternoon we reached the Wei-yüan battery. The Admiral and I went up on to it and tested the three big 5,000-catty cannons. We then went back to the Ching-yüan battery to have a look at the Portuguese bronze cannon, and make sure that the chains of the barricade were properly attached. The wooden barricade was then opened to allow my boat to pass. Lamps were already lit when I got back to my lodging.'

On May 18th he heard that on April 22nd he had been made Governor-General of Kiangnan and Kiangsi, the most coveted of all the Governor-Generalships. He was not, however, to go to his post till the opium business at Canton was settled. That day, having received a dispatch from the Emperor expressing doubt as to whether Jardine had really left China, Lin again assured him that he had made the most careful inquiries and had established beyond all doubt that Jardine left on January 30th. Moreover, he had also notified

[1] Island outside the Bogue, where opium was traded.

the other leading opium dealers, both members of the Jardine firm and others, that they must leave at once. But there was the question of what was to happen if they came back again, and Lin now asked that a special clause should be added to the opium regulations, making it clear that in future foreigners caught bringing opium would suffer the death penalty and that their cargoes would be confiscated by the Chinese state.

On May 19th Lin composed an 'Address to the Spirit of the Sea', to be used when making a sacrifice of apology to the Spirit for polluting the sea with the opium that he now proposed to liquefy and run off into the Canton estuary. It is an elaborate document[1] couched in the archaic sacrificial language which deities are supposed to demand and which Lin must certainly have taken the same sort of pleasure in composing as a former Balliol Classics scholar, long immersed in harassing Colonial business, might nostalgically derive if asked to compose a Latin address at some local academic function. 'On the seventh day of the fourth month of the nineteenth year of Tao-kuang', he says (but the date is expressed in archaic formulae) 'the Special Commissioner, appointed Governor-General of Kiangnan and Kiangsi Lin Tse-hsü, respectfully offering hard bristle [i.e. a pig] and soft down [i.e. a sheep], together with clear wine and diverse dainties, thus ventures to address the Spirit of the Southern Sea: "Spirit whose virtue makes you a chief of Divinities, whose deeds match the opening and closing of the doors of Nature, you who wash away all stains and cleanse all impurities . . . why should you raise any barrier against a horde of foreign ships? But alas, poison has been allowed to creep in unchecked, till at last barbarian smoke fills the market. . . . At this Heaven's majesty thundered forth; a special envoy came galloping".' The upshot was that without the expenditure of a single arrow, a store of tens of thousands of boxes was surrendered. 'If it had been cast into

[1] II. 107.

the flames, the charred remains might have been collected. Far better to hurl it into the depths, to mingle with the giant floods.' I tell you this, Lin explains, in order that you may warn your watery subjects in due time to keep away. Above all, he prays that the spirit by his cryptic influences may rid China of this baleful thing, tame the bestial nature of the foreigners, and make them know their God.

For God he uses the Hun word *Tengri*, 'Heaven', culled from ancient histories, and not very suitable to the rather limp Victorian deity of the opium smugglers.

Conscious that rumours might easily spread (as indeed despite all precautions they did) that he had not destroyed all the opium, but had kept back part of it as his own private perquisite, Lin had proposed to the Emperor on April 12th that the whole of the surrendered opium should be sent to Peking to be verified and destroyed, 'that there might be no doubt about the truth' of what he had asserted.

The fact that on May 19th, before a reply from the Emperor had been received, Lin (as shown by his composing an apology to the Sea Spirit) was still assuming that the opium was to be destroyed locally, shows that the offer to prove his veracity by sending it intact to Peking was a mere gesture which he did not expect to be taken seriously, implying as it did that the Emperor did not have full confidence in him. It must therefore have been rather a shock when five days later, on May 24th, he received a belated reply from the Emperor (it had been held up by the floods) saying that the offer to send the opium to Peking was accepted. The acceptance was not even accompanied by any assurance that the Emperor did not doubt Lin's word. Attached to it, however, was a notification that the names of Lin, the Admiral and other officials concerned had been sent to the Board of Civil Office to decide how their services should be rewarded. Next day, May 25th, there is the entry: 'At noon the Admiral, Yü Pao-shun (a member of Lin's staff) and others came to discuss arrangements for sending the opium to Peking.' On May 28th he drafted a memorial to the Throne submitting a proposal to send it by sea. The draft was sent to the Governor-General for revision and dispatch. It was apparently never sent to Peking, and was in fact already out of date; for on May 30th he received instructions that the opium was after all not to go to the capital. This *volte face* was due to the fact that one of the censors had pointed out the impracticability of the scheme. The delegates who conveyed the opium, he said, would find it extremely difficult during so long a journey to prevent pilfering; moreover the labour and expense involved would be immense. There was not the slightest reason to suspect Lin and his colleagues of deception, and it would surely be better to destroy the opium publicly on the spot. This would make a salutary impression both upon the inhabitants of the coastal region and upon the foreigners at Canton.

Criticism of Government measures, both by the official censors and by officials in general, was one of the most valued and jealously preserved aspects of Chinese administration. But it often happened that the critic only became aware of measures after they had already been put into force and criticism was no longer of any practical use. Critics were in an equally weak position elsewhere than in China. Parliament had no opportunity of expressing a view as to whether England ought to go to war with China until eight months after the war started.

In consequence of this abrupt change of policy the discarded apology to the Sea Spirit once more became relevant. 'Early this morning', he writes on June 1st, 'I sacrificed to the Sea Spirit, announcing that I should shortly be dissolving opium and draining it off into the great ocean and advising the Spirit to tell the creatures of the water to move away for a time, to avoid being contaminated. After I got back to my lodging-place it rained all day. In the evening I received confidential instructions sent from Peking on the

29th of the third month [May 12th] concerning a memorial by the Censor Pu Chi-t'ung.'

This memorial[1] contained a strong criticism of Lin's policy. Lin, the writer of it said, had been sent to Canton to put down the importation of opium for ever. But having confiscated all the opium that was on board the foreign ships at the moment, he had not made any proper plans for the future. The only effect of extracting from the merchants a guarantee that they would not ever bring opium again would be that instead of bringing their opium into the estuary they would keep well out at sea, get into touch with Chinese agents on shore and transfer their cargo to ships sent out by these agents. Lin must be told that the guarantee, on which he sets such store, is not a final solution of the problem, and that he must devise some better plan for stopping the opium traffic finally and completely. No reply by Lin to this criticism seems to be extant. His next report to Peking arrived on July 8th and seems to have been sent on June 13th. It concerned a fresh outbreak of smuggling at Namoa, on the northern borders of Kwangtung, and makes no reference to any general plan for stamping out the opium trade in the future.

On June 3rd the destruction of the opium began, and from now onwards he records day by day the quantity disposed of, just as in previous weeks he had recorded the quantity surrendered. On June 3rd, too, he had the distraction of receiving more news about examinations. At a special test of officials the staff of the Cabinet and of the Board of Civil Office had had to write an essay on the theme 'The Penal Code establishes the basic Law; the Rites follow human feeling'. In trying lawsuits Chinese magistrates were allowed in appropriate cases to give their verdict according to the traditional lore of the Book of Rites rather than according to the Penal Code. The two were sometimes at variance, for example revenge for the murder of one's father was a

[1] II. 106.

sacred duty according to the Rites, but was forbidden by the Code.

The three Boards of Revenue, Rites and War had to write an essay on the theme: 'Each shoots at his own target'. That is to say, the father must strive to be a model father, the son a model son, and so on. Finally, the Board of Punishments and Board of Works had as their subject: 'Of all inanimate things the mirror is the greatest sage'—I suppose, because it informs us about ourselves and self-knowledge is the greatest wisdom.

On June 7th there arrived at Macao the armed merchant-ship *Cambridge*, destined to be the first foreign-built ship in the Chinese Navy. She belonged to her captain, Joseph Abraham Douglas. She was a ship of 1,080 tons, which had cost, according to his own account, £15,600. Douglas freighted at Bombay in February 1839 with a full cargo of opium, cotton and other produce, signing bills of lading to deliver the cargo at Whampoa.[1] When he was in the Straits of Malacca he heard news of the plight of the English at Canton. On May 4th he arrived at Singapore, where he landed his opium, presumably selling it at the low price then prevailing because of the crisis at Canton. He then fitted out the *Cambridge* as an auxiliary man-of-war. He already had six eighteen-pound cannonades on board, and he now bought twenty-six eighteen-pound guns and four long-twelves, with powder and shot. He then engaged ten additional seamen, and set off for Macao, arriving on June 7th. Here he offered to protect the British ships in the Canton estuary, and as the sloop *Larne*, the only British warship on the China Station, had left on May 30th, there can be no doubt that Captain Elliot was grateful for the offer. Elliot proposed that the British Government should pay £14,000 for eight months' hire of the *Cambridge*; but there was no written agreement. On June 13th Douglas transferred most of his remaining cargo to an American ship, having, of course, to pay rent for storing

1 Ten miles downstream from Canton.

it. This enabled all his guns to be brought into action. Three days later Elliot appointed him Commodore of the Fleet.

But to return to Lin.

On June 13th he sent to the Emperor an account of the way in which the opium was being destroyed. This, like the delivery, required an immense amount of meticulous organization. Only the most trusted of his subordinates were used as superintendents of the work, and the coolies employed were stripped and searched when they knocked off from work each night. He tells the Emperor that the stench of foreign opium is atrocious; the idea that the foreigners do not simply scrape off the thickened juice and decoct it, but also use some 'strange and vile' process, is evidently true.

There were at the time many fantastic folk-beliefs about the making of opium. 'When a man dies', says an anonymous British Museum manuscript[1] of about 1842, 'the people [of the Philippines] throw him into a huge common gravel-pit and cover him with dead bodies of the serpent-eagle and with poppies. They then wait for several months till the blood and flesh of the man and bird have mixed with the poppies, whereupon they strain off the sediment, boil it and make a paste that they call *ying-hsiu*, which is opium. The English imitated this method and made the poison in order to destroy the Chinese with it.'

'The inhabitants of the coastal region', Lin informs the Emperor, 'are coming in throngs to witness the destruction of the opium. They are, of course, only allowed to look on from outside the fence and are not permitted access to the actual place of destruction, for fear of pilfering. The foreigners passing by in boats on their way up to Canton and down to Macao all get a distant view of the proceedings, but do not dare show any disrespect, and indeed I should judge from their attitudes that they have the decency to feel heartily ashamed.'[2]

[1] Oriental 7421.   [2] II. 155.

The entry for June 17th is: 'A fine day. Yesterday the American merchant King and others sent a note to Major Yang Ying-ko saying they had seen a proclamation announcing that orders had been received for the destruction of the opium on the spot and that foreigners were to be told that they might witness the destruction and obtain information about it. These people asked for permission to come and look, which I at once granted. This morning at the Hour of the Snake [9 a.m.] the foreigner King, with some ladies in his party, and also Bridgman, Captain Benson and others arrived in a small boat and were then brought in one of our war-junks to the Bogue. From a point above the destruction-tank they watched the melting of the opium, and then came to my pavilion, where they saluted me in the foreign way by touching their hats. One of my staff then conveyed to them suitable instructions and warnings, and after they had been given a present of things to eat, they retired. Today we melted 1,600 chests of "Company" opium. At the Hour of the Cock [5 p.m.] Teng, the Governor-General, and the Manchu Commander I-hsiang both arrived, and when night came we all dined together in my pavilion, the party breaking up at the Second Watch [9 p.m.].'

C. W. King (c. 1809–45) was a partner in the American firm of Olyphant and Co., which had scrupulously avoided all dealing in opium. He had already had some correspondence with Lin, claiming preferential treatment on the ground that he had never dealt in opium. But Lin pointed out (March 26th) that if the merchants (as King said) were all agreed on the necessity of surrendering the opium, everything would soon be normal again, and there would be no need to make special concessions to King about the restoration of his compradors, etc. Elijah Bridgman (1801–61) was the first American missionary to China. Along with another American, Wells Williams, he edited an excellent magazine, the *Chinese Repository*, to which we owe much of our knowledge of the period, at any rate as seen from the Western angle. Writing to the Emperor on July 5th Lin says:[1] 'I said to them through my interpreter "Now that the Heavenly Court has banned opium and that new regulations of a very severe kind have been agreed upon, you people who have not sold opium in the past and who will no doubt never think of bringing it in the future, must do more than that. You must persuade the foreigners of every country to devote themselves from now onward to legitimate trade, by which they can make immense profits, and not seek to enrich themselves in defiance of the ban, and so wantonly cast themselves into the meshes of the law." The foreigners listened attentively and respectfully, with heads bowed in sincere obedience. Their attitude certainly suggested whole-hearted acceptance of your Rule.'

The English account[2] of the interview says that 'Lin was bland and vivacious, without a trace of the fanatic's sternness with which he was credited. He looked young for his age, was short, rather stout, with a smooth full round face, a slender black beard and a keen dark eye. . . . Once he laughed outright when Mr King, on being asked which of the Chinese guild-merchants was the most honest, found himself unable to name one.'

Next day Lin received distressing news about a friend, Chung Hsiang, the Governor-General of Chekiang and Fuhkien, who during a tour of inspection had at Amoy on May 18th lost his seal of office. A thief had broken into his temporary headquarters and made off with it. Strictly speaking it ought never to have left his person, and his negligence was considered a grave matter. He lost his job, and when again employed was given a post of much less importance. His departure from Fuhkien deprived Lin of a great convenience, for it was Chung Hsiang who, through his special couriers, had enabled Lin to receive letters from his family in Fuhkien at high speed.

On June 10th Elliot complained that there were thirty or

[1] II. 160.   [2] *Canton Press*, July 20, 1839.

forty Chinese war-junks stationed near Kowloon Point.[1] This was making it difficult for the foreign ships to purchase supplies, and he feared that hunger might lead their crews to take some rash step. Lin replied that he was at a loss to understand why the presence of Chinese junks should make it difficult to obtain supplies. Neither he nor his colleagues had given any order that supplies were to be cut off. The foreign ships now anchored off Kowloon Point, whether they were ships that had surrendered opium or new-comers, or had been at Canton and were now on their way to the high seas, had no business to be loitering at the Kowloon anchorage, and by doing so inevitably invited the suspicion that they were there to dispose of opium. As a great concession he had now ordered the war-junks to anchor elsewhere for five days. During those five days the foreign ships must either put out to sea, or if they wanted to go up to Canton they must make their Customs declaration and proceed to Whampoa immediately. If they failed to obey, not only would the whole naval force of Canton be used against them but the coastal inhabitants, all of them sea-faring people, would rise up against them in a fury that it would be impossible to curb.

It was a weakness of Lin's methods that he more than once set time-limits of this kind and then allowed them to be ignored. Nearly two months later the foreign ships were still loitering off Kowloon Point; no vast Chinese flotilla had been mustered against them, nor was there the faintest sign of a popular rising.

June 23rd was the God of War's birthday and Lin, of course, went to his temple at dawn and burnt incense. On June 24th: 'In the afternoon the Governor-General brought wine and food to my lodging and I drank with him, the Admiral and the Intendant Wang Pao-shan. After lamps were lit we went to the archery-ground to watch practice with rockets, and then parted.' The bow was still the main Chinese weapon and the Chinese regarded our failure to make use of it as a sign of

[1] On the mainland, opposite Hongkong.

military backwardness. There was indeed one way in which the musket then in general use was inferior to the bow: it could not be used if it was raining. Percussion-guns, which could be fired in any weather, were only just coming in. It was also true, it may be mentioned incidentally, that in hand-to-hand fighting the Chinese spear, specially intended for the purpose, was far superior to that clumsy makeshift, the bayonet.

On June 27th there was another report about examinations at Peking. The subject for the poem was a line from the second of Li Po's two poems on 'Drinking alone on a spring day': 'With a zither across my knees I lean against a tall pine'; the rhyme to be *huai*, 'to cherish', because this word occurs three lines earlier in the poem. The results of an examination which touched him more closely arrived on July 2nd. His second son, Lin Tsung-i, born in 1824, had been placed tenth in the entrance examination to the Prefectural College at Foochow, the capital of Fuhkien. Numerous Canton officials called to congratulate him on the boy's success. On July 4th we find him still in the scholastic world: fifteen candidates in the Provincial Examinations called to present themselves to him, including Chang Hsiang-chin, a son of his friend Chang Wei-p'ing (1780–1859), the most famous of local poets.

On July 6th arrived at last a copy of the long-awaited Thirty-nine Regulations about opium offences, approved on June 15th. They were extremely complicated, dealing as they did with every conceivable kind of offence (import, wholesale dealing, retailing, smoking opium, inciting others to smoke and so on) and the printed text occupies twenty-two pages. Not only the actual culprits, but also the officials under whose jurisdiction the offence took place, were held responsible and, if proved to have been negligent, were punished by loss of rank or diminution of salary. Death was the punishment for all the major forms of offence (importing opium, wholesale and retail dealing, keeping an opium den, smoking). But in the case of smokers the death penalty did not come into force until eighteen months after the day on which the regulations reached any given district. Different classes of society were to be tried in different courts. Imperial clansmen, for example, had their own court, and Palace eunuchs were to be tried by a special Palace Court. The regulations, however, were concerned with rewards for those who assisted the Law as well as penalties for those who broke it. At least five pages are taken up by lists of elaborately graded recognitions and bounties, arrest leading to conviction and strangulation being discriminated from arrest leading to conviction and decapitation, the 'severer' of the two death penalties.

The drafting was not free from inconsistencies, ambiguities and omissions, and revised versions were issued from time to time.

The regulations arrived promptly at large places, such as Canton. But they took some time reaching smaller towns, and when they arrived were found to be incomprehensible there. They reached T'ai-ho in Kiangsu on August 13th. The Prefect, Chou Chi-hua, complained[1] to his superior that the regulations, though they went with such praiseworthy minuteness into every detail, were absolutely unintelligible to the common people, 'who with difficulty read them to the end'. He asks for permission to print a simplified version omitting, for example, what was to be the fate of incriminated Palace eunuchs, Imperial clansmen and other classes of people unknown at unsophisticated T'ai-ho. Lin and his colleagues published a manifesto in seventeen clauses, omitting all mention of rewards and simply giving a summary of the main offences and punishments.

On July 7th Lin went with the Governor-General to supervise the demolition of a number of terraces by means of which, it was suspected, Chinese were obtaining access to the foreign factories and the inhabitants of the factories

[1] l. 590.

access to the guild-merchants' quarters and the world outside. Next day he held a consultation with the Governor-General and Governor about the shops in the vicinity of the foreign factories, suspected (as we have seen) of being in many cases receiving-houses for opium, opium dens and so on. The entry for July 12th is: 'Sudden changes from fine to rain. Wrote a poem using the same rhymes as the Governor-General in a poem of his. Heard that at Kowloon Point sailors from a foreign ship beat up some Chinese peasants and killed one of them. Sent a deputy to make inquiries.'

This was the murder of Lin Wei-hsi, which did so much to embitter Chinese–English relations in the coming months. It seems that a party of English and American sailors landed on July 7th, got drunk and started a quarrel with some local peasants, one of whom died from his wounds on the following day. Lin again and again demanded that the murderer should be handed over; Elliot as often insisted that it had proved impossible to discover which of the sailors had dealt the blow. But of course the wider question of extraterritoriality was also involved. Until 1842 no Convention existed by which the English had the right to try their own delinquents according to their own laws, and Elliot was not empowered to make such a claim. To Lin it seemed self-evident that the failure of the English to hand over the culprit was simply a disguised attempt to assert extraterritoriality in direct defiance of the Manchu Penal Code. But he was not for the moment unduly perturbed; the entry for July 14th is: 'A fine day; wrote couplets on fans.' On the 18th and 19th he superintended the destruction of opium and opium pipes surrendered by Chinese, and on the second of these days received from the Board of Punishments a notification that a definition had been made, by which importers of opium from abroad, like wholesale dealers in China, were to be subject to the death penalty. This cleared up all remaining doubt as to whether the new regulations applied to foreigners as well as to Chinese. The 22nd to the 24th of July were spent in investigating the cases of Chinese opium offenders, including that of the 'cashiered Captain Wang Chen-kao' (see above, p. 18), whose dossier Lin had brought with him from Peking and whose case had now been lingering on for six months.

On July 28th he held an examination, as high officials arriving in a new place were entitled to do, of the students of all three Academies at Canton. Six hundred and forty-five young men answered the roll-call at what we should consider the uncomfortable hour of 5 a.m. Each Academy had its own essay-subject and theme for a poem. In the afternoon Tai Hsi (1801–60), the local Commissioner for Education, turned up, and Lin had a long chat with him. Anyone who has studied Chinese painting will have come across his name; he is in fact better known as a painter than as an educationalist. He was now about to hold the preliminary tests qualifying students to go in for the Provincial Examinations. Next day Lin returned Tai Hsi's visit, but was soon immersed again in trials of native opium offenders. On July 31st there were torrential rains. 'The water in the market-place was up to a man's waist', Lin says, 'and the square tank at my place overflowed.' Then follows a list of the newly appointed examiners for the Provincial Examinations in Yünnan, Kweichow, Fuhkien, Kwangtung and Kwangsi.

The report[1] of the Medical Missionary Society for 1839 lists among the cases it had handled: 'Case 6565. Lin Tse-hsü, the Imperial Commissioner.' It appears that during July Lin applied to Dr Parker, an American oculist and general practitioner,[2] for a translation of the Swiss jurist Emeric de Vattel's *Law of Nations* and a prescription for the care of opium addicts. A little later he asked, through an intermediary, for a medicine to cure him of hernia. He would

---

[1] *Chinese Repository*, VIII. 624.

[2] From 1854 to 1857 American Commissioner to China; born 1804, died 1888.

not come to Dr Parker or allow the doctor to visit him. It was explained to Lin that medicine would be of no use, and that he must wear a truss. 'The truss sent answers tolerably well', writes Dr Parker in his notes. There is no allusion to all this in Lin's diary.

Vattel's book on international law, published in 1758 and partly founded on the even earlier Latin work of Christian de Wolff, a disciple of Leibnitz, was completely out of date; but H. Wheaton's *Elements of International Law* (1836) was unlikely to have reached Canton. No doubt what Commissioner Lin wanted to find out was how he stood in the matter of Lin Wei-hsi, the Chinese villager killed by a foreign sailor on June 27th, and also whether in general it was the European practice for foreigners to submit to the laws of the country in which they resided. On the latter question Vattel gives the clearest possible ruling: 'Les étrangers qui tombent en faute doivent être punis suivant les lois du pays.'[1] On the other hand, Lin's demand that the English should fix on somebody and hand him over as the murderer was certainly not justified by any passage in Vattel or any other legal authority.[2]

On August 1st, 2nd and 3rd he was busy[3] writing a series of communications to the Emperor. The first accompanied the draft of his new version of the letter to Queen Victoria. It was to a large extent rephrased and also brought up to date by references to the handing over and destruction of the opium. The threatening clause about the lives of the foreigners being in the Emperor's hands is slightly toned down, becoming 'Our Heavenly Court has inscrutable divine and awe-inspiring majesty'. Some of Lin's newly

---

[1] Vol. I, p. 185 of the 1775 Amsterdam edition.

[2] In a proclamation that exists only in English (*Chinese Repository*, VIII. 214) Lin refers to the possibility that the dead man's ghost may take revenge, unless appeased by a victim. According to Earl Swisher (*China's Management of the American Barbarians*, p. 821), parts of *The Law of Nations* were translated by Parker and sent to Lin.

[3] II. 168.

acquired knowledge about foreign parts is utilized; he refers to the Queen as ruling over 'London, Scotland, Ireland and other places'. As I have said above (p.28), this second version, perhaps because less abstract and general than the first, is less impressive. In his covering note, Lin reminds the Emperor that when he saw him at the end of 1838 he had mentioned a project for publishing an appeal to foreigners with regard to the opium trade. When he reached Canton he was to talk it over with the Governor-General and submit a draft for the Emperor's revision. Subsequently the Emperor agreed that it would be better to deal first with what could be handled on the spot, that is to say the surrender and destruction of the opium, and defer the appeal to foreign rulers till the new regulations about opium offences had been published. Considering the question of how the appeal was to be sent, Lin notes that the Portuguese at Macao were near at hand, and a communication to them presented no difficulty. The Americans, however, were a more difficult problem. They had no national ruler, but only twenty-four local headmen, and it would be too great an undertaking to get into communication with all of them. By far the most important body of traders were the English. 'They are ruled at present', says Lin, 'by a young girl. But I am told that it is she who issues commands, and on the whole it seems that it would be best to start by sending instructions to her.' The French, Dutch, Spaniards, Filipinos, Austrians, Germans, Danes and Swedes, he says, come in such small numbers as to be relatively unimportant. After the appeal to the English ruler has been approved at Court and dispatched, the administrators and merchants of the other foreign countries can be approached, and if they express the desire for a similar communication to be sent to their rulers, it can be drawn up and submitted to the Emperor for approval.

In a second communication to the Emperor, also sent on August 3rd, Lin points out a defect in the drafting of the new regulation about the application of the opium laws to foreigners. The expression 'if they enter the Mouth' (i.e. the Bogue) was used. But as Lin points out, the smugglers disposed of their opium at Lintin or other places in the open estuary, long before reaching the Bogue. For 'enter the Mouth' he proposed to substitute the words 'come to inner territory', i.e. enter Chinese domains.

The third communication, sent jointly in Lin's name and that of the Admiral, concerned corruption in the naval patrol forces at Canton. Lin says that to enforce the laws against opium-dealing and the export of silver at Canton, it had proved necessary, owing to the ramifications of the estuary and its many islands, to establish a service of naval patrols. On board these ships there had to be not only officers, sergeants and so on, but also hired detectives. Among such people the most scrupulous and law-abiding were not always the best at arresting criminals, nor was ingenuity in tracking down crime any guarantee of honesty. Nowhere was the difficulty of handling such agents more acute than at Canton, and of all types of offence at Canton, none was more ticklish to deal with than those connected with the opium traffic. One had to resign oneself to the fact that the agents used in the suppression of the trade could themselves never for an instant be regarded as above suspicion. A case in point was the former naval officer Wang Chen-kao (see above, pp. 18 and 56) against whom, despite his energy and success in patrol work, complaints were made that he had set up an opium store.

In 1838 the junior officers in charge of patrol were dismissed and the whole business put in the hands of the headquarters of the local military and civil districts. The cases of Wang Chen-kao and a number of others were reviewed, but no solid evidence against them was forthcoming. Lin himself, after the destruction of the foreign opium, at last had leisure to apply himself to this question; but though he found that both the patrol officers and the detectives had a very bad reputation, it was impossible to procure satisfactory evidence against them. However, at the trial of the helmsman Feng A-jun and others it came out that it had been their habit, when conveying seized opium, to stick to what they described as 'any odd bits and pieces', and distribute them among the other patrol-boats. Moreover, if in any secluded creek they found a ship selling opium, they let the offenders escape in return for a bribe paid in foreign silver. Wang Chen-kao and his associates were then examined again. This time, although there was in their deposition a great deal of quibbling and prevarication, they did not attempt to deny all complicity in these transactions.

The importance of this document will become apparent shortly, when we come to that hitherto mysterious episode, the Battle of Kowloon.

In the diary during the first half of August there is very little echo of Lin's struggle with the foreigners. On the 6th he looked over the papers sent in by the Academy students, on the 9th he attended a little ceremony at the Meeting Hall of Fuhkienese resident at Canton and put up in front of the image of the Queen of Heaven an inscribed board on which was written 'He tamed the treasure-boats from far away', presumably an allusion to Lin's feat in securing the surrender of the opium, and at the same time an acknowledgement of the Queen of Heaven's assistance. On August 10th, he summoned to a re-test sixty students, twenty from each Academy, of whom all but four presented themselves. The subject of the poem they had to write was 'For one evening the miasmic mists by the wind have been rolled away'. The rhyme had to be 'Han' in view of the fact that the subject was a line from a poem addressed[1] to the great writer Han Yü when he was exiled to a malarial district in the south. On the 13th he witnessed the destruction of 20,000 catties of opium in a magnificent new tank specially designed for the purpose. They were from Ch'ao-chou, two hundred miles north-east of Canton. After nightfall he read the essays and

[1] By Chia Tao. *Complete T'ang Poems*, XXI. 86.

poems of the fifty-six Academy students. On the fourteenth he published the results of the examination. The first place should, by merit, have gone to a boy of sixteen, called Feng Yü-chi. But he had come only to the revise-test and not to the original examination, and was placed second.

It was a busy day, as Lin had arranged to set out with the Governor-General on August 15th to pay the long-promised visit to the island of Hsiang-shan and to Macao, which lies on a peninsula of that island. Western writers have tended to regard this visit to Macao as the result of a sudden outburst of rage against the English. Nothing could be further from the truth. Lin's original instructions were that he was to visit the various ports in the Canton region. On April 24th he had received a special reminder[1] that he was to 'go in person to the Bogue, Macao and other places, and estimate what measures the situation demanded'. The afternoon of August 14th was spent in paying farewell visits. Next day he started off for Hsiang-shan with the Governor-General, having first sent off a letter to his family at Foochow through the agency of his fellow-townsman Ts'ai Chin-hsi the glass-dealer 'who keeps a curiosity and Canton goods shop at the entrance to Lang-kuan Lane, at Foochow'. They reached the town of Hsiang-shan next afternoon and Lin lodged at the local Academy. On August 17th he replied at length to a note in which Elliot said that 'in obedience to the clear instructions of his Sovereign' he was unable to hand over any offender to Chinese justice, but that if he succeeded in finding out who killed Lin Wei-hsi, the murderer would be duly executed. Lin took this to mean that after the demand for the surrender of the murderer, Elliot had written to England asking for instructions and had already received a reply. 'Your Sovereign', Lin retorted, 'is myriads of leagues away. How can you in this space of time possibly have received instructions not to hand over the culprit? . . . If the principle that a life is not to be paid for with a life is once admitted,

[1] II. 91.

what is it going to lead to? If an Englishman kills an Englishman or if some other national, say a Chinese, does so, am I to believe that Elliot would not demand a life to pay for a life? If Elliot really maintains that, after going twice to the scene of the murder and spending day after day investigating the crime, he still does not know who committed it, then all I can say is, a wooden dummy would have done better, and it is absurd for him to go on calling himself an official.' Lin warns him that if he fails to hand over the culprit, Elliot himself will be held responsible for the murder.

Lin's contention that any blockhead could long ago have discovered who struck the fatal blow seems to me utterly unreasonable. The only weapons that had been used were sticks. The victim, as I have said above, did not die till next day. At the inquest held by the Chinese local authorities he was found to bear the mark of a heavy blow with a stick across the chest.[1] Many blows had been struck, and it was clearly impossible to ascertain which of the seamen concerned had struck the blow that proved fatal. And actually, in default of expert medical evidence, it was by no means certain that the blow was the cause or at any rate the sole cause of death. A healthy man would not normally die of a blow with a stick across his chest.

Lin in his note to Elliot also mentions that in order to bring him to his senses he has been obliged to give orders that the English at Macao are to be cut off from all supplies. There was, as he subsequently pointed out to the Emperor, a precedent for this: the same thing had been done when in 1808 Admiral Drury attempted to seize Macao, on the pretext that the French were intending to do so.

I want to say something more here about the general question of extraterritoriality, and the extent to which the English demand for it was justified. We are apt to look at the matter from the angle of the later nineteenth century, when English law was certainly far less harsh than Chinese

[1] II. 177.

and English prisons were infinitely superior. But it is doubtful whether in 1839 Chinese prisons, insanitary and in every way abominable though they were, compared very unfavourably with English prisons. As regards harshness of the law and wide application of the death penalty it must be remembered that according to English criminal law of the period a man could still be executed for stealing any sum over a shilling.[1] One very bad feature of Chinese trials had, however, no parallel in Victorian England. I refer to the use, fully sanctioned by the Manchu dynasty Code, of torture in order to produce confessions and evidence by witnesses. If those who use torture to obtain evidence really believe or have ever believed in the past that it can yield valid information, this is surely one of the strangest aberrations of the human spirit! But in China, and no doubt elsewhere, confessions of guilt, produced by whatever means, served a subsidiary, propaganda purpose: they suggested to the masses that the magistrate concerned had not acted arbitrarily or harshly. For who was he to contradict the accused man's assertions about his own crime?

On August 21st Lin notes that some ten English families have in the last few days left Macao and taken refuge on board ship. Cut off, in theory at any rate, from supplies, notified by the Portuguese that they could no longer be harboured, and uncertain about the intentions of Lin and the Governor-General, who had brought several hundred soldiers with them, the English clearly had no choice but to leave Macao. Whether, once on board ship, they would be able to obtain supplies and hold out till the crisis had blown over, or would have to withdraw to Manila, 640 miles away, remained to be seen.

On August 22nd Lin complained in a note to Elliot that his repeated demands for the surrender of Lin Wei-hsi's murderer had been ignored and that finally a representative sent on August 17th to impress upon Elliot the urgency of

[1] Cf. G. W. Keeton, *The Development of Extraterritoriality in China*, p. 118.

the matter had been grossly insulted. Lin then insists once more on the principle that 'a life must be paid for with a life', irrespective of whether the murderer is a Chinese or a foreigner. If a culprit could be shielded as Elliot was shielding the murderer of Lin Wei-hsi, murder would become rampant. Lin then turns to the opium question. Contrary to Elliot's repeated protestations, the opium trade was again in full swing. In recent trials of Chinese one defendant after another had confessed to having recently bought opium from foreign ships, and Chinese patrols had reported having sighted foreign ships off Ch'ao-chou, Namoa, Lien-chou, Lei-chou and the island of Hainan—all places where they had no right to be—and had found notices stuck up giving the price in foreign silver at which opium could be purchased. When pursued by Chinese patrol-boats, the foreign ships had opened fire. Chinese agents sent to arrest Chinese who were in league with the foreigners had been seized, held on board foreign ships and forced to release their prisoners. This, says Lin, is a final warning that if the murderer of Lin Wei-hsi is not immediately handed over and the newly-arrived opium all surrendered, Elliot will find the whole might of the Dynasty arrayed against him.

On August 25th Lin presided at Hsiang-shan over the trial of a certain Huang Mien-sheng, accused of selling provisions to foreigners at Macao. On the 27th, after an early luncheon, he inspected the battery of guns at Hsiang-shan that fired explosive shells. On returning to his lodging he learnt that since the order making it illegal to supply the foreigners at Macao with provisions, the evacuation had been going on steadily. Fifty-seven families had already retired to the merchant-ships, and it was expected that by the end of the day there would be no more English left at Macao.

Once more, just as six months before when the season's opium was surrendered, Lin felt that he had definitely got the upper hand. 'No doubt', he reported[1] a few days later

[1] II. 178.

to the Emperor, 'they have on their ships a certain stock of dried provisions, but they will very soon find themselves without the heavy, greasy meat dishes for which they have such a passion. Moreover the mere fact that they will be prevented from going ashore and getting fresh water is enough by itself to give power of life and death over them.' But on the same day as he wrote this, unknown to Lin, the situation suddenly turned once more in the smugglers' favour. In answer to an appeal by Elliot to Lord Auckland, the Governor-General of India, the twenty-eight-gun frigate H.M.S. *Volage*, commanded by Captain H. Smith, arrived off Kowloon point, bringing the news that a second frigate, the *Hyacinth*, would follow in a week or two. The Chinese naval forces had nothing that they could put up against ships of this kind, and were now entirely at the smugglers' mercy.

I have spoken sometimes of the Chinese Navy. But there was, in fact, at this period no such thing. There were merely a series of local navies acting under the orders of the local Governor-General. Nor was there any such thing as an Admiralty. There was indeed a Board of War, but its chief function at this time was to control the military examinations by which officers entered the service, and to deal in general with matters of personnel—promotions, degradations and so on; military operations being in the hands of the Supreme Council. The position of President of the Board of War was usually given as a decorative sinecure to supposedly deserving elderly officials. Our own War Office has sometimes been accused of a tendency to evolve in a somewhat similar direction, but the process has certainly not gone anything like so far as in China.

On September 1st Lin at last found himself able to answer a communication from Peking received on July 10th. As his reply sheds an interesting light on current Chinese beliefs about foreigners and on Lin's failure (afterwards to some extent rectified) to obtain, even after six months at Canton, anything but the most fanciful notions about them, I shall try to summarize the chief points in his very long communication.[1]

Was it true, the Emperor asked, that foreigners coming on ships were in the habit of buying Chinese children, mostly girls, and in some cases as many as a thousand or more at a time? If this was happening, it must mean that these children were to be killed and their corpses used for purposes of black magic. It certainly did not merely mean that the countries in question were short of inhabitants. Lin replied that since coming to Canton he had sometimes heard a curious local expression 'buying little pigs', and had a feeling it was a secret term which really meant trafficking in human beings. In April when he was superintending the opium surrender, he saw on one of the foreign ships a couple of boys aged about ten, who did not look at all like English children. He sent one of his staff to make inquiries about them and learnt that though their hair was not curly and their features were pleasant, they had patterns tattooed on their arms, which is a foreign, not a Chinese custom. They spoke a little Cantonese, but seemed unwilling to talk. An interpreter then questioned them in foreign languages, and they stated that they were from India and were the children of sailors. 'But I could not help feeling', says Lin, 'that they had been carried off, somewhat as the wasp carries off the young of the caterpillar.' Later on he learnt that out-of-work Chinese, particularly in bad years, did sometimes take service with foreigners and were carried off by them to foreign parts to work for wages in mines and plantations. But they were free to return, if they wanted to, after three years. As for children, it is possible that one or two may have been bought as pages or the like; but certainly not in large numbers, nor to be used in black magic. In this connection, says Lin, the section on England in the *Hai-lu* ('Record of the Seas') is worth quoting: 'England is

[1] IV. 167.

several thousand leagues in circumference. It is so short of inhabitants that they rear all the children who are born. Even prostitutes who have children never destroy them.' The *Hai-lu*, I should explain, is a little book supposed to have been dictated by a sailor who, thirty and more years ago, had worked on European ships. It was printed at Canton in 1820. Other books, Lin continues, confirm that abroad the population is very sparse, so that a great value is set on every human being, and as it is also well known that they prize women even more than men, it is improbable that they would kill little girls for purposes of black magic. . . . It has been suggested that foreign opium is made by mixing poppy-juice with human flesh.[1] But I have ascertained, says Lin, that it is mixed with the corpses of crows. Now it is known that foreigners expose their dead and let the crows peck away the flesh. That is why the crows shown in pictures in foreign books are of such enormous size, sometimes being several feet high. Consequently they could certainly obtain sufficient flesh from crows, without having recourse to human flesh.

On September 2nd Lin set out for Macao, accompanied by Teng, the Governor-General, reaching Ch'ien-shan, just north of Macao, the same day. Here he received instructions, sent from Peking on August 12th, that he would be expected, as soon as the business at Canton was disposed of, to proceed to Nanking to take up his duties as Governor-General there and in particular to deal with the reorganization of grain-transport. There was a sad irony about this; for two days later the opium trouble, so far from being disposed of, flared up into an armed conflict that was to last for three years.

On September 3rd Lin entered Macao from the north and, at the barrier that separated Macao from the rest of Hsiang-shan island, he was met by the Portuguese Governor and a guard of a hundred soldiers 'dressed up in their foreign uniforms, who marched fully accoutred in front of my

[1] See above, p. 49.

carrying-chair', Lin says in his diary, 'playing foreign music'. At the temple of the God of War, situated on the outskirts, he burnt incense before the image of the god, and was presently joined by the Governor, with whom he conversed through an interpreter. He then gave presents all round. 'To the foreign officials', the diary says, 'I gave coloured silks, folding-fans, tea and sugar-candy; to the foreign soldiers, beer, mutton, wine, flour and four hundred pieces of silver from abroad. Then we entered the gate of S. Paulo and going south reached the Niang-ma Tower, where I burnt incense on front of the image of the Queen of Heaven, and sat down for a while. Starting off again we went the whole length of the Southern Ring Street [the Praya Grande?] from south to north, getting a general view of the foreign houses. The foreigners build their houses with one room on top of another, sometimes as many as three storeys. The carved doors and green lattices shine from afar like burnished gold. Today the men and women alike were all leaning out of the windows or thronging the side of the streets to see me pass. Unfortunately foreign clothes are no match for foreign houses. The bodies of the men are tightly encased from head to toe by short serge jackets and long close-fitting trousers, so that they look like actors playing the parts of foxes, hares and other such animals on the stage. Their hats are round and long, like those of yamen runners, and even at the height of summer are made of felt, velvet or other such heavy material, so that to catch their sweat they have to carry several kerchiefs inside their hats. When they meet a superior they salute him by raising their hats and withdrawing their hands into their sleeves.[1] Their hair is very curly, but they keep it short, not leaving more than an inch or two of curl. They have heavy beards, much of which they shave, leaving one curly tuft, which at first sight creates a surprising effect. Indeed, they do really look like devils; and when the people

---

[1] The withdrawing of hands into sleeves had presumably been picked up from the Chinese.

of these parts call them "devils" it is no mere empty term of abuse. They also have devil-slaves, called black devils, who come from the country of the Moors and are used by the foreigners to wait upon them. They are blacker than lacquer, and were this colour from the time of their birth. The foreign women part their hair in the middle, and sometimes even have two partings; they never pile their hair on the tops of their heads. Their dresses are cut low, exposing their chests, and they wear a double layer of skirt. Marriages are arranged by the young people themselves, not by their families, and people with the same surname are free to marry one another, which is indeed a barbarous custom.

'I left Macao at the Hour of the Snake [9 a.m.]. Next day [September 4th] was spent on board ship travelling along the western side of the estuary, in the direction of the Bogue.' By nightfall he was off Jung-ch'i Point, about thirty miles from Hsiang-shan. That day at Kowloon, about eighty miles to the south-east, the first battle of the Opium War was being fought. Lin probably did not hear about it till several days later, and it is not mentioned in the diary. As we shall see, he first mentions it in a report sent to the Emperor a fortnight later.

Contemporary accounts of the battle, of which we possess at least six, differ in small ways according to whether they are by supporters or detractors of Captain Elliot, or again are hostile to or admirative of Captain Douglas. They all agree, however, that Chinese warships stationed near Kowloon were preventing Chinese villagers from supplying the English ships with food. A number of small English boats with armed men on board were sent to protest to the Chinese Commander and try to obtain food. Eventually, when after repeated requests no promise of being allowed to buy provisions could be obtained, the English boats opened fire and several of the Chinese ships were driven ashore. The English suffered four casualties, but no English boat was sunk. One of the casualties was Captain Douglas, who was wounded in the arm. Henceforward there was no difficulty in obtaining provisions; but they were slightly more expensive, and this may perhaps give us a clue to what had really been happening. It is hard to suppose, in view of the notorious corruption of the Canton Navy at this period, that it interfered with the provisioning of the English ships merely out of a patriotic desire to frustrate the enemy. I cannot help thinking that when, on August 31st, an order appeared forbidding the peasants to sell food to the English, the Chinese patrol-boats tried to 'squeeze' out of the peasants, in return for turning a blind eye upon their trading activities, a larger bribe than they were prepared to pay; in consequence of which the English for a time got no supplies. After the battle, however (if my theory is correct), the patrol ships were disinclined to risk another encounter with the English and were willing to accept from the peasants a much smaller 'squeeze', with the result that food was now available at only a slightly increased price.

Lin did not tell the Emperor about the battle till September 18th, but it will be convenient to discuss what he said here, rather than adhere woodenly to chronology. On the evening of September 18th, then, he sent a long report on the situation at Canton, together with a dispatch about the Battle of Kowloon, by the local commander Lieut.-Colonel Lai En-chio. This dispatch contains hardly a word of truth either as to how the hostilities started or in regard to the action itself. According to Lai, his representative was just about to deliver a reply to the English request for food 'when, without any warning, the foreigners opened fire'. He claimed that, in the action which followed, a two-masted English ship was sunk and casualties inflicted which, if one adds up the various mentions of them, would certainly amount to at least forty or fifty. Lin himself refers in his report to the Chinese having 'obtained a victory over superior forces'.

Lin was regarded by both the Chinese and the English as

a man of unusual integrity, and it seems at first sight surprising to find him not merely transmitting but even himself
endorsing a military report so flagrantly mendacious. In
order to understand how this was possible, it is necessary
to know something about the whole system of reports to
the Throne on military engagements. Any action, whether
successful or unsuccessful, was immediately followed by a
wild scramble to get mentioned in the official report on the
battle as suitable for decoration, promotion, or other
awards. The claims were usually based on alleged casualties
inflicted on the enemy, and as the authorities at Peking had
no way of checking up on enemy losses, the figures given
were determined by what officers thought would entitle them
to the reward they had in mind. Naval warfare lent itself
particularly well to fictitious claims of this kind. No officer
who claimed to have sunk a foreign ship was expected to
give its name or identify it in any way, except perhaps by
mentioning how many masts it had. Occasionally the farce
was enacted of sending to Peking as 'evidence' a few spars
or pieces of rigging; but it must have been obvious to everyone concerned that these proved nothing.

It was not usual for the high official on the spot, who
forwarded military dispatches to Peking, to investigate the
claims contained in them, unless these claims were contested
by some other high official and an inquiry demanded.
Indeed any Governor-General or Governor who on his
own initiative threw doubt upon such claims was likely to
find himself becoming very unpopular, and to be accused of
deliberately damping the loyalty and enthusiasm of the armed
forces. If a protest against a false claim to victory was lodged
at all, it was generally months after the event, by a censor
who had no first-hand knowledge of the battle, and who
produced as 'the true facts' counter-rumours that were even
wilder than the dispatches he was criticizing.[1]

[1] Compare the Censor Lo Ping-chang's criticisms, made August 1841, of
the recommendations for promotion, etc., made on behalf of officers and

Lieut.-Colonel Lai En-chio, it may be mentioned, went on concocting false reports with impunity till the end of the war, and early in 1843 succeeded to the post formerly held by Admiral Kuan, having been recommended as 'the most outstanding and trustworthy of our naval commanders', greatly distinguished by his services against the English in the autumn and winter of 1840.

One result of this long-established system of false claims, both military and otherwise, was the destruction of any real confidence between the Emperor and his high provincial officers. We have already seen (p. 45 above) that Lin found it advisable to offer to send to Peking the opium confiscated from the English, and that this offer was at first accepted, the Emperor evidently not regarding it as entirely out of the question that even Lin, his most trusted Minister at that period, was deceiving him and had in fact either not secured the surrender of the opium at all, or had disposed of it to his own profit.

To what extent Lin himself was aware that the reports he sent on this and subsequent battles were largely fictitious, it is hard to say. They were apparently believed by the Chinese Government both at the time and long afterwards, and it is worth noting that when his conduct of affairs at Canton was being investigated in December 1840, the sponsoring of false military reports was not one of the charges brought against him.[1]

The same, however, is not true of the reports sent by his successors. By the summer of 1841 the Emperor had become convinced that for a long time past the authorities at Canton had been systematically deceiving him, and on July 30th of that year he ordered[2] Liang Chang-chü (1775–1849), who

troops who had in May of that year surrendered the forts behind Canton without firing a shot (III. 498).

[1] It was in the margin of his report on the Battle of Kowloon that the Emperor wrote his often-quoted comment: 'You and your colleagues will never get into trouble with me for taking too high-handed a line. My only fear is lest you should show weakness and hesitation.'   [2] I. 417.

was Governor of Kwangsi from 1836 to 1841, to give him a clear and detailed account of what had been happening at Canton. Kwangsi, the Emperor pointed out, was a neighbouring province and Liang must have received independent accounts. He warned Liang that he was making secret inquiries 'in other places', and would be able to check up on Liang's information.[1]

But we must return to Lin's voyage back from Macao. Soon after midnight on September 5th he arrived at the village of Hu-men, on the east side of the entrance to the Bogue. On the 10th he received the *Peking Gazette* and learnt from it of a general shuffle of high officials, caused partly by the sacking of Chung Hsiang, the Governor-General whose seal of office had been stolen. He read, too, that in the recent test of censors, the subject of the essay had been 'How best to give full effect to the recently promulgated opium regulations'. On September 13th he notes that as he is likely to have to stay at Hu-men, the seat of Admiral Kuan's headquarters, for some time, he has brought all the people at his residence in the Academy at Canton to join him there. 'Today', he adds, 'the naval units at the Bogue held their manœuvres. It was a grand sight, really rivalling, in a remote way, the review during the banquet of examiners at the Provincial Examinations.'

Elliot had returned to Macao on September 15th, and on the 16th he announced, through the Chinese Prefect of Macao, that his only desire was for peace and amity, and that he wished to discuss with the Chinese authorities how outstanding differences could best be settled. His return to Macao seems to have been due to a hope that the Portuguese Governor might be persuaded to act as mediator. About September 18th the second frigate, the *Hyacinth*, joined the

---

[1] After the signing of the Peace Treaty in 1842 the Emperor's sources of information widened. It was owing to information received from Sir Henry Pottinger that Lin's friend Yao Ying was imprisoned for seven months, on a charge of having claimed mythical successes on the coast of Formosa.

Volage, and to Captain Douglas's consternation Elliot informed him that 'having now two of Her Majesty's ships on the Station, he did not require the further services of the *Cambridge*'. Instead of the £14,000 for eight months' hire, as originally promised, Elliot now proposed giving him £2,100. As the *Cambridge* had been used to protect the merchant fleet for nearly two and a half months, something more like £3,600 would have been the proper proportion of the sum originally named. Captain Douglas, however, accepted on the understanding that Elliot would 'urge the Government to make good the whole payment for the contract of the *Cambridge*'.

On September 22nd Lin writes: 'This afternoon the Governor-General called and we went by boat together to Shakok[1] and then on board the Admiral's boat looked over the lists of the "braves" newly recruited by each warship. Over eighty ships, including fire-boats, were drawn up in two lines. We then invited the Admiral and General Huang to picnic with us at the Shakok battery, to which we took wine and things to eat. After the moon rose we climbed to the mirador on top of the Shakok Hill and spent some time there enjoying the moonlight. After that the Governor-General and I went home, taking advantage of the tide.' It was the full moon of the Chinese eighth month, the great time for going to a high place, looking at the moon and writing poems. In Lin's very long and very allusive poem[2] he boasts that 'A vast display of Imperial might has shaken all the foreign tribes, and if they now confess their guilt we shall not be too hard upon them. . . . This year, on this night, we have managed to dissipate our sorrows. But next year on this night shall we be together or not? This poem remains in preparation for thoughts after parting; for as soon as the present business is settled, I shall return to my native fields.' 'Tonight', the entry ends, 'I saw Elliot's

---

[1] On the eastern side of the entry to the Bogue.
[2] II. 548.

reply to my letter sent through the Prefect of Macao.' In this letter Lin lays down three conditions for a settlement: (1) The murderer of Lin Wei-hsi must be surrendered; (2) The opium-receiving ships must all leave China at once, as must also the known opium dealers, whose names were on the black-list so often transmitted to Elliot; (3) Any ship found still loitering will suffer the fate of the *Virginia*.

It must here be explained that on September 12th a Chinese patrol ship had boarded the Spanish brig *Bilbaino*, anchored off Macao, under the mistaken impression that she was the English opium ship *Virginia*. For months on end Lin with typical obstinacy continued to maintain, despite overwhelming evidence to the contrary, that the *Bilbaino* was the *Virginia*, while at the same time, with typical acuteness, triumphantly detecting trivial inaccuracies, inconsistencies and illogicalities in the repeated protest of the Spanish consignee Goyena and the testimony of those who supported him. For example, Goyena used the argument that 'as the *Virginia* still existed it could not have been she who was burnt'. 'If he knows that she exists, he must also know *where* she exists', comments Lin. 'Why does he not deign to tell us?'

Elliot became involved because, in common with the Dutch, Portuguese and Americans, he signed an affidavit that the ship burnt was the Spanish ship *Bilbaino*, and had no connection with the *Virginia*. This blunder of the Chinese gave him a useful controversial handle and we find him months later (January 3rd, 1840) still quoting it as a justification for firing at sight on any Chinese patrol ship.

In stating his third condition, Lin refers to the Battle of Kowloon. It was, he says, the English, not the Chinese, who fired the first shot. He hopes that the defeat they suffered has taught them a lesson. Since then Elliot had suggested that on the question of future trade some compromise might be reached. But he had also said that before allowing English ships to enter the Bogue he must wait for an answer to his letter asking for his Sovereign's instructions. Before any negotiation could be opened, Lin insisted, he must know the date when Elliot's letter left for England, the date when the answer was sent, and the length of time that must elapse before it reached China. If these three conditions were fulfilled there ought to be no difficulty in arranging for a resumption of legitimate trade.

In his reply, referred to in the diary, Elliot professes to be ready to end the opium trade entirely, as commanded by the Emperor. He adds that he wishes Lin would not call his notes to the English 'instructions'. This, however, was the name ordinarily given to letters addressed to inferiors and Elliot, virtually a consul, clearly *was* inferior to Lin whose rank was something like that of our Viceroy of India.[1]

On September 28th Elliot dealt more fully with the points raised by Lin. He offered to allow Chinese officials to search the ships; if any opium was found, the whole cargo, legitimate and illegitimate, would be surrendered. New ships on their arrival would sign a guarantee that they were not carrying opium and would not ever in future do so 'within the Inner Seas'. (This phrase was slipped in so that the smuggling might still be carried on from ships stationed in the 'outer seas', at a distance from the coast.) With regard to the murder, Elliot states that American sailors were also present. This complicates the inquiries, and the culprit has still not been identified. As regards notorious opium dealers—they will start for home as soon as there is a north wind. But there are two wrong names on the list; Sam Matheson is a boy in his early 'teens and Mr Henry has never dealt in opium. Finally, his letter to England, asking for instructions on various matters, was sent on May 29th, and an answer could not be expected until December. Before it came, he would be obliged to go on preventing English

---

[1] It must be said, in fairness to Elliot, that he had received instructions to take a firm line about these matters of etiquette.

ships from entering the Bogue.[1] In a postscript Elliot adds that he proposes to offer a reward of 2,000 dollars for information about the murderer.

There was such a spate of notes and replies at this time that it is impossible to deal with them all. Lin, also on September 28th, quotes the case of a Chinese, accused of opium dealing, who confessed on September 5th to having bought opium from one of the English ships. He insists on the original form of guarantee, making foreign opium offences subject to Chinese law.

Writing to the Emperor on October 6th Lin defends his policy of enforcing a guarantee. The Censor Pu Chi-t'ung (see above, p. 47) had argued that people so dishonest as the English would have no scruple about signing any guarantee demanded of them, and would then go on selling opium just as before. But it is evident, Lin points out, that on the contrary they take such pledges very seriously. Otherwise they would not be so reluctant to sign.

On October 10th he heard about the subjects set at the Provincial Examinations in his home-town, Foochow. One of the essay subjects was the saying of Mencius: 'The great man is one who in manhood still keeps the heart of a child.'

On October 11th he went to watch naval exercises at Shakok. The marines, drawn up in battle formation and standing in the water, 'went through the motions of slashing and striking. Then they hurled lances and shot arrows from the tops of the masts, showing great agility'. He got back at the Hour of the Monkey (3 p.m.). 'At night', he says, 'it rained, and this gave the fields where the late rice had in the last few days been coming into ear, an added freshness and sheen.'

The entry for October 13th is: 'A fine day. Looked through the documents used in compiling the *History of the Custom-house at Canton*.' This was a work edited by Liang T'ing-nan,

---

[1] The letter referred to (No. 150 of the Elliot–Palmerston Correspondence) contains no request for instructions about permitting ships to enter the Bogue.

the head of the Academy whose premises Lin had made use of in Canton. It gives the history of customs dues, general trade, tribute-ships, the Chinese guild-merchants, the foreign merchants, and so on, down to the end of 1838. Liang had handed over[1] these papers to Lin about eight months ago, and must certainly have been beginning to wonder whether the great man was ever going to find time to look at them.

On October 14th he received two equally gratifying, though very diverse, pieces of news: nine of the Academy students whom he had in his private examination put in the top class, had been successful in the Provincial Examinations, and an English captain, the first to do so, had, in defiance of Elliot's orders, asked to be allowed to sign the guarantee and go through the Bogue to Canton. The ship was the *Thomas Coutts*, belonging to the firm of Marjoribanks and commanded by Captain Warner. She had brought a cargo of cotton, rattan and pepper from Bombay. The natural inference, at once drawn by Lin, was that if one English ship found no difficulty in signing the guarantee, the others were merely hesitating because they were carrying or intended to carry less innocuous cargoes. Captain Warner, it is said, had taken legal advice and been told that Elliot had no right to prevent ships from signing the guarantee and entering the Bogue. He now became Lin's 'model foreigner', whose only fault was that he was unable to persuade the other ships to follow his example.

On October 20th Lin reminded Elliot that as a great concession he had agreed that even ships which had not signed the guarantee might be allowed to enter the Bogue if on their being searched, it was found they had no opium. Now, however, the situation has been changed by the fact that the *Thomas Coutts* has signed the guarantee and proceeded to Whampoa; 'with what frankness and correctness!' Lin exclaims. It is now clearer than ever that ships which will not sign the guarantee are afraid to do so because they are

[1] VI. 9.

still engaged in selling opium. As regards the murder, Elliot has already detained five men. If he cannot himself find out which of them committed the murder, he must hand over all five to the Chinese authorities for trial. If Elliot fails to do this, he himself will be arrested and put on trial.

It must here be observed that the five sailors had been tried before an English jury on August 12th and found guilty of riotous behaviour. The indictment for murder was rejected. Two of them were sentenced to three months' imprisonment and a fine of £15; the other three to six months' imprisonment and a fine of £20.

On October 22nd Lin writes: 'A constant succession of notes from Macao. I hear that the receiving ships of the bad foreigners have for some days past been leaving their anchorage, and will soon all be gone. But the merchant ships are still asking to be searched (instead of signing the guarantee) and I must think out what regulations I must make about this.' Later in the day, however, he seems to have changed his mind, for he wrote to Elliot threatening to arrest him if he continued to prevent the ships from signing the guarantee.

'It is strange to think', he writes on October 24th, 'that they must by now be wearing lined furs in the north! Here one sweats even in thin silks. What a difference of climate! But at the first puff of cool wind or shower of rain one is very apt to catch cold. Some people came in a boat from Canton inviting me to a conference with the two super-intendents of the Examinations. But I cannot possibly get away from here while all this business is on my hands, and I had to refuse.' On the same day he wrote to Elliot totally rejecting the idea of a search of the ships in lieu of a guarantee. He argues that to search a ship properly would take five days so that as there are now forty ships at Kowloon, the whole business would take two hundred days. Till the search was complete it would be impossible to allow the merchants' families to return to Macao, severe restrictions would continue to be put on their purchase of food, and there could be no question of giving them back their compradors and carpenters; whereas if they would only sign the guarantee, as the *Thomas Coutts* has done, all their usual privileges would at once be restored to them.

On October 25th the sole entry is: 'Fine weather. A great many official papers to deal with.' One of these was a report[1] to the Emperor about the case of a Canton bookseller who had printed a spurious 'Communication' to England about the making of opium, attributing it to Lin. There is no suggestion in the report that the forged 'Communication' contained anything outrageous or improbable. But according to the Code anyone forging communications alleged to have come from an official of the First and Second Ranks must receive a sentence of a hundred blows with the rod and three years' banishment. The bookseller had been found guilty and the sentence pronounced. But the man alleged that though he had three brothers, they had all been adopted into another branch of the family. (Consequently if the sentence of exile was carried out, there would be a lapse in the Ancestral Sacrifices.) This was being looked into. The document in question was probably a spurious version of Lin's letter to Queen Victoria. It seems, indeed, that a spurious version of some kind was still circulating at the beginning of the twentieth century; for Backhouse and Bland, in their *Annals and Memoirs of the Court of Peking* (1914) quote a passage that does not occur in either of the authentic versions.

Next day, October 26th, Lin hears that the Americans have bought one of the empty receiving ships, loaded it with cotton, signed the guarantee and sailed up to Canton. To members of his staff and the Prefect of Macao, who were conducting negotiations for him, Lin wrote: 'My deputies are in a hurry to wind up their mission and get home. The Prefect is in a hurry to get the ships their passes. The English are in a hurry to get back to Macao. But I, the

[1] IV. 170.

Commissioner, am in a hurry to get the full guarantee signed first. . . . The English continually say that they have complied with every request. But I ask, have they signed their guarantee, have they handed over the murderer, not to mention everything else?'

On October 27th Lin charged his representatives (Yü Pao-shun and the rest) with allowing the English to procrastinate and quibble about the guarantee. 'I am here', Lin says, 'as the representative of the Emperor, and if these foreigners are allowed to band themselves together[1] and resist His commands there will be nothing for it but to go to Peking and await punishment; my position here will be too humiliating to endure.' On the same day he repeats his objections to a search of the ships as an alternative to the guarantee, and explains that the English are, without his permission, beginning to return in considerable numbers to Macao. Chinese troops have been stationed at the Barrier, and any English who do not leave at once will be surrounded and arrested. He also complains of a fresh act of violence: on September 16th off the coast near Kuang-hai, about fifty miles south-west of Macao, some foreigners who arrived in four boats shot a Chinese and threw his corpse into the sea. They then boarded a Chinese boat, sword in hand, wounded three other Chinese and cut off the pigtails of seven others. Quite apart from these acts of violence—what were they doing at Kuang-hai, miles away from the only authorized route for foreign ships? He also quotes a case of opium selling off the north coast of Hainan Island, over two hundred miles away from Macao.[2] In his reply Elliot naturally pointed out that these cases had occurred at a distance from Canton, beyond the area which he controlled, and though he was horrified that such things should have happened there was nothing he could do about it.

---

[1] Alluding to a recent conference of the British merchants.

[2] A captured foreigner appears to have said he was acting on behalf of Captain Parr of the *Vixen*.

These cases are never alluded to again, and Lin may have found that he had been misinformed.

On October 28th Lin declared that he does not now believe and never did believe Elliot's story about this letter to England, asking for permission to let the ships enter the Bogue. Daniell, the consignee of the *Thomas Coutts's* cargo, who readily signed the guarantee and came up to Canton, must surely know better than Elliot what are the wishes of the English Government, seeing that he was once on the Select Committee of the East India Company, and has just come from England? The note ends with the menacing announcement that the Chinese naval and military forces have already been fully mobilized at Canton and will shortly be arriving at the mouth of the Bogue, where detailed plans would be made for a general assault. It was evident from this note that Lin now intended, unless 'the murderer of Lin Wei-hsi' was handed over immediately, to fulfil the threat to 'annihilate the English' that he had made in his note of September 28th.

On October 29th he heard that a second English ship, the *Royal Saxon*, had signed the guarantee. She had come from Java with a cargo of rice. Lin wrote to his representative at Macao: 'Make sure that the captain, the owner of the goods and his two principal partners have all signed, and be so good as to affix a careful translation. If everything is in order, make him stamp his seal on sealing-wax, as was done in the case of K'o-kuang's guarantee [I suppose K'o-kuang was one of the Americans who had signed—possibly Cogham or the like]. If he cannot write the Chinese translation for himself, do it for him. . . . His family, as a mark of special favour, are to be allowed to live in Macao. Only be sure that no other foreign families pass themselves off as belonging to him.'

In view of Lin's threat to annihilate the English, the *Volage* and *Hyacinth* beat slowly up the estuary against a heavy wind, arriving at Chuenpi, on the east side of the mouth of the Bogue, on November 2nd. Eight miles away a large force of Chinese war-junks and incendiary-boats could be clearly seen.

On the morning of November 3rd Lin conducted the trial of three Chinese, accused of abetting the foreigners in opium dealing, and applied for permission from Peking to carry out the death sentence. He also sent an optimistic report to the Emperor, claiming to have driven away all the opium-receiving ships and all the foreigners on the black-list. Even the difficult matter of getting the English to sign the guarantee seems, he says, nearer a solution, and two ships, the *Thomas Coutts* and the *Royal Saxon*, have already signed. 'Early in the afternoon I heard that at Lung-k'ung¹ an English warship sent a note to Admiral Kuan, which he did not accept. Whereupon the warship opened fire and attacked him. The Admiral returned the fire and destroyed the ship's fore and aft masts. Some Englishmen were hurled into the sea, and at this point the warship retreated.' Next day (November 4th) he writes, 'After my meal, I went to Shakok and had a talk with the Admiral. Then we both went and looked at the damage done by the enemy guns, discussed repairs and rewarded and consoled the wounded, each according to his deserts. Fishermen brought in four foreign hats that they had found afloat; also shoes and other objects, all of them belonging to English who had fallen into the sea and drifted about.'

The note referred to was one from Captain Smith of the *Volage* to Admiral Kuan, calling upon him to withdraw his forces. As Lin no doubt learnt from the Admiral himself, Captain Smith's note, after some initial delay, had been answered by the Admiral, who said he could not retire till a time had been named when the murderer of Lin Wei-hsi would be surrendered. It was evident to Captain Smith that this time the Admiral at last intended to carry out Lin's repeated threats, and make an all-out attack on the merchant ships, still crowded with refugees, for the protection of whom

¹ A mile or so from the Chuenpi battery.

Smith was responsible. It was at this point that (on November 3rd) he opened fire.

I shall not attempt to discuss in detail the discrepancies between the Chinese and English accounts of how much damage each side sustained in the encounter that followed, known to history as the Battle of Chuenpi. So dense a pall of smoke enveloped naval actions at this period that mistakes about damage inflicted on the enemy were easy to make. One point only need be stressed here: this was intended by Lin and the Admiral to be the battle of extermination with which Lin had threatened the English on September 18th. It cannot be doubted that the Admiral's plan was to board the English merchant ship that was supposed to be harbouring the murderer, seize an expiatory victim and then sink or burn this and all the other English merchant ships. Nothing of the kind was effected, and after sustaining considerable damage the Chinese fleet retired to the west side of the entrance to the Bogue.

Lin's report on the battle to the Emperor, not sent till November 21st, is at variance with the entry in his diary. On November 3rd he told the Emperor that the *Royal Saxon*, which had signed the guarantee, was making for the Bogue 'when two English warships, arriving at Chuenpi at midday, forced her to turn back. One was Captain Smith's ship (the *Volage*), which previously made trouble at Kowloon; the other was the more recently arrived ship commanded by Captain Warren (the *Hyacinth*). Admiral Kuan, being told of this and thinking it an odd procedure, was investigating the matter, when Smith opened fire on him.'

During the battle that followed, Lin continues, 'the Admiral stood erect before the mast, drew his sword, and grasping it in his hand directed operations, shouting in a loud and menacing voice that anyone who attempted to retreat would at once be beheaded. A fragment of enemy shell brushed the mast and ripped a splinter from it, which grazed the Admiral's arm. The skin was broken and the wound showed red; but the Admiral, heedless of his own safety, still stood sword in hand.' This account, derived perhaps from one of the Admiral's officers, reads like a passage from a contemporary heroic ballad or play rather than a piece of sober reporting, and it was no doubt written to distract attention from the fact that the largest naval force which could be handled as a unit had been repulsed by two English frigates. There is, however, no need to doubt that the Admiral behaved with exemplary courage. Elliot himself describes him as 'manifesting a resolution of behaviour honourably enhanced by the hopelessness of his efforts'.

On November 7th Lin writes: 'I hear that at Kuan-yung (south of Chuenpi) where the coastguards are stationed on the shore, bad foreigners who for several days past have been coming and spying, have now been driven away or captured. Some who were wounded fell down the cliff, but escaped, leaving their muskets behind. I also hear that fishing-boats at Lung-k'ung have again hooked out foreign hats from the water, making eleven, including those that were found before. Today from the Hour of the Monkey to that of the Boar [3–9 p.m.]. I personally examined and obtained confessions from (Chinese) opium offenders.'

On November 12th he writes, 'This afternoon the Governor-General came and we discussed what can be done about exterminating the lair at Kowloon [i.e. the English merchants]'. Lin probably still clung to the hope of being able to set the ships on fire.

November 14th: 'Fine. Rose early to go with the Governor-General to the Ching-yüan Battery at Heng-tang[1] to console the Admiral. He has lost his son and heir, Kuan Kuei-lung, who died on the eighth day of the eighth month at Wu-sung (fourteen miles north of Shanghai) where he was Brigadier. He had at the time of his death already been pro-

---

[1] The Wantung of English accounts. Here used as a general name for the middle Bogue. The forts here referred to were on Anunghoy Island, about ten miles north-west of Chuenpi.

moted to the post of Deputy Commander at Chinkiang. We found that the Admiral was living near the three recently constructed batteries—the Ching-yüan in the middle, the Wei-yüan on the left and the Chen-yüan on the right. They have, between them, about a hundred and twenty large cannon and certainly look very formidable. . . . In the evening I got a note from the Ta-p'eng camp, saying that on the night on the 6th [i.e. November 11th] we had a great victory at Kuan-yung [just south of Chuenpi].' On the 15th he loyally celebrated the Empress's birthday, and on the 16th heard of another great Chinese victory which had resulted in all the merchant ships leaving Kowloon Point and anchoring at various points to the south-west.

Actually, Captain Smith had ordered the ships to move to anchorages where he could more easily defend them. Eleven merchant captains were against the move, and there was some delay in carrying it out. The English accounts only record a certain amount of desultory firing in the days succeeding the battle of Chuenpi. Lin's diary records three Chinese victories (including the Chuenpi battle). The number was doubled in a communication from the Emperor dated December 13th,[1] and the Six Smashing Blows against the English warships still figure in Chinese history books.

On November 19th Lin received a communication from the Emperor dispatched on October 29th, a week before the Battle of Chuenpi, in which Lin was reminded that his real position was Governor-General of Kiangnan and Kiangsi, and it would not be possible to keep him indefinitely at Canton. On the other hand the routine affairs of Kwangtung and Kwangsi really represented a full-time job and, for the present, Governor-General Teng could not be expected, in addition, to deal single-handed with the opium business. He and Lin must make a joint effort to end the opium trade in a fundamental and lasting way and, as the saying went, 'by one supreme effort gain lasting repose'.

[1] II. 119.

On November 30th Captain Douglas sold the *Cambridge*, the ship which, as will be remembered, he had armed and hired out to Elliot at the time when the British were left entirely without defence. It was bought by the American firm Delano for £10,700. The guns and other equipment were, however, dismounted, sold to the British Government, and in the end duly paid for. Ten days later he left for England with his wife and two servants, paying £550 for the passage. He left, then, with a great deal of money, but also with a financial grievance; and after quickly running through the considerable sums he had received he spent the rest of his life dunning Elliot and the Government for more.[1] But the interest to us of the Douglas affair is that early next year Commissioner Lin bought the *Cambridge* from Delano, and she became the first foreign-built ship in the Chinese Navy. Her function seems, however, to have been chiefly that of a training ship and a model for Chinese shipbuilders.

On December 4th Lin wrote a report, on Governor-General Teng's behalf, on the lampoons (in the form of ballads) that had recently been circulating at Canton. In these he was accused of exploiting his zeal in arresting opium offenders in order to curry favour with the Court, of obtaining information through *agents provocateurs,* of conducting trials in a harsh and inhumane way and of accepting bribes. Worse still, they represented the whole opium-suppression policy as endangering the economy of the State, and the new code of punishment as an ill-considered setting aside of the standing dynastic Code. The Emperor replied that he had absolute confidence in Lin and Teng, and that they must not let popular outcry of this kind deter them from carrying out their task. The authors of the lampoons should be arrested and punished with the utmost severity.

The fact was that vast numbers of the Cantonese, quite apart from the opium dealers, made their living in ways

[1] My information about Douglas is taken chiefly from an anonymous pamphlet called *A Case of Individual Sacrifice and of National Ingratitude*, 1847.

connected with foreign trade, and they were hard hit by the stagnation of trade that the conflict caused by the new laws had now provoked. There was at this time much more indignation against the Government's opium policy than against the foreigners. It was not till May 1841, when English troops looted and raped in the villages north of Canton, that hatred of the English began.

On December 5th Lin writes: 'We have decided that from the first day of the eleventh month [December 6th] all English ships are to be debarred from trading at Canton. A proclamation to this effect was issued several days ago. From the fifth month till now fifty-six ships of various nationality have signed the guarantee and entered harbour; among them one English ship. Thirty-two English ships have refused to sign and have consequently not been allowed to come into harbour. One English ship (i.e. the *Royal Saxon*) signed, but was prevented by English warships from entering harbour.'

On December 11th, a new phase in the struggle having commenced, Lin left Hu-men village and returned to the Academy at Canton. On December 14th he reported to the Emperor that in accordance with his instructions he had put a stop to all English trade. In these instructions,[1] received on November 19th, the Emperor had said that if the English again went back on their promises, they were to be 'cut off from their rhubarb and tea'.

On December 16th he interviewed the survivors of the *Sunda*, an English ship that had been wrecked off the coast of Hainan island on October 12th. 'I went to the Governor-General's place early in the morning, where I found the Governor and the Head of Customs. We lunched together and afterwards went to the Temple of the Queen of Heaven, where the fifteen survivors of the wreck, including the foreigner Chia-li-ch'en [Carson?] were brought to me, and I talked with them face to face for more than two hours. I also gave them things to eat, upon which they all raised their hats

[1] II, 115.

and thanked me. I then ordered members of my staff to get ready a boat and escort them to the Bogue.'

The *Sunda's* surgeon, Dr Hill, published an account of the interview in the *Canton Press*.[1] He tells us that Lin showed the survivors two English books into which Chinese translations of certain passages had been inserted. One was A. S. Thelwall's *The Iniquities of the Opium Trade with China*, published at London early in 1839. The book makes an eloquent appeal for the suppression of opium production in India, and it no doubt had a considerable effect on the general reader, calling his attention to an evil the existence of which was quite unknown to him. But public men knew of the evil and in most cases deplored it. Their difficulty was that they did not see how the Government of India could manage without the revenue that it derived from opium or how the tea trade (from which the home Government derived vast revenues) could be carried on unless tea were paid for by opium. Thelwall's book could only have had any political influence if he had faced these difficulties, which he entirely fails to do.

The other book produced by Lin lacked its title-page; but Dr Hill thought it was by John Davis (1795–1890), afterwards Governor of Hongkong. If so it was probably his *The Chinese*, published in London in 1836. This is an extremely well-informed work, showing great appreciation of Chinese literature and drama, and of Chinese institutions and customs in general. There is not a trace of the bantering and at the same time patronizing attitude towards the Chinese that became common in the second half of the nineteenth century.

Lin then showed Dr Hill the English translation of the second version of his letter to Queen Victoria. 'It was written', Dr Hill says, 'in their usual high flowing strain, at which I could scarcely command my gravity, which he observing immediately asked if it was all proper. We said it was only a few mistakes at which we smiled, whereupon he

[1] January 11, 1840.

requested us to . . . correct any error we might find in it. . . .
Some parts we could make neither head nor tail of. . . .'

We possess, so far as I know, only one specimen of the
English produced by Lin's linguists. It is a proclamation
dating from June 1839, and is printed in the *Chinese Repository*.[1]
To give it an enhanced literary dignity it was deprived of all
punctuation. I will only quote the opening sentences:
'Great imperial commissioner's governor's of two Kwang
provinces lieutenant-governor's of Canton earnest proclamation to foreigners again issued. For the managing opium on
the last spring trade for present time till the opium surrendered to the government than ordered be opened the
trade same as before.'

That evening (December 16th), he received a note from
Elliot saying that his sincere desire for peace and his consistent obedience to the laws of China were well known to
Lin and his colleagues, and it grieved him deeply that the
present imbroglio should have arisen. He hoped that it
might be possible to settle outstanding difficulties in such a
way that the English merchants and their families might be
allowed to reside again at Macao and conditions found in
which legitimate trade might be carried on pending the
arrival of instructions from his Sovereign.

Lin's reply was naturally withering. After recapitulating
events since the surrender of the opium, which had amply
shown how little regard Elliot had either for peace or for the
laws of China, Lin asks sarcastically whether Elliot had
'waited for instructions' from home before twice opening
fire on Chinese warships and committing all the other
arbitrary acts which had led to the cessation of trade. 'The
basis of your own laws is the promotion of trade, and in
causing the cessation of trade by disobeying Chinese law,
you are infringing the whole purpose of the laws of your
country. Are you ready to answer to your own Government
for this grave crime?'

[1] 1839, p. 167.

On December 21st, Lin hears that Elliot has been badgering the Prefect of Macao, through whom communications from Lin arrived, to find out whether there has been any reply to his note. Evidently the reply had been held up for a few days. 'One can see what a fret he is in', observes Lin. Only about a third of the English merchants dealt in opium, and the rest were probably beginning to press very hard for a resumption of trade.

December 22nd was the day of the Winter Solstice: 'At dawn I set up an altar in my lodging and burnt incense, looking towards the Palace at Peking, and kowtowing my best wishes for a felicitous Solstice.'

On the 24th, handicapped by a bad attack of catarrh,[1] he answered a note from the Portuguese Governor of Macao, presumably about trading conditions. On December 26th a newly arrived Englishman called Captain Gribble was returning, in a Chinese boat, from a visit to the virtuous ship, *Royal Saxon*, where he had been making arrangements about taking a house at Macao, when a Chinese patrol ship came up. Gribble, who had heard hair-raising stories about the reckless behaviour of patrols, particularly, for example, the burning of the *Bilbaino*, fired at the Chinese marines, without waiting to discover what they wanted. He did no damage, but was at once arrested and put into prison at Canton. An endless interchange of notes ensued, till finally on January 7th (1840) Captain Towns of the *Royal Saxon* was authorized to come to Canton and fetch Gribble away.

On December 29th it was bitterly cold, and though Lin was wearing his lined furs he caught a severe cold and had to stay in bed. The doctor was sent for and he was given some medicine. Next day the doctor came again; several letters from Peking and the *Peking Gazette* kept him amused. On December 31st he was well enough to write on some fans and deal with business. On January 1st he received orders

---

[1] Lin's *kan-mao*, which was chronic, may have been something like hay-fever.

from Court to find out whether the Customs at Shao-chou[1]
were letting opium through; he passed this on to the
Governor-General and Governor. 'Today', he notes, 'is
New Year's day abroad [it was the twenty-seventh day of
the eleventh month in China]. It falls ten days after the
Winter Solstice. The Spaniards, Portuguese, people of
Manila, English and Americans count today as the first
day of the first month of 1840. The foreigners in the
factories outside the city wall exchange good wishes
when they meet, but everything else goes on as usual.'

It was about this time that Lin bought the *Cambridge* from
the Americans. Denuded of her armaments she was now
merely a rather large merchant ship, which the Chinese did
not know how to navigate, so that she had eventually to be
towed up to Canton. On January 13th Lin received instructions to stop all trade with the English, which in fact he had
already done on December 5th. 'All their ships', the
Emperor said, 'must be driven out of the harbour without
any further attempt to secure the guarantee; nor is it worth
while trying to get them to hand over the murderer. What
has become of the *Royal Saxon* is also not worth inquiring
into. It must be explained to the other nations that the
English, by their crimes, have brought this punishment on
themselves; but the other foreigners, so long as they obey the
law and do not give assistance to the English, are not
implicated, and can continue to trade as usual.' It was also
announced by Peking that Admiral Kuan had received a
resounding Manchu title in recognition of his services at
Chuenpi.

From January 6th to the 10th Lin suffered from
rheumatism in the right arm, and being dissatisfied with his
usual doctor sent for a Dr Tu, who was attached to the
Provincial Treasury. On the 8th he heard that his eldest son's
wife had given birth to a daughter. Lin was asked to give the
girl a name, and chose Fragrant Bell, in imitation of the

[1] On the North River, 140 miles north of Canton.

name of the famous T'ang poet Po Chü-i's daughter—
Golden Bell. The 'fragrant' was appropriate because Po
Chü-i called himself the Recluse of the Fragrant Mountain
(Hsiang-shan); also because she was born on a day the signs
of which lacked the element 'metal', which needed reinforcing. Lin mentions more than once at this time ingenious
schemes for speeding his letters to Foochow. For example,
he would pay the messenger two dollars at Canton, on the
understanding that if he delivered the letter by a certain date
the addressee would pay him another two dollars. A further
dollar was to be given for each day that the letter arrived
earlier than the appointed date, while half a dollar was to be
deducted for every day that the messenger was behind time.

On January 18th Captain Warner of the *Thomas Coutts*
signed the following undertaking: 'I, the English ship's
captain Warner, having received from their Excellencies the
Commissioner, the Governor-General and the Governor a
communication addressed to the Sovereign of my country,
undertake to convey it with all respect and care and see that
it reaches the addressee. What I have here undertaken, I
will faithfully perform.'

That is the last we hear of Lin's famous letter to Queen
Victoria. We know from shipping records that the *Thomas
Coutts* arrived safely at London, but it is certain that the
letter was never delivered to the Queen. Captain Warner may
have transferred it to a mail-packet that was taking the new
Suez overland route. The mails on this route were sometimes robbed, and the letter, like so many interesting
documents, may one day be rescued from the sands of
Egypt.

On January 22nd the Prefect of Macao reported that George
Thomas Staunton was being sent to replace Elliot, owing to
the dissatisfaction of the Queen with what Elliot had been
doing. 'Staunton', comments Lin, 'came to Canton when
he was young and was formerly Taipan [President of the
Select Committee]. He took part in the tribute-mission of

the 21st year of Chia-ch'ing [the Amherst mission of 1816], and is now over seventy.' He was in fact only fifty-nine; but in an unsigned letter to the *Canton Register*[1] he is referred to as 'venerable'. 'I am sorry to see the London papers name Sir George Staunton as the expected High Commissioner to China', says the writer of the letter. 'Sir George is a man of the days when tea was everything; national honour nothing.'

On the question of the Opium War Staunton held an odd combination of views. He was a member of the Anti-Opium League, and began his speech at the debate in the House of Commons on the China question (April 7, 1840) by saying that he was 'as strongly opposed as any member of the House to the opium trade'. He ended it by saying he 'thought it was a just and fitting war and he would support the Government'. The whole speech somewhat reminds one of those of the Knights at the end of *Murder in the Cathedral*.

It was, however, not Elliot but Lin himself who was on the eve of losing his position. On January 26th he received news that his term as Special Commissioner was at an end. Instead of being nominal Governor-General of Kiangnan he was now to replace Teng as Governor-General of Kwangtung and Kwangsi. The salary was considerably smaller than that of the Governor-General of Kiangnan and the position was usually thought less important. But Lin was still an official of the First Rank, and had no reason to regard himself as in disgrace. The present Governor-General, Lin's great friend Teng, was to be Governor-General somewhere else; but there was some indecision about where he was to go.

From February 3rd to September 10th there is a gap in the diary, or at any rate in the printed text of it, and we have to fall back on other sources, particularly Lin's correspondence with the Emperor.

On February 6, 1840, Lin was notified that an important memorial had been laid before the Throne by the Mayor of Peking, Tseng Wang-yen. A committee consisting of Lin

[1] Supplement, July 21, 1840.

himself, the Governor of Kwangtung, the commander of the land forces, the Hoppo (head of Customs) and other local officials was to consider Tseng's proposals and report on their practicability. What Tseng recommended was a total cessation of foreign trade. He asserted that the ships of all the foreign nations had been in the habit of bringing opium. If allowed to go on trading they would dump their opium on the English ships outside the Bogue and then bring other goods to Canton, get rhubarb and tea in return, and transport them on behalf of the English. Only by depriving the English entirely of rhubarb and tea could they be brought to heel. Some people believe that the English have stocks of these commodities sufficient to last them ten years. This is to ignore the fact that though rhubarb roots probably keep for a long time, tea deteriorates after two or three years. It is also essential, says Tseng, to prevent any Chinese ships going out to sea at all; otherwise they may bring goods to foreign ships or be lured into their service. Fishermen must content themselves with getting what fish they can in inland waters. Cut off from supplies the foreign ships will be bound in the end to come close to shore and try to get hold of provisions. Expert swimmers are then to be called upon to volunteer. They will swim out to the ships at night, catch the crews completely unawares and massacre them on the spot. In a postscript, Tseng calls attention to the necessity of limiting the trade of the Portuguese at Macao so as to ensure that they are not carrying for the English.

The committee, owing to its divergent official duties, was difficult to bring together, and Lin was not able to report for some weeks.

Meanwhile a long correspondence[1] had been going on between Captain Elliot and Captain Smith of H.M.S. *Volage* on the one hand and Pinto, the Portuguese Governor of Macao, on the other. On January 1st Elliot asked for permission to store cargo at Macao. Pinto replied that he had

[1] II. 442 seq.

summoned his Senate, who had agreed with him that in view of the very delicate situation of the Portuguese *vis-à-vis* the Chinese Government (the Portuguese were merely tenants at Macao) he could not accede to Elliot's request. On February 4th Captain Smith notified the Governor that he was about to station a warship (the *Hyacinth*) in the harbour at Macao, to protect the English, in view of menacing placards put up in Macao by the Chinese authorities. Pinto replied that an English warship had no right to enter the harbour, and demanded its withdrawal. Smith asked if the Portuguese were willing and able to protect those who lived under their flag? If not, he must again evacuate the English from Macao, and in that case would, of course, withdraw the *Hyacinth* from Macao harbour. Pinto replied that the admission of foreign warships was absolutely forbidden by the terms of Portugal's relation to China. The English seemed to think only about the hardship of having to live on board ship if they left Macao, and not at all about the difficulties in which they had involved the Portuguese. He threatens to publish to all the world what the English have done in the last nine months, that all nations may judge for themselves. 'You are not only breaking the laws of our country, but also those of England. I pray that God may protect you. Don Adriao Accacio da Silva Pinto.'

This correspondence was forwarded[1] to the Emperor with the comment: 'At this crucial phase of our effort to ward off the foreigners, we must constantly find out all we can about them. Only by knowing their strength and their weakness can we find the right means to restrain them. For that reason I have got hold of six letters that passed between the Portuguese and the English and have secretly had them translated by people who can read foreign languages. I enclose fair copies, and respectfully hope that you will cast an eye over them.'

Lin's own attempt to improve his knowledge of the West

[1] II. 195.

probably began in the summer of 1839, during the lull that followed the destruction of the foreign opium. We have seen that in July he asked for a translation of Vattel's *Law of Nations*, and in December he possessed translated extracts from Thelwall's *The Iniquities of the Opium Trade*. He also had extracts from Hugh Murray's *Encyclopedia of Geography*[1] translated. In the summer of 1839 he set his translators to work on making extracts from European newspapers and periodicals published at Macao and Canton.[2] These extracts, which terminate in November 1840, were probably brought to Lin in batches. They do not seem ever to have been printed in book form, but the original MS of them is preserved at the Nanking Library and they have recently been printed.[3] There are four short comments by Lin. Two of them merely question the accuracy of statistics about Chinese military and national expenditure. To an article trying to show (contrary to what had been asserted by Thelwall) that Chinese hostility to Christianity had a long history and was not due to the fact that Christians were now importing opium, Lin added the comment: 'It appears that the Jesus-religion preached by Matteo Ricci was Catholicism, whereas the Jesus-religion preached afterwards by Verbiest[4] was Christianity. The two terms "Catholic" and "Christian" must express some such difference.' It would certainly have taken a long time to sort out this muddle for him. To a review (dated September 5, 1840) of a book containing translations of many of Lin's communications to Elliot, of his letter to Queen Victoria and of his recent proclamation inciting the Chinese to murder any Englishman they could lay hands on, Lin adds the note, 'This is a book I ought to get from Macao'.

A few years later great use was made of these press cuttings by Chinese writers on foreign affairs; but there is very little sign that Lin studied them closely. Some of them deal with

[1] 1834.   [2] Chiefly the *Canton Press* (organ of the anti-opium party).
[3] II. 365 seq.   [4] Belgian Jesuit, died 1688.

events in Afghanistan, and the profusion of foreign names, both of places and persons, very sketchily transliterated would make them difficult for anyone to understand who had not some previous knowledge of the Afghan campaigns. Equally unintelligible to anyone not already in the know are many of the passages about institutions and events in England. Here is the account[1] of the proceedings in Parliament on April 7th when, on a vote of censure, the Whig Government only escaped defeat by a margin of nine votes: 'There has been a debate between those who support the State and want to fight, and those who support the people and do not want to fight. The discussion lasted three nights, and there was a great deal of talk. It came to an end yesterday at four in the morning. Each Minister managed to have nine parts' paper tickets of support; and so just avoided a general dispute. . . .' After three more lines in this style, the despairing translator breaks down. 'Here', he says, 'there are four or five sentences that I cannot understand.'

About February 19, 1840, Lin received a letter[2] from the Emperor reminding him that he was now a substantive not merely a ranking Governor-General. He had the two provinces of Kwangtung and Kwangsi under his control. All affairs both civil and military were dependent on him and there could be no *p'ang-tai*, which is the Chinese equivalent to 'passing the buck'. 'If measures are not taken to root out this evil once and for all, you, Lin Tse-hsü, will be called to account.' This was the first sign of the Emperor's increasing impatience.

On February 20th Lin appealed to the Portuguese to drive the English out of Macao and not to wait till Chinese troops were sent to do so, in which case the Portuguese would survive as little as the English. He hoped they were not being influenced by rumours that twelve English warships from England and twelve from Bombay were shortly going to arrive. This was mere idle boasting on the part of Elliot and

[1] II. 506.   [2] II. 125.

the rest, and need not be taken seriously. Even supposing they came, they could not bring ammunition and provisions to last for more than a short time. Moreover the crews would arrive worn out after so long a journey, and the Chinese land and sea forces would have no difficulty in disposing of them.

This was written three days after Palmerston's instructions with regard to the English expeditionary force were sent to the Indian Government. The assurance that the fleet would not come was weakened, the Portuguese must have felt, by the boast of what its fate would be if it did come. But both arguments were probably only used in order to allay the fears of the Portuguese that if they sided too definitely with Lin the English force, when it arrived, would make war on them as well as on him; and it does not follow that this passage represents Lin's considered opinion.

On April 8th, in the course of a long report to the Emperor, Lin mentions that various rumours are circulating at Canton. One is that the English are collecting warships at several ports. These will join up and come in a body to make trouble. That story has only been put about to scare us, says Lin, and need not be taken seriously. Another story of the same kind is that only one or two ships are coming, but they will be full of arms and ammunition which will be used to convert the merchant ships that are still hanging about into warships. Others say that the opium traders have taken cargoes of other products to their port (i.e. Singapore), exchanged them for the opium they dumped at this port last autumn and intend to bring it here and entice people to flout the law. Against this we shall have to take strict precautions. In any case, whether more warships are coming or not, the *Volage* and *Hyacinth* are still here, and this alone is enough to prove that the English are still bent on resistance.

Lin then says that he and the Admiral have drawn up a plan for enlisting fishermen and Tankas,[1] the most hardy and

---

[1] Boat-dwellers.

venturesome classes at Canton, as volunteers. At present the foreign ships give them exorbitant prices for vegetables, sometimes paying them in opium. They must be recruited and sent out in fire-boats, officered by a few regulars, hide till night comes and then, when wind and tide are favourable and everyone asleep, set fire first of all to the Chinese boats that are moored round the English ships. A reward would be given for each ship set on fire, and a double reward if they succeeded in setting fire to an English merchant ship. A very successful first attack of this kind was reported by the Admiral as having taken place on February 29th. Twenty-three Chinese ships intended for carrying away opium and supplying provisions to the English had been set alight.[1]

On April 26th the American Consul Delano[2] wrote to Lin saying that, according to English and other newspapers, the English fleet when it arrived in June would announce a blockade of the port of Canton. At present the admission of American ships to the port and permission to unload were subject to considerable delay. He would be obliged if the process could be speeded up; otherwise American ships with their cargoes still unloaded might get caught in Canton harbour when the blockade came, and American merchants suffer ruinous loss.

To Lin, who was still trying to persuade himself that no British fleet would come, this letter was very annoying. He replied that the delays in clearing American ships were due to the fact that a very strict search had to be made, in case these ships might be carrying cargoes on behalf of the British. The story about the British blockading Canton in June was the most impudent lie imaginable. Canton is a Chinese port. How can the English blockade it? You Americans are not subject to the English. Why should you take on so at the mere mention of the English not allowing ships to pass? However if when June comes you dare not trade, just

---

[1] One of the 'traitors to China' captured on this occasion 'was wearing foreign trousers and foreign shoes'.   [2] II. 363.

because the English tell you not to, our officials will be only too pleased; it will save them a lot of trouble. Lin concludes by reminding Delano that since the English were excluded from trade the Americans have been making profits many times greater than ever before, and it was absurd for them to be talking now about 'ruinous loss'.

About May 4th the committee appointed to investigate Tseng's proposal (see above, p. 94) for total abolition of all foreign trade was at last able to report. Writing on its behalf Lin points out that although other countries besides England have in the past imported opium, the opium was produced solely[1] in territory controlled by England, and it was impossible to treat Holland, Spain, the Philippines, Denmark, Sweden, Prussia, Austria and Hamburg on the same footing as England. When they protested, as they were bound to do, the authorities at Canton would find it impossible to justify such treatment. On the other hand, preferential treatment of the other nations tended to foment ill-feeling between them and the English, which was all to China's advantage. Lin then proceeds to quote from the classics. Westerners often imagine that Chinese statesmen continually interspersed their dispatches with 'Confucius said. . . .' 'Mencius said. . . .' and so on. Such appeals to Confucian authority are, however, rare in eighteenth- and nineteenth-century official documents, and Lin hardly ever indulges in them. But here, very much apropos, he quotes from an old chronicle[2] the story of the Ch'u minister Tou Po-pi who said to the ruler of Ch'u that if Ch'u assumed a threatening attitude towards small neighbouring states, the effect would be that 'they will unite to oppose us and may prove difficult to separate'.

As for the proposal to prevent any Chinese ships at all going out to sea, it must be remembered, says Lin, that the inhabitants of Kwangtung are essentially a seafaring people. There is even a local saying, 'Seven to fishing; three go to

[1] He forgets about the Turkish opium sold by the Americans.
[2] *Tso Chuan*, year 706 B.C.

the plough', and again 'Three parts mountain, six parts sea', leaving only one part out of ten for agriculture. To stop all seafaring would bring ruin to a large proportion of the inhabitants.

About rhubarb, Lin says, Tseng is misinformed. It is now known that the quantity consumed by the English is very small and it is a thing which, contrary to what was formerly believed, is in no way essential to them. Their consumption of tea is very large, and in order to prevent their getting it the amount sold to other nations should be restricted to what those nations normally export. Trade with Macao, Lin maintains, has already been regulated on much the same lines as those suggested in Tseng's memorial.

On the same day Lin sent reports about the proposed erection of fresh batteries at Kowloon Point and farther north at Kuan-yung, about the consequent reorganization of the military district in which these places lay, and about the progress of the now somewhat time-worn campaign against Chinese opium offenders. In urban districts, Lin reports, the opium evil has been pretty successfully eliminated. But in remote country places the task has proved much more difficult. The more stringent the search for opium becomes, the more ingenious the means used to dispose of it. Sometimes it is hidden in back apartments where the presence of women deters the agents from carrying on a proper search. Or else it is buried in the precincts of temples or in forests, or even put into chests disguised as coffins, and laid in bogus tombs. Then again officials know that if they fail to make arrests they cannot at the worst be accused of anything more serious than negligence; whereas if they make wrong arrests, they may find themselves standing trial for the much more serious offence of exceeding their powers. Finally there is the difficulty of getting hold of spies and *agents provocateurs*. Such people, says Lin, are useless unless they have previously been intimately connected with the traffic. They will certainly not take to working with the Government merely out of enthusiasm for the anti-opium movement; they will only do so if it pays them better to help the authorities than to carry on the traffic. This makes them very expensive, and the local authorities are hard put to it to budget for so heavy an item.

Lin, it will be noticed, does not mention the system generally employed in the West for obtaining spies at a reasonable figure: namely, to use persons over whom, owing to some personal failing or past crime, the authorities have a blackmail hold.

On June 21st the main body[1] of the British expeditionary force, consisting of about twenty warships (including several steamers) and transports carrying some four thousand British and Indian troops, arrived off Macao. The Chinese naturally supposed that they were going to attack Canton; and when on June 24th and 25th they sailed out to sea again and disappeared, there was naturally great relief. It was assumed that they had found Lin's new batteries and other defence preparations too tough a proposition, and had decided to go back to wherever they came from. In a report sent on June 24th,[2] before he learnt of the warships' departure, Lin tells the Emperor that a number of new ships have arrived. They seem to be rather heavily armed, but no doubt they are principally loaded with opium. By day they secretly launch small boats from their decks which carry opium hither and thither, hoping to find retail purchasers. At night they anchor with skiffs collected round them to keep a look-out 'in case we use fire-boats against them. That is all they are doing, and as Your Majesty rightly observed, there is really nothing they can do.' The only trouble is that they are selling opium at temptingly low prices.

He further reports that since the very successful attack with fire-boats on February 29th, when twenty-three ships

---

[1] The *Alligator* (twenty-six guns) had arrived on June 9th; the *Madagascar* steamer on June 16th.   [2] For the date, see II. 216; line 10.

were destroyed, a similar attack had been made on June 8th, combined with an ingenious deception of the kind we should call a Secret Operation. A number of agents who could speak some English were dressed up as peasants and, arriving in the sort of skiffs used for bringing provisions, supplemented the work of the fire-boats. Some foreigners dressed in white leapt out of the ship *Pa-li*(?) gun in hand. Four of them were killed and the rest burnt alive, along with the ship. Another ship, with opium chests on board, was also burned. A third, with masts and sails on fire, weighed anchor and escaped, and the foreigners managed to put out the fire. Eleven supply-boats were burnt and nine mat-sheds near the shore.

After recounting still more exploits and dwelling on the heavy losses incurred by the English, the report goes on: 'The foreign official who is in charge of troops on the *Druid*, John Churchill, also died of illness on that ship.' This was Lord John Churchill, who died on June 3rd, several days before the battle. It is possible that the Chinese did succeed in burning some boats belonging to 'traitors to China' who were bringing provisions to the English ships or fetching opium. This being a secret business, the fate of such boats would not figure in the English reports. But these reports do not admit that any English ship was destroyed, and claim that long-boats put out from the warships and had no difficulty in taking the fire-boats in tow and grounding them on shore.

Another report, sent by Lin on the same date, illustrates once more the greatest weakness in China's administration— the lack of any proper police system and, in the present case, particularly of any efficient body of river-police, a thing of great importance in a country where transport was so largely by water. In England a proper London police force had existed for about ten years; but the creation of county police forces was still optional and had not been widely carried out; so that it is doubtful whether England was at this period substantially ahead of China.

On April 7th a Chinese merchant, duly armed with a certificate that he had paid the necessary duty, was bringing a cargo of iron nails from Shao-chou, 140 miles north of Canton, to Fatshan, ten miles west of Canton. Spies in the service of the anti-smuggling force indicted him as a smuggler, and near Ch'ing-yüan, ninety miles by river from Canton, armed agents boarded the boat and confiscated the greater part of the cargo. When the captors were already on the way back to their headquarters, it was discovered by a further agent that the merchant had with him a certificate. He was forced to throw it into the river and sign a document stating that most of the cargo had fallen overboard and been lost. Three days later, near Samshui (twenty-five miles from Canton) the rest of the cargo was confiscated by another band of agents. The merchant's firm complained to the local authorities, who sent the case up to the Governor. At the trial that followed the anti-smuggling agents, as one may call them, confessed that they had sold the nails and shared out the proceeds between them. They were deprived of their rank and put on reduced pay.

About July 13th, in a report about the movements of foreign warships, Lin mentions that there are among them three 'cart-wheel ships that put the axles in motion by means of fire, and can move rather fast. They are used for patrol-work and carrying mails; one of them came to Canton some while ago.' He is here referring to the steamer *Jardine*[1] which sailed from Aberdeen and arrived at Lintin in September 1835. Here her machinery was put in order for steaming, and it was intended to run her as a conveyance for mails and passengers between Macao and Canton; but on her first voyage Chinese forts fired at her, thinking no doubt that she was some new form of incendiary vessel, and in the end her machinery was removed. But Lin was very much mistaken in thinking that the steamers now arriving were equally harmless. Owing to their great speed, shallow draft

[1] See *China Review*, Vol. III, p. 189.

and the fact that they were not dependent on wind or tide they proved to be one of the crucial factors in the war.

Lin goes on to assure the Emperor that the defences in the Canton estuary are now so strong that nothing is to be feared from an English attack. It is, however, the season of strong south winds and in case any enemy ship should take advantage of this to sail north, a special warning[1] has been sent to the authorities on the Fuhkien, Chekiang, Kiangsu and Chihli coasts, instructing them to be on the look-out. A few days later, in a dispatch that reached Peking on August 3rd, Lin enclosed a copy of an explanatory proclamation issued in Chinese by the Commander-in-Chief of the British naval forces, Sir James Gordon Bremer, as a pendant to his public notice that the river and port of Canton were in a state of blockade. It began by saying (no doubt under Elliot's inspiration) that the high officials of Canton, Lin and Teng, in defiance of the Chinese Emperor's instructions that the English were to be treated with justice and moderation, had suddenly subjected the Superintendent of Trade and the English in Canton to the most perfidious violence, all the time deceiving the Emperor by shamelessly mendacious reports. The Sovereign of England has been obliged to appoint special envoys whose business it will be to acquaint the Emperor with the true facts. Further on in the document Bremer says: 'The high officials Lin and Teng by false representations to the Emperor induced him to issue a decree putting a stop to trade with England, causing heavy loss to thousands and ten thousands of good men, both Chinese and foreign.' There are, of course, the usual assurances that life and property will be rigidly respected, so long as no resistance is offered to British arms. It naturally occurred to Lin that similar accusations against him might well have been conveyed to the neighbourhood of Peking by one of the English ships. He had indeed received information from the Americans that the English fleet was making for

[1] III. 363. Sent about July 20th.

Chekiang and Kiangsu; and some people were saying that they were on their way to Taku,[1] the nearest seaport to Peking, Lin says to the Emperor. They will not be able to do any harm, as these places have been warned to be on their guard and are fully prepared. But supposing they were to get as far as Tientsin and ask for a resumption of trade. They might well presume on Your Majesty's long-continued indulgence to the extent of assuming that their plea would not be rejected out of hand. They would no doubt pretend that the present ban on trade is an arbitrary measure carried out unbeknown to you by myself and my colleagues. But if their plea is expressed in a respectful and obedient manner . . . I wonder if it might not be possible to use the precedent of. the twenty-first year of Chia-ch'ing [1816] when the Amherst embassy was sent back again from the north to Canton. The Governor-General of Chihli might escort the English spokesmen by the inland route, stage by stage to Canton. 'That would be a way of "dispersing their teeth and claws", and would make it easier for us to keep them within due bounds. If the plea that they present has reference to the doings of myself and my colleagues, I request that a high official may be sent here to investigate the charges. This will impress them with the entire justice of our Heavenly Court's procedure, increase their respect for us, and deprive them of all excuse for their conduct.'

The above passage foretells with uncanny precision exactly what did happen. The English plenipotentiaries, as we have seen, duly arrived off Taku on August 10th, bringing a letter[2] from Lord Palmerston, demanding among other things that the high officials at Canton (meaning Teng and Lin) should be called to account for their treatment of Elliot and the British colony. The only wrong surmise was that the

[1] The fleet anchored eleven miles from the mouth of the Pei-ho and consequently sixteen miles from Taku itself, on August 10th.

[2] See Morse, *International Relations of the Chinese Empire*, Vol. I, pp. 621–6. For the Chinese text see IV. 48 of the corpus. See also my appendix, p. 248, below.

plenipotentiaries would be brought back to Canton by the inland route; they naturally went south with the fleet. Everything else happened exactly as in Lin's anxious day-dream. The Governor-General of Chihli, Ch'i-shan, went south by land and river, superseded Lin as Governor-General at Canton and headed an inquiry into his conduct.

But Lin's gift of prophecy has led us to anticipate. We must go back to the time, late in June, when the English fleet, after spending a few days near Macao, disappeared into the blue.

Their first objective was to capture Ting-hai, on Chusan Island, at the tip of the southern arm of Hangchow Bay. Lin had, as we have seen, warned the authorities at Hangchow and Ningpo that English warships were at large and might be making for the north. But he does not seem, judging from the following extract, to have given any description of their appearance or to have explained how they could be distinguished from merchant-ships. In general appearance, of course, the difference was not so marked then as it is today. 'Before the war', says an account[1] derived from a Mr Wang, who was sub-Prefect of Ting-hai, 'whenever a foreign ship arrived everyone from the Commandant, the Prefect and sub-Prefect down to chair-carriers and office lacqueys all took bribes from the foreigners and unless satisfied with what they got would not let them trade. At first not more than one or two or at the most three or four ships came. But the greater the number of ships, the greater the amount taken in bribes, so that so far from being apprehensive when more ships came than usual, their one fear was lest the number should decline. . . . One day it was announced . . . that a far larger number of ships had arrived than ever before. At first the officials and their subordinates were rather puzzled. But the explanation soon occurred to them, and they guffawed with joy. Obviously the ships had assembled here because of the cessation of trade at Canton. "Ting-hai",

[1] IV. 630.

they said, "will become a great trading centre, and we shall all make more and more money out of them day by day".'

What actually happened (July 5th) can best be read in Lord Jocelyn's *Six Months with the Chinese Expedition* (1841): 'The ships opened their broadsides upon the town, and the crashing of timber, falling houses, and groans of men resounded from the shore. The firing lasted on our side for nine minutes; but even after it had ceased a few shots were still heard from the unscathed junks. . . . We landed on a deserted beach, a few dead bodies, bows and arrows, broken spears and guns remaining the sole occupants of the field.'

Some Western and even some modern Chinese accounts give the impression that Ting-hai surrendered without putting up any resistance. That is quite false; the town rejected a demand for unconditional surrender and when attacked put up such resistance as was possible. But it had not from the first any chance of withstanding the concentrated fire of fifteen warships; as well might one expect Hiroshima to have hit back at its attackers. The military commander, Chang Ch'ao-fa, died of his wounds;[1] the Prefect Yao Huai-hsiang and the Chief Constable Ch'üan Fu committed suicide rather than submit.

Only the town and its immediate neighbourhood were occupied. An eye-witness[2] says of the people there: 'They have in a thousand instances received great injustice at our hands. While we have been issuing proclamations, talking sweet words . . . our soldiers and sailors have been plundering them and forcibly carrying off their poultry and cattle. . . . We are now going to break open all the unoccupied shops and houses and take possession of them for governmental purposes. As they will no longer bring poultry and vegetables to market, we are going to forage their farms. . . .

[1] On August 2nd, at Ningpo.
[2] Quoted in the *Chinese Repository*, 1840, p. 325.

As they will sell us no fish, we are going to take measures to prevent them fishing at all.'

It perhaps is significant that what seems to be the earliest printed use of the Indian term 'loot' as an adopted English word occurs in reference to Ting-hai: 'Silks, fans, china, little shoes . . . the articles of a Chinese lady's toilette—lay tossed in a sad and telltale mêlée; and many of these fairy shoes were appropriated by us as lawful loot.'[1]

With regard to looting, I am concerned in this book with the impact it made on its victims. I by no means wish to imply that the English expedition behaved worse than was or is usual in war, or that the Chinese themselves would have behaved better under similar circumstances. The system of 'security placards', by which households purchased theoretical immunity from plunder by giving up their live-stock gratis, does however seem unusually cold-blooded. Whether it was invented *ad hoc* or had previously been used in India I do not know.

Karl Gutzlaff, the Prussian buccaneer missionary inter-preter, was made magistrate of Ting-hai. Better known to Chinese history and legend is his magistracy at Ningpo in 1841 and 1842, about which I shall say something in a later part of my book.

But to return to Lin's reports to the Emperor. On or about July 13th he also gave an account of his measures against 'planting booty', that is to say trumping up false charges by hiding incriminating articles, such as opium, opium pipes, etc., in innocent people's boats or luggage, after the manner of Joseph's silver cup in the Bible story. The report may well have struck the Emperor as rather trivial, for it reached him on August 3rd, at a time when he was already preoccupied with far more serious matters, having heard on July 20th of the fall of Ting-hai.

Late in July Lin had apparently still not heard about Ting-hai, for in a report[2] which reached Peking on August

[1] *Six Months with the Chinese Expedition*, p. 61. [2] II. 219.

21st he makes no reference to it. He is indeed in an optimistic mood, and reports that although there are still some English warships in the estuary, they do not dare to approach the Bogue. 'These foreign ships', he says, 'only have confidence when they are in open waters on the high seas, where they can manœuvre at will. Once inside a river-mouth they are like fish in a cauldron; they can at once be captured and destroyed.' They are, however, says Lin, quite aware of this and are determined not to take the risk of entering the river. They are in constant fear of our fire-boats, and even at night keep continually on the move. Their only object is to intimidate us into reopening trade. But we cannot let them loiter here indefinitely and shall sooner or later have to take military measures against them.

It is in a report sent on August 16th that Lin first refers to the loss of Ting-hai. Up till now, he says, we have never provoked hostilities, leaving it to them to get themselves into trouble, for it was not worth our while to embark on a combat by sea. But now that they have committed this dastardly crime on the Chekiang coast, they must be well aware that there can be no further question of reopening foreign trade, and they have also become far more aggressive at Canton, where they have seized fourteen of our salt transports, killing a steersman and wounding a sailor. 'This has led to a great outburst of popular indignation, and at Macao our sailors, acting on indications given by local peasants, arrested a white foreigner called Stanton, and two black foreigners called Chan-li and Ch'i-t'u, and brought them to our officials for investigation.'

No one seems to have bothered about the fate of the two Indians; but there was a tremendous outcry about the disappearance of Mr Stanton.

Vincent Stanton was an adventurous undergraduate who, on hearing that a tutor was wanted by an English family at Macao, left St John's College, Cambridge, without taking a degree and set out for China, at the age of twenty-three.

Like so many of his contemporaries he was intensely religious and we are told[1] that 'in the absence of an ordained clergyman he performed divine service at the British chapel established at the house of the second Superintendent', Alexander Johnston.

On August 5th he went to bathe at Cacilhas Bay, southeast of the Barrier, and was arrested by Chinese soldiers who jumped out from behind rocks. He was taken to one of the Bogue forts and there handed over to Canton officials. When parting from him one of the poorest and hungriest-looking of his captors pressed upon him a handful of copper cash, saying he might need to buy food. While in prison at Canton he was well treated and allowed to have Chinese books and an English Bible and Prayer Book sent to him.

It was popularly believed that Commodore Bremer, the Commander of the English fleet, had been captured. This was not surprising (despite the fact that Bremer was at this date on his flagship, far away to the north), for Bremer was rapidly becoming a stock figure in Chinese legends about the war. He was believed to be a giant with an enormous head. He was killed at the Battle of San-yüan-li on May 30, 1841 (so legend said); though in point of fact he had left China for India on March 31st. When he reappeared in July it was concluded that there must be several Commodore Bremers. Lin soon realized that Stanton, on the contrary, was a person of 'only very moderate importance', and would probably have released him at once, had not Captain Smith, who, now that Elliot had gone north, was in charge of British interests at Macao and Canton, made the mistake of getting the Portuguese to demand the release of Stanton, on the ground that the kidnapping had taken place on their territory. This infuriated Lin, who regarded Macao not as Portuguese territory, but as a corner of China where Portuguese were allowed to reside. To release a foreigner at the bidding of other foreigners was beneath China's dignity, it would

[1] J. E. Bingham, *Narrative of the Expedition*, Vol. II. p. 51.

'show weakness' and consequently make the English more presumptuous than ever. The request met with a sharp refusal, followed by the dispatch of several thousand Chinese troops to the vicinity of Macao, nominally to protect the Portuguese against the predatory designs of the English.

But to return to Lin's report of August 16th. He announces that next day he is going to hold a final inspection of the regular troops and new militia, and when he has satisfied himself that they are all completely trained and know their jobs nothing will remain but to 'select a day, marshal them and send them all out to sea, to engage in a final battle of annihilation'.

In a postcript he says that he has been fortunate enough to secure a foreign letter about conditions at Ting-hai, and has had it translated.¹ It gave the names of the leaders in the attack on Ting-hai—not quite correctly, for Admiral Elliot, cousin of Charles Elliot, who figures among them, did not arrive till after the fall of the town. It duly records, however, that his ship, the *Melville*, struck a rock at the entrance to the harbour and was badly holed. Lin understood from the letter that 'an officer of rather high rank called Oglander was killed by our troops'. This was Brigadier-General Oglander, who died on the way from Macao to Ting-hai and was buried near the town on July 11th.

'Every ship', Lin further gathered from the letter, 'brought with it a supply of opium to use in payment for provisions; but they are already very short of food, and at any moment the wind may change to the north, all of which makes them very anxious and depressed.' It was probably not true that the English warships had officially-sanctioned supplies of opium on board. But it is not unlikely that individual sailors had small amounts, which they hoped to sell to the Chinese. The fleet had certainly been followed by a number of opium ships, for a letter from Ting-hai dated

¹ This may refer to some letter from Ting-hai printed in one of the local English newspapers.

July 11th, and printed in the *Canton Press* on August 1st, says: 'Several opium vessels are lying outside, but the Admiral will not allow them to come into the harbour.'

'I hear too', says Lin, 'that they have made a certain Gutzlaff "prefect" of Ting-hai. He speaks Chinese, and steps should be taken to thwart his machinations.' Militia should be recruited and disguised as local peasants, or local peasants should be trained as militia and infiltrate the place, pretending that they have come in response to the appeal to refugees to return, and are now willing to accept English rule. When sufficient numbers of them have accumulated in the city, on an agreed date they must rise and turn on the foreigners, whom they could butcher as easily as chickens or dogs. But, of course, great secrecy must be maintained beforehand.

Next day, August 17th, Lin went to the Lion Reach, about twenty-eight miles downstream from Canton, to hold an inspection of newly-raised forces, prior to the final battle of extinction, which was to take place the moment wind and weather were favourable. But Captain Smith got in first. The kidnapping of Stanton and the dispatch by Lin of large new forces to the neighbourhood of Macao made him feel that he must strike an immediate blow to protect the English there. Near the Barrier at Macao nine Chinese warships were lying in the bay and about 1,500 troops were concentrated on shore. 'The *Hyacinth* and a steamer [the *Enterprise*] were sent in to attack and under cover of their broadsides Captain Smith landed marines . . . and a party of Bengal volunteers. A few volleys of musketry soon drove the Chinese from their position, and two of the junks having been sunk . . . the remainder made the best of their way round the opposite point to join their flying soldiers.'[1]

Reproducing information supplied by 'the officials military and civil in charge of the defences of Macao' and confirmed by the Prefect of the neighbouring district Hsin-an, Lin

[1] *Six Months with the Chinese Expedition*, p. 128.

reported to the Emperor a great victory, in which the English had been driven off with considerable damage to their ships and heavy losses in men. A second victory on August 31st was also reported, in which great damage was done to a ship called *Chia-li* (Charlie?). The report says nothing about the size of the ship, and as there was no English warship with a name at all like this, it may be that what happened was a brush between Chinese war-junks and a long-boat called *Charlie*, launched from one of our warships.

As in the case of the Battle of Kowloon, the subsequent course of events seems in itself to suggest that the Chinese claims were untrue. For it is certain that after the Battle of the Barrier, as this action may be called, the English at Macao were never again threatened or molested.

Late in July one of the censors petitioned that all the coastal provinces should be told to enlist and train naval militia. Lin, in common with other Governors-General, was ordered to report on what could be done locally in this line. He and his colleagues reported that the fishermen and boat-dwellers of the region were renowned for their reckless courage in braving the dangers of wind and wave, and had gained the soubriquet of water-devils. There were supposed at various places near Canton to be astonishing divers who could walk about at the bottom of the sea and remain hidden there all night. They were also supposed to be able, when submerged, to pierce holes in the bottoms of ships and sink them. Last year, Lin says, he and his colleagues hoped they might be used against the opium ships, and a number of them were hired for this purpose. They were repeatedly put to the test; but it turned out that the most they could do was to bob about in shallow water. Not one of them could stay under for any length of time. Some of his Manchu colleagues, Lin says, had a similar experience when 'water-braves' were assigned to the Manchu marines under their command; the performances of these recruits fell lamentably short of what had been claimed for them.

However, if we do not recruit these coastal people, the English will get hold of them and use them for transporting opium. At the worst we can at least console ourselves with the reflection that every 'water-brave' we keep in our pay means one less ruffian in the pay of the English. In fact what we propose to do is more or less what the censor recommends.

Lin goes on to point out that an adequate supervision of the whole of Kwangtung's 1,400 miles of sealine is clearly impossible. Large numbers of irregulars have already been recruited; but picked up here, there and everywhere they are very difficult to form into disciplined units. Many are sure to turn out to be unusable and will have to be weeded out, paid off and dismissed.

This very negative and discouraged communication, which probably reached the Emperor after September 28th, when he dismissed Lin, must have confirmed him in his opinion that Lin was no longer the right man to tackle the situation at Canton.

On September 10th the diary begins again. We find him, as before, minutely recording examination news, and never failing on the first and fifteenth day of the moon to worship and burn incense; for he was as strict in his fortnightly devotions as the opium smugglers were in their Sabbatarianism. One is reminded that he had on his hands all the affairs of Kwangtung and not merely its sufferings at the hands of foreigners by the fact that on September 13th he received instructions to inquire into the doings of a mixed band of insurgents from Kwangtung and Fuhkien who had recently crossed the borders of the neighbouring province of Kiangsi. On September 14th, after sacrificing in the morning at the Temple of the Fire Spirit,[1] he hears in the afternoon that

---

[1] Outside the Eastern Gate. Worshipped during the second and eighth Chinese months. Lin's offerings cannot be said to have had a good effect, for as he notes in his diary there were fires at Canton on September 21st and 22nd.

English warships reached Tientsin[1] on August 13th and presented a petition. The fact was reported to the Palace, and Ch'i'-shan,[2] the Governor-General of Chihli, was ordered to allow them to state their grievances, and 'he was also to send any State document or whatever else they had brought with them to the Emperor at Peking'.

On September 18th Lin got back a report he had sent on August 21st, commented on[3] as follows by the Emperor: 'You speak of having stopped foreign trade, yet a moment after admit that it is still going on. You say you have dealt with offenders against the opium laws, yet admit that they are still at large. All this is merely an attempt to put me off with meaningless words. So far from doing any good, you have merely produced a number of fresh complications. The very thought of it infuriates me. I am anxious to see what you can possibly have to say for yourself!' The report that produced this outburst was received at the Palace on August 21st, the day after the Emperor got Lord Palmerston's letter,[4] in which Lin and Teng were accused of having systematically deceived the Emperor about what was going on in Canton. Later on the Emperor Tao-kuang denied that his loss of confidence in Lin had anything to do with the complaints against him made by the English Minister; but it is hard to believe that this was altogether true.

The report which provoked the Emperor's scathing comments was negative and despondent, and yet in a way complacent. Despite the order putting a stop to trade the English ships, says Lin, are still hanging about. The severe penalties attached to opium offences have considerably reduced the Chinese demand for it. But the English, in their determination to get remaining stocks off their hands, are selling at very low prices, and Chinese purchasers are still

---

[1] i.e. the county of Tientsin, not the town itself, which is sixty-seven miles from the coast.   [2] See below, p. 121.   [3] IV. 55.
[4] Transmitted to him by Ch'i-shan. It was not addressed to the Emperor. but to the 'Chinese Emperor's Minister'.

operating from unfrequented creeks at depth of night. However, many of them have been caught and 'we are beginning to break their villainy, though it must be confessed that secretly, in inner rooms, a good deal of smoking still goes on. . . .' I intend, before the year and a half's grace runs out, to make a most strenuous effort to obtain arrests. Every offender will be arrested and every arrest will be followed by an inquiry. In this way, by applying the principle of 'incriminating to end crime'[1] I hope gradually to extirpate the evil, root and branch.

Lin had now been extirpating opium smoking for nearly two years, and it is no wonder that the resigned and leisurely tone of this report dismayed the Emperor.

On September 21st Lin took part in holding the preliminary tests of candidates wishing to compete in the Provincial Examinations, tried a case of robbery referred to him by the local officials of Hsing-yeh in Kwangsi province and dealt with a Cantonese opium offender. On September 24th he sent off four reports to the Emperor. One of these would appear to have been his famous apologia,[2] which reached Peking on October 24th. It is of great length, but I will try to resume its principal points, as it formed the basis upon which Chi'-shan's subsequent inquiry into Lin's conduct was founded. The English, Lin says, despite all appearances to the contrary, are at the end of their resources. They have been hiring ships and soldiers at all their ports, and have spent enormous sums both on this and on cannon-balls and gun-powder, as well as on provisioning their forces. Such a rate of expenditure cannot go on much longer. A proof of how hard up they are is that at Ting-hai they have put up notices announcing that opium is for sale at one foreign dollar per catty (1⅓ lb.) which is far less than they pay for it.

Again, foreigners keep warm in winter by wrapping themselves up in rugs; they do not use furs, and it would be

[1] A maxim from the *Book of History*; Legge's Chinese Classics III. 2. 542.
[2] IV. 66.

against their nature to do so. The climate in Chekiang is very severe and it is certain that they will not be able to hold out at Ting-hai through the winter. Foreign letters from Ting-hai to Canton complain of the dampness and unhealthiness of the climate, and say that large numbers of the English have died of disease. As soon as the north winds set in they are certain to go back to the south.

Since the English established their blockade of our ports other foreigners have been complaining bitterly, and are about to send warships to bring the English to their senses. But the fact that they are in a hopeless position makes them try to cover up their weakness by adopting an even more arrogant and bullying attitude than before. However, when all their villainous devices have failed they will have nothing for it but to bow their heads and submit. . . .

It is not true that the measures against opium led to their sending soldiers here. From the moment that, years ago, they began to import opium they already harboured bellicose intentions against us. But the case is like that of a cancer: if it is not dealt with in time the poison will spread to the rest of the body. The opium question should have been dealt with twenty or thirty years ago, when there were relatively few smokers. Treated at this late stage of the disease, the poison has inevitably broken out elsewhere. That is the explanation of the happenings at Ting-hai.

But to go back to the confiscation of the opium—Elliot of his own accord sent a note asking to collect it. This may be verified by reference to the English and Chinese versions of the note, duly impressed with the foreigner's seal. When the opium was destroyed certain foreigners were invited to look on, and they recorded what they saw in a document of several thousand words, and in it they expressed their admiration for the way in which the laws of our Heavenly Court were administered.

Lin then recalls that subsequently the English, unlike other foreigners, refused to sign the guarantee, and later seized a Chinese town 'killing and wounding the officials both civil and military. Since that dastardly outrage there can be no further question of anything but subduing them by force. Some of your advisers fear that our ships and guns will prove no match for those of the foreigners, and that some means must be found of temporizing with them. Unfortunately their appetites are insatiable; the more they get, the more they demand, and if we do not overcome them by force of arms there will be no end to our troubles. Moreover there is every probability that if the English are not dealt with, other foreigners will soon begin to copy and even outdo them.'

At this point the Emperor wrote in the margin: 'If anyone is copying it is you, who are trying to frighten me, just as the English try to frighten you!' Lin goes on to suggest that, as the National Exchequer has for long past been receiving huge sums levied by the Customs at Canton, at least one part in ten ought to have been set aside to pay for the ships and guns needed for the defence of the city. At the side of this the Emperor writes: 'A pack of nonsense!'

The Superintendency of the Customs at Canton was a Court appointment, this being presumably a hang-over from the days when foreign trade was thought of as tribute. The Customs dues were paid into the National Exchequer, but the Superintendent (the 'Hoppo' of the English sources) was expected to make considerable presents to the Court, as a condition of being allowed to keep his job. Thus a suggestion by Lin about how the Customs dues ought to have been used was a criticism of the private servants of the Emperor, and so of His Majesty himself. Considering the revolutionary nature of the proposal it is certainly surprising to find it thrown off so casually, and it is not to be wondered at that the Emperor regarded the suggestion as a stupid impertinence. Lin does indeed continue: 'Your Majesty will wonder that in a memorial the real purpose of which is to ask that I may be punished for my misdeeds, I still venture to make this humble suggestion. But if in making it I can in any degree serve my country, I am ready to take the consequences, even if they should turn out to be that I am "pulped from head to heel".' Lin then offers, if the Emperor will grant this as a special favour, to go to Hang-chow and serve with the forces that are being mustered there to recover Ting-hai. In Kwangtung, he says, every port and inlet is now so well fortified that about that province at least the Emperor need feel no anxiety.

At the end of Lin's dispatch the Emperor wrote: 'the passages I have marked are all to be scrutinized and reported upon'. On the same day (October 24th) he gave orders that the dispatch was to be given to Ch'i-shan (already appointed as Lin's successor) who was to report upon the marked passages.

The diary entry for September 25th is: 'Overcast. It being the birthday of my late grandmother I made offerings to her spirit in the early morning. In the afternoon it rained; in the evening I replied to petitions.' On the 26th he went at dawn to the temple of the God of Literature and burnt incense. He then went with the Governor to the Examination Hall and they paid their respects to the two superintendents of the Provincial Examinations. 'The eighth day [October 3rd] is fixed for the announcement of the results.'

On October 1st, he writes: 'Coming back to my office I found a mandate sent on the twenty-second day of the eighth month [September 17th] by express messenger, five hundred leagues a day, informing me that the English rebels have gone to Tientsin and presented a petition to be forwarded to the Emperor by Ch'i-shan, the Governor-General of Chihli; the English have been permitted to go back to Canton and "beat on the barrier".[1] Orders have also been given for Ch'i-shan to proceed to Canton as High Commissioner and investigate various matters.'

Ch'i-shan[2] is chiefly known to Western readers from the

---

[1] Sue for peace.   [2] Huc's Ki-Chan.

lively but unreliable pages of Huc's *Travels in Tartary, Tibet and China*, translated by William Hazlitt, junior, son of the famous critic. Ch'i-shan was born about 1783. He counted as a Manchu, but was of Mongol descent. He inherited the rank of Marquis in 1823, and held a long succession of high posts. In 1831 he was appointed to the most coveted of all Governor-Generalships—that of Chihli, the province in which Peking stands. In the early summer of 1838, when, as we have seen (p. 13), a number of high officials were asked to report on how to deal with the opium question, he opposed[1] the introduction of the death penalty for opium offences. 'In Fuhkien and Kwangtung', he said, 'seven or eight out of every ten persons smoke opium. There would have to be hundreds of thousands of executions, or even more.' Instead of organizing a wholesale massacre of opium smokers, many of whom are people who in every other way are of the highest respectability, the proper course, Ch'i-shan said, would be to take efficient steps to prevent the import of opium. Smoking would then cease of its own accord, without recourse to a policy which would fill every court in China with capital charges. He and Lin were thus from the beginning on opposite sides in the opium controversy that had been raging in official circles since 1836.

On October 2nd, as commonly happened when he received agitating news, he had one of his attacks of catarrh, which (as I have said) were possibly something in the nature of hay-fever. He sent for Dr Liu Shih-tse, a Nanking man who was attached to the Customs Superintendency. 'Tonight', he says, 'the Examination results were posted up, but I was not well enough to go.' On October 4th he was able to go at dawn to make offerings to the Queen of Heaven at the club for Fuhkien residents at Canton; but Dr Liu was sent for once more. On the 5th he is a little better, but on the 6th is dissatisfied with Dr Liu and sends for Dr Ku. On the 7th a banquet to successful candidates is held, but he cannot

[1] I. 515.

go. In the afternoon he gets another communication from the Emperor, but apparently does not feel strong enough to deal with it for several days. On October 9th he is much better. He still sends for Dr Ku to feel his pulse, but takes no medicine. At night he begins to draft his reply to the Emperor's last two dispatches, and continues to work at it next day. The dispatch[1] which arrived on October 1st announcing Ch'i-shan's appointment and ordering coastal authorities not to fire at English ships that anchored outside Chinese ports—referring, of course, to the British fleet returning from the north to Canton—was comparatively easy to deal with. He had merely to say that the Emperor's will must be done. The dispatch sent from Peking on September 18th and received on October 7th was more perturbing. The Emperor wanted to know why in the same dispatch (that of August 16th; see above, p. 113) Lin spoke in one place of 'selecting a day on which to engage in a final battle of annihilation' and in another place of it 'not being worth our while to embark on a combat at sea'. It is obvious, says the Emperor, that Lin, being afraid that the troubles along the Fuhkien and Chekiang coasts and the arrival of the British fleet in the neighbourhood of Tientsin will be attributed to his mismanagement of the situation at Canton, decided on this move in order to get in first. But if he thought that a switch-over from a defensive to an offensive policy was necessary he ought to have sent an express message informing the Emperor of what he was going to do, and asking for authorization. 'As it is, your messenger did not hand in the dispatch till today.[2] This is all most irregular and I have given orders that you are to be severely reprimanded.' If there has been a decisive action, Lin is to report on it at once and this time by express courier. . . .

[1] IV. 69.

[2] i.e. on September 18th, Lin's dispatch having taken thirty-three days to arrive. An express message by relay riders should not have taken more than eighteen days. Like other communications of this kind, the whole is in the third person; but it is often more convenient to use the first person in English.

Lin replies by summarizing the course of events since September 1839. The battles of Kowloon, Chuenpi and the Barrier, and the routing of the '*Charlie*' on August 13th, were all purely defensive; it was the English who fired the first shot. The last two were only small reverses for the English. 'If I did not send a message by express courier, it was because there was no large-scale victory to report.' How it was that he announced to the Emperor his intention of launching a great naval onslaught and thus reversing the defensive policy that had hitherto been followed, without first obtaining leave to change over to the offensive, Lin does not attempt to explain. Nor does he explain why this intention was not carried out. Presumably the Admiral dissuaded him.

On October 13th worse was to come. The Governor of Kwangtung, I-liang, called and showed him an express letter that he had just received. It was dated September 29th, and was addressed to 'I-liang, Acting Governor-General of Kwangtung and Kwangsi'. In this casual and humiliating way Lin learned that he had been cashiered, and that his Governor-Generalship was temporarily in the hands of his inferior, the Governor of the one province of Kwangtung. It is a curious coincidence that Captain Elliot, too, nearly a year later, first learnt of his recall in an equally casual way. Picking up the *Canton Press* on July 24, 1841, he saw an announcement that Palmerston had recalled him and that a new Plenipotentiary would be sent. It was not until nearly a week later that the official intimation arrived.

The diary betrays no perturbation; and indeed Lin had probably for some time past regarded his loss of the Governor-Generalship as a foregone conclusion. On October 14th he went to a party given in honour of the two Examination Superintendents, and next day himself entertained them. A possible sign of agitation was that on the 16th he wrote a large number of poetical couplets for the decoration of pillars. As we shall see, he tended in crises to calm himself by exercises in calligraphy. On the 17th he went with a large party, including the two Examination Superintendents, to Whampoa to look at some foreign ships, and also went aboard a new Chinese warship of the Complete Victory class. On the 19th the Military Examinations (corresponding to the civil Literary Examinations) began, and Lin went to watch tests in shooting arrows on horseback. On going home, he wrote more couplets. On the 20th came the expected notification from the Board of Civil Office. Lin was to come to Peking and there await the decision of the Board. Ch'i-shan was to be Governor-General in Lin's stead, the duties of this office being carried on by the Governor I-liang till Ch'i-shan arrived at Canton. In the decree[1] effecting these changes (dated September 28th) the Emperor insisted (see above, p. 117) that Lin was being put on trial solely because of his failure to carry out his mission at Canton, and not because he had been influenced in any degree by the charges against Lin made by the English in their petition. 'At the Hour of the Cock', Lin writes in his diary, 'I wrapped up my seals of office, that of Governor-General and that of Commissioner of the Salt Gabelle, and sent them to the Governor to take charge of. He and his subordinate then came to call.' October 21st: 'Today is the anniversary of my ancestor Jung-lu's death. I made offerings to his spirit and saw no visitors, but spent the time arranging my books.' On the 23rd he went to a farewell dinner given to him by his colleagues at the Governor's Office, where he learnt that his friend Teng, the former Governor-General, had also received orders to go to Peking and await trial. On the 24th he went round paying farewell visits. 'For several days', he says, 'the local shop-keepers and other residents have been climbing up on to the shafts of my palanquin— such throngs of them as to block the street. I speak words of good cheer and send them away. All their presents—shoes, umbrellas, incense-burners, mirrors and the like—I give

[1] IV. 61.

back. But twenty or thirty laudatory inscriptions I have accepted and deposited at the Temple of the Queen of Heaven.' On the 25th he divides his luggage into three parts, one to go by sea to Foochow, one to go to the house of the Superintendent of Customs, Yü-k'un, for him to take and use whatever he requires, one to be put on to the boat. He had already arranged to start for Peking at 5 a.m. next day when he heard that on October 3rd it had been decided that he was to remain at Canton, so as to be at hand during the investigations that were to be made there—meaning those to be carried on by Ch'i-shan when he arrived. 'I shall have to hire a lodging of some kind immediately', he writes laconically, 'so as to be able to move in tomorrow.'

He found accommodation at the Guildhall of the salt-merchants, and moved in immediately. His dependants were to follow on October 28th. At this point he records some of the laudatory inscriptions that he has deposited at the Temple of the Queen of Heaven, beginning with those offered by local tradesmen, such as tea- and silk-merchants. They are chiefly quatrains of four syllables to the line, such as:

> The people were drenched with his favours,
> The foreigners feared his might.
> For his services, he remains in Canton
> Benefiting all the Regions of the South.

Last comes a eulogy in eight lines offered by twenty-five leading local gentlemen. Among them were the great poet Chang Wei-p'ing (see above, p. 53), and a young man of thirty called Ch'en Li, who was then tutor to Chang Wei-p'ing's sons, but was afterwards to become one of the most learned and prolific scholars of the nineteenth century. The most interesting of his works to us today is perhaps his history of Chinese music (*Sheng-lü T'ung K'ao*), a book that I possess and have constantly consulted during the last thirty years.

On October 30th Lin spent the day arranging his books in his new lodgings. Next day he wrote calligraphic inscriptions to hang on the pillars. The whole of November 2nd was spent in 'making characters', *tso-tzu*, which I take to mean practising calligraphy. From now till November 28th 'making characters' is practically the only activity that he records. However, on November 21st his great friend the former Governor-General Teng returned from Fuhkien, having been ordered, like Lin, to make himself useful at Canton; and the two were henceforth constantly together. On November 29th there is the eventful entry: 'The Minister Ch'i-shan arrived today. I sent someone to welcome him. He left the Capital on the ninth of the ninth month; so it has taken him two months to get here.' This leisurely method of travel was typical of Ch'i-shan's easy-going temperament. 'In the evening', Lin adds, 'Liang Pao-ch'ang[1] also arrived. As he started from the Capital at mid-autumn [September 10th], it has taken him the best part of three months to get here.' There is certainly a tinge of censure in these remarks. On November 30th Ch'i-shan called, but 'I did not see him'. This may merely mean that Lin was not at home. On December 3rd Lin 'wrote characters' and put together twenty-five of the English originals of Elliot's notes to him, to send to Ch'i-shan. This meant, of course, that Ch'i-shan had begun his inquiry into Lin's dealings with the English, and wanted to check up on whether the Chinese translations of Elliot's notes were accurate. For this purpose he had at his disposal Pao P'eng,[2] a former comprador of the opium dealer Lancelot Dent. Pao claimed to know English, though it is doubtful whether his knowledge went beyond pidgin-colloquial. Ch'i-shan was also trying to get into touch with Elliot, who had arrived back from the north on November 20th and was now sole Plenipotentiary, his cousin Admiral Elliot having retired owing to illness on November 29th.

[1] He had come to Canton to be Provincial Treasurer.
[2] See below, p. 241.

On December 4th Lin writes, 'I hear that Yü Pao-shun has gone down to the Bogue to make arrangements with the foreigners'. Yü had been one of the principal members of Lin's staff. On December 8th Lin writes: 'Ch'i-shan wants to take over my old files; so today I looked them through, put them in proper order and sent them to him. Yü Pao-shun has come back from the Bogue. He says the English are ready to return all the boats that they have seized.'

It must have been not much more than a week after this that Ch'i-shan concluded his conscientious but certainly rather rapid investigation into the charges against Lin. His report[1] reached Peking on December 30th and is therefore unlikely to have been sent from Canton later than December 13th. He must have been working at it intensively from about December 4th to December 12th, but he found time to think of other things. On December 10th, having discovered that the young Englishman Vincent Stanton was still in gaol at Canton, he had him released, brought to his own official residence for two days to be fed up, so that he might make a better impression, and then restored him to his friends.

Ch'i-shan's report begins with the general verdict that hostilities occurred in the first place because Lin had in more than one note[2] to Elliot promised to ask the Emperor for permission to give the English some kind of compensation for the loss of the surrendered opium, but in the end had only offered[3] five catties of tea per chest of opium, which did not represent more than one per cent of the value, and in the second place from the demand for a guarantee never to sell opium again and to submit to the death penalty if caught doing so.

As regards Lin's report[4] to the Emperor received on October 24th—his famous apologia—and the passages in it

---

[1] I. 409 and IV. 73. Both versions are abridged in places.
[2] e.g. on March 18th (II. 243).
[3] Offered on August 31, 1839; refused by Elliot (II. 176).
[4] See above, p. 118.

marked by the Emperor: the assertion of Lin that 'Elliot of his own accord sent a note asking to collect it' is disproved by the fact that Elliot's note was sent five days after Lin deprived the English of their compradors. It is evident that Elliot's surrender of the opium was forced from him under strong pressure, and was not offered of his own free will. Another point I have been asked to investigate, says Ch'i-shan, is whether the Sovereign of England sent a letter to Lin, which he did not communicate to the Emperor. This is untrue; the story must have arisen from the fact that the King of Luzon did once write to Lin.[1] As regards the passage in his report (see above, p. 113) about foreign letters from Ting-hai complaining of the climate and saying that large numbers of the English had died of disease—I learn from I-li-pu, the Governor-General of Kiangnan, that the English there have ample supplies of food, and that though there have been several hundred deaths from illness these have occurred almost exclusively among the rank and file; not more than one or two officers have died. At present everything is all right again, and it is quite false to represent them as being in great straits.

Before Lin's arrival at Canton, Ch'i-shan says, officials paid no particular attention to foreign writings, as they were concerned almost exclusively with business matters. But Lin, wanting to understand the foreigners better, purchased a great number of them from various quarters. The 'document of several thousand words' describing the destruction of the opium, referred to in Lin's report, was found after long inquiry to have been meant satirically.[2] But when it was discovered that it was not the admiring and laudatory piece that it appeared to be, it was burnt; so that further investigation is impossible.

1 About the *Bilbaino* case. No such letter survives; possibly it was from the Governor of Manila.

2 Lin was presumably referring to the laudatory and respectful article in the *Canton Press*, July 20, 1839. The satire Ch'i-shan heard about may have been some different document.

Ch'i-shan's report also raises a number of other, less important points. What it very well might have done, but does not do, is to question the veracity of Lin's reports about naval engagements.[1] This question had not been raised by the Emperor, for the simple reason that their truthfulness was not then and has never since been doubted in China, except by historians writing under direct Western influence.

During the second half of December written negotiations were going on between Elliot and Ch'i-shan without any result. Elliot was still sticking to the general demands outlined in Palmerston's letter, only made more concrete by the substitution of 'Hongkong' for Palmerston's 'large and properly situated island'. Warlike measures were decided upon, and on January 7th Lin records in his diary: 'A fine day. The English attacked the forts at Shakok and Taikok.' These were the forts on each side of the entrance to the Bogue. After naming some of the Chinese officers who were killed and saying that the losses of the ground troops were over two hundred, he notes that the Chinese marines had hardly any casualties. I am not going to try here, or in connection with the subsequent actions, to give a detailed description of the operations. This has been done in many standard accounts of the war. I will only add from Western sources such details as are indispensable to an understanding of what happened. One must, for example, note here that the forts were not merely attacked, but taken, and that on the same day, a little higher up the Bogue, practically the whole of the Chinese fleet that was guarding the Bogue was destroyed. On January 8th 'a little boat with an old woman and a man in it'[2] was sent out by Admiral Kuan to ask for a truce. On January 10th Lin hears that the English fleet is stationed off Anunghoy island, forming an arc round the Middle Bogue forts, Chen-yüan, Wei-yüan and Ching-yüan. This news was already out of date; for though on January

[1] See above, p. 72.   [2] Bernard, *The Nemesis in China*, p. 97.

8th the fleet had approached the forts, intending to capture them during the course of the day, it was suddenly withdrawn owing to the reopening of negotiations. 'For several days on end', Lin writes on January 15th, 'Canton River has been in a state of alert; but today I hear that the foreigners in the Bogue have withdrawn a little.' On January 20th Lin notes that both Ch'i-shan and the Governor of Kwangtung have received copies of an express confidential message dated January 6th. 'Ch'i-shan', says Lin, 'at once came to my lodging, letting himself in at the back door. We talked for a short time, and then he left me. Soon afterwards I went to return the visit; but when I got to the gate, I turned back.' The confidential message referred to contained a peremptory order by the Emperor that there was to be no further parleying of any kind and that orders had been given for reinforcements from Hunan, Szechwan and Kweichow, four thousand in all, to proceed immediately to Canton. Ch'i-shan was to call in Lin and Teng to advise him and with them make plans for annihilating the English the moment they attempted to land.

Perhaps what Ch'i-shan came to say was this: 'If I break off the negotiations, after signing only yesterday a preliminary arrangement, the English will seize the remaining Bogue forts and will have Canton at their mercy within a few days. If I continue the negotiations, it will be in direct defiance of these orders from Peking. All the same I mean to go on negotiating, in the hope of keeping Elliot in play till our reinforcements come from Hunan and Yünnan. Then we shall soon be able to announce a victory, and my having taken an independent line will be overlooked.' Lin presumably dissented violently, and Ch'i-shan broke off the conversation.[1] Presently (as I see it) Lin felt he must try once more to prevent Ch'i-shan from taking a course which would be regarded as open rebellion, and would probably lead to

[1] One would take a rather different view of Ch'i-shan's relations with Lin if one believed in the genuineness of the famous 'letter to his family', II. 563.

Ch'i-shan's execution. But having got as far as the door, he had the feeling that argument was useless, and turned back. On that same day Elliot duly announced the conclusion (presumably on January 18th) of a preliminary arrangement, the main feature of which was the 'cession of the harbour and island of Hongkong to the British Crown'.

On January 24th, Chinese New Year's Day, Lin first paid New Year calls and then 'went to the Kuang-hsiao Monastery to study the inscriptions'. This was the monastery where the Sixth Patriarch of the Meditation Sect, Hui-neng, was supposed to have been ordained. There were plenty of inscriptions there; but one wonders whether going to a monastery to 'study inscriptions' was not Lin's 'cover' term for a secret interview, possibly with someone who might help to prevent Ch'i-shan from political and indeed actual suicide.

The further details of the convention (known as the Convention of Chuenpi) were to be settled at a meeting between Ch'i-shan and the English leaders. It was to be held at the Lotus Flower Wall,[1] about twenty-six miles downstream from Canton. On January 25th Lin writes: 'Ch'i-shan left his office at dawn to go to the Lotus Flower Wall. I sent someone to see him off.' On the 26th he reads in the *Peking Gazette* that Chou T'ien-chio (Governor-General of Hupeh and Hunan) has been sent to serve as a common soldier at I-li, on the north-west frontier. Chou was a zealous but harsh official, whose severities had often been applauded by the Emperor. In 1840 he was accused of allowing his subordinates to use unauthorized forms of torture. It was apparently in 1837 that he arrested the Lazarist missionary Father Jean-Gabriel Perboyre, who after a long imprisonment was executed at Wu-ch'ang on September 11, 1840, presumably just before Chou T'ien-chio's fall. The execution was legal, as the spreading of 'false doctrines' was a capital offence. It is of some interest

[1] Generally called Lotus Flower Hill (*Kang*).

that this, the only martyrdom of the period, seems to have taken place at the hands of an official who was notoriously and exceptionally savage in his administration.

On January 27th Lin writes: 'I hear that today Ch'i-shan gave a great banquet to the English rebels at the Lotus Flower Wall, on the banks of the Lion Reach. At the Hour of the Snake [9 a.m.] there arrived eighteen foreign officers, two interpreters and two foreign boys, together with three French foreigners.[1] They were escorted by fifty-six foreign soldiers and sixteen musicians, drumming and fifing. After they had been presented to Ch'i-shan, four mats were spread for Manchus and Chinese, while the place of honour was given to the rebel foreigners. The Acting Governor of Canton, Yü Pao-shun, and the Brigade-Commander Chao Ch'eng-te attended at the banquet, being given places at each end, on east and west. To the foreign soldiers and musicians hot food was served, while the sailors and others were given mutton and wine. After the meal all the foreigners came to the front of Ch'i-shan's tent and expressed their thanks. Then suddenly they began giving a great display of gunnery, both small arms and artillery. When that was over, they went back to their ships. But Elliot and Morrison[2] went to Ch'i-shan's boat and talked privately with him for over an hour. They have agreed to meet again tomorrow.'

This account agrees closely with those of eye-witnesses on the English side. Six months later, at his trial, Ch'i-shan played down the whole affair. There had been no such thing as a formal banquet, he said. The English had had nothing to eat, so he gave them some light refreshments.

On January 31st Lin writes: 'Ch'i-shan came. He had a great deal to say about the fierce fire power of the foreign rebels' guns and high quality of their mechanical contrivances. He also spoke in very extreme terms about the utter useless-ness of our marines.' It was just at this time that Ch'i-shan

---

[1] Officers of the French frigate *Danaide*, which had just arrived at Canton.
[2] i.e. J. R. Morrison, the interpreter.

was writing the famous report[1] that reached Peking on February 16th. Translations of it figure in many Western books, and I will here only summarize four of the main points.

(1) *The Forts*

These are either on small islands or have channels in their rear, so that they could easily be blockaded by foreign ships and the defenders starved out. All the forts are sited on the assumption that the attackers will approach by the route they have been used to following in peace-time. Unfortunately Canton can be approached by other channels, far out of range of the forts.

(2) *The Guns*

These are quite inadequate in number and are all placed in front of the forts, the sides of which are quite undefended. Many of the guns are obsolete in type and are not in working order. Recently we have got hold of a cannon-maker who has produced a design for a better type of gun; but we have only just begun to experiment with casting guns of this type.

(3) *The Troops*

The soldiers we are using as marines are unused to going in ships and suffer badly from sea-sickness. The troops normally employed for patrol purposes are in some cases of very poor quality. Hearing that after the fall of Shakok the troops threatened to disband unless given a gratuity, I asked Admiral Kuan if this was true. He confirmed the story, and said that he had to pawn his own clothes in order to scrape together enough to give each man two foreign dollars.

(4) *The Cantonese*

Apart from actual traitors, in the service of the foreigners, the people in general are so used to foreigners that they no longer regard them as creatures of a different species, and in

[1] IV. 91.

fact get on very well with them. Some small present, such as a mechanical contrivance, is enough to win over most Cantonese completely.

The first three points are all to a considerable extent meant to be reflections on Lin, who had been responsible for the defences of Canton since 1839. As regards the chief alternative channel, by-passing the Bogue, Ch'i-shan had been misinformed. It was definitely of minor importance because it was in places only five feet deep, and large war vessels could not have used it. But even so, it was by no means undefended; the flat-bottomed, shallow-draft steamship *Nemesis* explored this western route on March 13th and 14th,[1] 1841, and had to cope with a considerable number of forts and defence-posts. Moreover in some places the channel had been blocked with stakes and rafts. The uselessness of the Chinese marines had, of course, been constantly emphasized by Lin, and he had made strenuous though apparently unsuccessful efforts to reform them.

To the readiness of Chinese civilians to assist the English, before the period (end of May 1841) when the pillaging of Chinese villages began[2] the experiences of the *Nemesis* also bear witness. Villagers were only too happy to assist in pulling away the impediments that blocked the river. But that, no doubt, was partly because local communication was chiefly by water, and the staking of the river was a nuisance to fishermen and peasants.

After Ch'i-shan left, Lin went 'studying inscriptions' again; this time at the Temple of the Five Genii and at the Monastery of the Six Banyan Trees. The 'Five Genii' were five old men who in ancient times arrived at what afterwards became Canton riding on five rams and each carrying in his hand a stalk of grain, symbol of future abundance. The rams changed into stone, and the Genii disappeared into the sky. The temple, however, only dated from the middle of the

[1] Bernard, *The Nemesis in China*, p. 139 seq.   [2] See above, p. 112.

eighteenth century. The Monastery of the Six Banyan Trees stands near the Hua T'a (Decorated Pagoda). There was certainly something to look at there—the name-board of the monastery, written out in large calligraphic characters by the great poet, painter and calligrapher Su Tung-p'o (eleventh century A.D.)

On February 2nd Lin records that 'Tsung-i and Kung-shu began to attend school'. These were his second and third sons, now aged seventeen and fourteen. The eldest son already held a Civil Service post. The second seems to have come to Canton from Foochow in the spring or summer of 1840. As we shall see, their studies were destined to be constantly interrupted.

On February 9th Lin writes: 'I respectfully read the Emperor's decree of the fifth of the first month (January 27th) and learnt that Ch'i-shan's conduct in allowing parleys to take place instead of carrying out the destruction of the English rebels, is to be investigated by the Board of Civil Office, as is also his failure to hold the forts at Shakok and Taikok. Admiral Kuan loses his cap-button and is to retrieve his failure by future services.'

The English, hearing that the Admiral, for whom they had a great admiration, had 'lost his button at Shakok', took the statement literally and began looking for it. They did indeed find a button of some sort on the battlefield, and sent it to the Admiral.

February 10th: 'Ch'i-shan went to the Bogue, and I sent someone to see him off.' February 11th: 'At dawn I went with Teng to Lieh-te[1] and Erh-sha-wei[2] to see how things [i.e. defences] are on Canton River. I came back at the Hour of the Snake [9 a.m.].' February 13th: 'Ch'i-shan came back from the Bogue; but I did not see him. I went with Teng to the Po-ni-hsün[3] and neighbouring places to see how things on

---

[1] Seven miles downstream from Canton.
[2] About eight miles south-west of Canton.
[3] A police-post on the West River, about twenty miles west of Canton.

the river are getting on. I came back at the second drum [9 p.m.] and heard that orders had been given for I-shan to assume the title of Rebel-quelling General. He is to come to Canton and, assisted by Lung-wen and Yang Fang as Deputies, he is to destroy the foreigners.'

I-shan was a cousin of the Emperor's; Lung-wen was also a Manchu grandee. Yang Fang was a Chinese; a professional soldier who had distinguished himself in a long series of campaigns, particularly against Moslem risings in the West. He was now over seventy, and so deaf that conversation with him had to be in writing. He was typical of those ancient military figureheads who are so often brought on to the scene in times of desperate crisis, in the hope of reviving morale. Everyone had heard of how Yang Fang routed and captured the fanatical Mohammedan leader Jehangir (in 1828); and the news that he was on his way had some of the desired effect. Yang Fang was at Ch'ang-sha, the capital of Hunan, when about February 9th he received orders to go at once to Canton.

Just before he started, he wrote to the Emperor: 'The essential points now are on the one hand to recover Ting-hai and on the other to allow the English to have a place to store their merchandise, on an out-of-the-way shore of some small island.' He probably already knew of the cession of Hongkong, and did not want to have to tackle the job of trying to get it back again. Passing through Nan-ch'ang, the capital of Kiangsi, he visited Pao Shih-ch'en (see above, p. 16) from whom so many statesmen travelling between Peking and Canton sought or at any rate got advice.

Pao Shih-ch'en's advice[1] to Yang Fang on the present occasion was to this effect: *We* cannot compete with the English either in ships or guns. But the other foreign countries are equipped as the English are, and though no one country is capable of standing up to the English, if they united they could certainly inflict a crushing defeat. Our

[1] IV. 465.

policy should be to fan the grievances of the nations whose trade has been stopped owing to the behaviour of the English, and get them to join in an attack. These other nations should then be rewarded, according to the amount of help they have given in achieving this victory, by Customs concessions, and so on. Yang Fang was evidently much impressed by this advice, and offered[1] to arrange for the reinstatement of Pao, who had been Prefect of a neighbouring district, but had lost his job.

On February 21st Lin writes: 'A thousand regular troops from Hunan and the same number from Yünnan are now arriving in batches at Canton.' In the afternoon the Manchu General Hsiang-fu, in command of the Hunan troops, called on him, partly perhaps to arrange for some of the soldiers to encamp in the grounds of the salt-merchants' Guildhall, where Lin was staying. Next day the Manchu General Yung-fu, from Kweichow province, also called.

On February 23rd Lin writes: 'I hear that two steamers belonging to the rebel English, with several small boats, sailed straight up to T'ai-p'ing-hsü[2] in the Bogue, opened fire and set alight a number of peasants' houses, and also the Customs House.' Lin does not mention that a battery was destroyed; on the other hand the English accounts say nothing about damage to 'non-military targets'. Both accounts are no doubt true as far as they go. On the 24th he went with Ch'i-shan and other high officers to inspect the defences of the Inner River, and spent the night at Lieh-te, seven miles east of Canton. The tour of inspection went on next day, and ended early on February 26th at the Ta-huang-chiao, about eight miles south of Canton.

'I got home at the Hour of the Monkey [3 p.m.]', writes Lin, 'and when night came heard that the Bogue forts and those on Wantung Island were being invested, preparatory to attack, by the English rebels. I at once went with Teng to

[1] IV. 476.
[2] Behind Anson's Bay, between Anunghoy and Chuenpi Islands.

Ch'i-shan's office and at the Hour of the Rat [11 p.m.] we heard that the Wantung, Yung-an and Kung-ku[1] forts have fallen. All night I could not sleep.' February 27th: 'I hear that the Bogue forts Chen-yüan, Ching-yüan and Wei-yüan[2] have been taken.' Admiral Kuan and Major Mai T'ing-chang both fell. The ships of the English rebels are already making straight for Wu-yung,[3] in the Inner River.

'I also hear that the President of the Board of Punishments Ch'i Kung has been ordered to come here as Governor-General and Intendant of Grain. General Ch'ang-ch'un, commandant of the station of Nan-kan-chen in Kiangsi, arrived in Canton today with two thousand soldiers. He came to see me.'

The most reliable account of the Admiral's death is that of Captain Hall of the *Nemesis*, transcribed by W. D. Bernard:[4] 'Many of the Chinese officers boldly and nobly met their death. . . . Among the most distinguished and lamented was poor old Admiral Kuan, whose death excited much sympathy throughout the force; he fell by a bayonet wound in his breast, as he was meeting his enemy at the gate of Anunghoy. . . . Kuan's body was recognized and claimed by his own family[5] on the following day, and was of course readily given up to them. A salute of minute-guns was fired to his honour from the *Blenheim*.'

Legend readily attributes the death of a hero to treachery on his own side. Stories were soon spread that his soldiers had refused to apply fuses to the guns of the fort. When Kuan tried himself to fire a gun, he found that water had been allowed to get into the fuse hole. He applied for reinforcements from a neighbouring camp, but none came, and so on. These stories are unconvincing. We know from the English accounts that the fire from the forts, though not very

[1] The first on the northern of the two Wantung islands in the Middle Bogue. The other two were on the west side of the Bogue, opposite Wantung (?).
[2] On Anunghoy Island, on the east side of the Middle Bogue.
[3] Twenty miles downstream from Canton.
[4] Bernard, p. 121.   [5] By a trusted servant, according to Chinese accounts.

effective, was brisk; and it is certain that, given the vastly superior fire power of the English, the arrival of reinforcements would only have added to the number of the Chinese casualties.

As we have seen from the mention of Kuan's sixtieth birthday on April 29, 1839, he was by Chinese reckoning sixty-two when he died; that is just short of sixty-one for us.

February 28th: 'I hear that yesterday the English rebels broke resistance at Wu-yung. The regulars from Hunan were stationed there, and had heavy losses, their Commander Hsiang-fu being also among the killed.' It will be remembered that Lin had made Hsiang-fu's acquaintance only seven days before. 'There are also', Lin continues, 'a hundred trained militiamen, taken from those at the disposal of the Intendant, who came along afterwards from Hsiang-fu's camp. But they had not reached Wu-yung at the time of the attack, and are in fact encamped in the grounds of my house. Today I decided to send my dependants inland.[1] In the afternoon Ch'i-shan, I-liang and Teng all came to talk things over. They stayed to dinner and did not leave till the third drum [11 p.m.].'

After capturing the Wu-yung fort, a party of about a dozen men, led by Captain Hall of the *Nemesis* steamer, boarded the *Cambridge*, the ship formerly belonging to Captain Douglas and purchased a year ago by Lin. 'She mounted', Captain Hall says,[2] 'altogether thirty-four guns, of English manufacture; and it was surprising to see how well the Chinese had prepared for action, the guns being in perfect order, fire buckets distributed about the decks, and everything clean and well arranged.' The Chinese wounded were removed from the ship and 'principally with a view to strike terror into the Chinese' she was set on fire and when the flames reached her powder magazine, she blew up with a tremendous explosion. It may, perhaps, have been some time

[1] The 'Inner City' of the text is a misprint.
[2] Bernard, *The Nemesis in China*, p. 129.

before anyone dared break this news to Lin, for there is no mention of it in his diary.

March 1st: 'Today my dependants embarked on the boat that is to take them upstream to where they are to live for the present. I went to Erh-sha-wei[1] to have another look at the river channels. In the afternoon I went to the Foochow and Ch'ao-chou Club on the southern bank to arrange about recruiting volunteers from Ch'üan-chou[2] and Chang-chou.[3] Coming home at the third drum [11 p.m.] I learnt that Ch'i-shan, owing to his having yielded without permission to the demands of the English rebels, has been deprived of the rank of Grand Secretary and of his Peacock Feather; and that his conduct is to be the subject of strict investigation by the Board of Civil Office. This evening Teng moved into my house, where he is going to live with me.'

The removal of Lin's family to Nan-hsiung, far away up-river, had naturally left him with a lot of spare rooms on his hands.

Ch'i-shan did everything in his power to gloss over the cession of Hongkong to the English; for example by maintaining that he had only ceded a small corner of the island. But the news that proclamations had been put up all over the island announcing that the inhabitants of Hongkong were now British subjects, coming as it did after the Emperor had forbidden negotiations of any kind, was too much for him. The Edict depriving Ch'i-shan of his rank and decorations is dated February 16th, and was evidently sent to Canton at record speed.

March 2nd: 'I hear that the English rebel ships have already forced their way to the fort at Lieh-te.[4] Early in the morning I went to talk things over at the General Office in the Monastery of the Giant Buddha.'[5] March 3rd: 'I went

[1] Seven miles downstream from Canton.
[2] The Chinchow of contemporary English texts.
[3] In southern Fuhkien. The volunteers were, of course, men from these places who lived at Canton.
[4] Seven miles east of Canton. The 'Howqua's Folly' of the English accounts?
[5] At that period no longer used as a monastery but simply as a Munitions Office. It was in the south-east corner of the Old City.

early to the General Office, and then to the Foochow-Ch'ao-Chou Club to recruit volunteers. At the Hour of the Sheep [1 p.m.] I went to the General Office, and did not come back till the second drum [9 p.m.].' Next day he goes again to the Club on recruiting business, enlists 560 men, and parades them in two files, one to the east, one to the west, just inside the Yung-ch'ing Gate, one of the southern gates of the New City, on the way to the Execution Ground. On March 5th Yang Fang, the immensely famous but deaf and aged General, arrived from Hunan. Lin went at once to see him. He remarks that for some days past the people of Canton have been in a very nervous state and large numbers of them have fled from the city (as indeed Lin's family had done). But the news of Yang Fang's arrival has done a lot, he says, to restore confidence. It was probably after his arrival that Yang Fang received the Emperor's letter,[1] addressed to himself, I-shan and the Manchu Deputy Commissioner Lung-wen and containing the ominous warning: 'If any of you have the two words "reopen trade" still in mind, then you are completely betraying the purpose of your mission to Canton.' This crossed Yang Fang's dispatch, written when he set out from Hunan, in which he had rashly proposed that the English should be given 'a place to store their merchandise, on an out-of-the-way shore of some small island'. (See above, p. 137.)

March 6th: 'Early this morning the Hunan regulars and militia asked me to sacrifice to [i.e. to dedicate] their battle-standards.' Later in the day, as almost every day at this period, he had a meeting with Yang Fang. On March 8th Lin hears that the Lieh-te and Erh-sha-wei batteries have fallen and that the English have sent several small armed ships to reconnoitre the Ta-huang-chiao, the confluence of channels to the south-west of Honam Island. On the 9th and 10th he hears that the English ships are being withdrawn to a point lower down the river. A momentary truce had in fact been arranged.

[1] I. 414.

On March 12th he hears that, as the penalty for having
ceded Hongkong without permission, Ch'i-shan, deprived of
his various posts, is to be conducted to the capital in chains,
in charge of the Manchu General Ying-lung. All his property
is to be confiscated by the State.[1] His confidential assistant
Pao P'eng[2] (so well known to the English as Lancelot Dent's
comprador) is also to be brought to the capital for trial.
Ch'i Kung is to be Governor-General, his duties being
performed till he arrives at Canton by the present Governor
I-liang. No time was lost in carrying out this decree. Next
day (March 13th) Lin writes: 'Today Ch'i-shan and Ying-
lung set out for the north. I went to the T'ien-tzu Quay[3] to
see them off. At the Hour of the Monkey [3 p.m.] I heard that
the fort[4] at Ta-huang-chiao has been captured by the English
rebels.'

To see off someone who is in chains must give one a
queer feeling. Moreover it must have seemed certain then
that Ch'i-shan was going to his death. He was indeed, after
a long imprisonment, condemned to death by beheading
on August 8th, but he was soon reprieved, and held a series
of high appointments till the time of his death, in 1854, at
the age of well over seventy.

March 16th: 'Today the rebel foreigners tried to push on
into the City River, but when they were passing Phoenix
Hill[5] our regular troops sank two of their dinghies and
shattered the mainmast of one of their warships; after which
they retired.' The English accounts do not mention any
damage. Next day Yang Fang reported a victory and awards
were made to the officers concerned.

However at about this time Yang Fang sent a secret
dispatch[6] which could hardly have been more pessimistic.
He points out eight main difficulties of the situation, as

---

[1] For lists, see III. 316 and 433. [2] See below, p. 241.
[3] On the south-east part of the river front.
[4] The 'Macao Fort' of English accounts?
[5] The 'Bird's Nest Fort' of English accounts; on the west side of Honam
Island. [6] III. 483.

follows: (1) The Chinese naval forces have been completely destroyed and no naval operation is possible till a new fleet has been built. (2) The great mobility of the attackers, owing to their complete command of the waterways, makes defence of shore-batteries almost impossible. (3) The local troops are unreliable. They are discouraged by repeated reverses, and their morale is undermined owing to infiltration by collaborators. (4) Though the success of March 16th by Kiangsi troops showed that foreign ships can be driven back, the other reinforcements from outside—the troops from Szechwan, Yünnan and Kwangsi—are still unfamiliar with the terrain; there is only 'a loose connection between the men and the soil'. (5) The Cantonese tend to flee at the first sign of danger; nine houses out of ten are already empty. (6) The Old City could easily be held, but the Governor-General's office and the office of the Superintendent of Customs are in the New City, the walls of which are flimsy; moreover it is completely open to attack from the river. (7) Yang Fang is himself unfamiliar with the environs of the town, and has been unable to visit them owing to the continuing emergency at Canton itself. (8) The result of the evacuation of Ting-hai by the English in February has been that they have been able to send large reinforcements to Canton.

There appears to be nothing for it at the moment, says Yang Fang, but to trick the English into withdrawing their ships from Canton. As all they now ask for is a renewal of trade, to start them trading again might be a way of getting them under control. No one would deny that we should be justified in meeting deceit with deceit.

On the 18th Lin writes: 'At the Hour of the Snake [9 a.m.] warships and steamers of the English rebels pushed their way into the City River and fired shells and rockets, twenty or thirty of each; but they failed to start any fire. I inspected volunteers from Foochow and allotted them their posts. Then I went to the troops on and below the City walls, examined the positions they had taken up and bade them keep strict guard. I hear that a first detachment of Szechwan regular troops—four hundred men—arrived today.'

The above is a very incomplete account of what happened on March 18th. Actually the English landed at Canton and re-occupied the foreign factories, which they held till May 21st. Negotiations with Yang Fang followed, and on March 20th both he and Elliot issued proclamations saying that trade at Canton was reopened.

On March 19th Lin writes: 'Both Yang Fang and the Governor of the province, I-liang, came here and we spent all day discussing what was to be done. Yang Fang has come to live with me. Today the English rebels sent a note to Yang Fang begging for the reopening of trade.' March 20th: 'Yang Fang sent the Governor of Canton, Yü Pao-shun, to the foreign boats with an answer to their note.' March 22nd: 'The warships of the English rebels are one after another retiring downstream. The five hundred additional troops from Yünnan who were ordered to proceed to Canton have now all arrived, and five hundred from Hunan have also got as far as Fatshan.'[1] This entry shows that the Chinese were taking the armistice less seriously than Captain Elliot, who appears to have believed that the Chinese were at last ready for peace.

On March 22nd Yang Fang sent to Peking an account of the present situation at Canton. He did not dare tell the Emperor either that the foreign factories had been re-occupied or that trade with the English had been resumed. That merchant ships were coming up to Whampoa and discharging their cargoes must, of course, soon have been known in Canton, and ultimately the Emperor was bound to hear of it. But only a few people intimately connected with trade or foreign affairs could distinguish the ships of one foreign nation from those of another, and by various fictions,

1 Ten miles upstream from Canton.

which it would be tedious and confusing to discuss here,[1] Yang Fang tried to give the impression that the English were still excluded from trade. He admits that Elliot has sent him a document proposing conditions for reopening trade; but in order to avoid the accusation of having entered into negotiations in the manner that had landed Ch'i-shan in chains, he pretends to have done no more than glance at the note.

As we shall see, the Emperor was for the moment completely deceived, and even went so far as to say—an extraordinary statement for any Chinese Emperor to make—that these local matters could best be handled by those on the spot. Till the reinforcements had all arrived and taken up their posts, the Emperor went on, the main thing was to prevent the British from putting out to sea and so avoiding annihilation.

March 30th: 'In the afternoon I went to the Kuang-hsieh Archery Ground to inspect the five hundred Foochow militia already enlisted.' On April 1st eight hundred Hupeh troops arrived, and their Commander An Te-shun called.

On April 3rd, without waiting for a reply to his dispatch of March 22nd, Yang Fang (who had now left Lin's house and gone to live at the Examination Hall) wrote an even more imprudent dispatch[2] to Peking, with the object, apparently, of reinforcing the fiction that though other nations were now trading at Whampoa, the English were still excluded. He did this by quoting what purported to be a plea by the Indian merchants to be counted as non-English and consequently to be allowed to trade. There seems, however, to be no reason to doubt that the Indian merchants (chiefly Parsees) had, like everyone else, been trading briskly since March 20th. To make a sharp distinction between them and the English was impossible; several Parsees, for example,

---

[1] Yang Fang's report, which arrived at Peking on April 6th, is translated by Earl Swisher, *China' Management of the American Barbarians*, p. 61.
[2] IV. 101.

were members of English firms. Moreover there was a further complication. The term (*chiang-chiao*) used to describe Indian merchants appears at Canton to have been currently applied also to Englishmen bringing cargoes from India. Thus Lin himself in his note[1] to Elliot of May 2, 1839, applies it not only to the Parsee merchant Dadabhoy, but also to Dent, Henry, Inglis and other English merchants. If the Emperor had fallen into this trap and someone had pointed out that Dent (who was still in China) was trading again, the reply would have been ' "Indian Merchants", have been allowed by the Emperor to trade, and Dent is an "Indian Merchant".' On April 8th Lin hears that Chou T'ien-chio, the sadistic Governor who has been cashiered and ordered to go to the north-west frontier to serve as a common soldier, has now been told to go to Canton and make good by serving his country there in the present crisis.

On the evening of April 10th Lin got a letter from I-shan, the new Commissioner, and Lung-wen who was to be Yang Fang's colleague, inviting him to come to meet them, so that they might have the benefit of his advice before actually arriving at Canton. On April 12th, accompanied by Teng, he set off by boat for Fatshan.[2] At Fati, just above Canton, 'the rice-fields on both banks were one mass of grey-green, looking like a hair-carpet. We got to Fatshan at the Hour of the Cock [5 p.m.] and moored in front of the Customs House. . . . We heard that I-shan passed Samshui at noon.' April 13th: 'Early this morning we moved up to Huang-t'ing.[4] Here we heard that I-shan and Lung-wen, in their two boats, have both got stranded on a sandbank and are waiting till the tide turns. This happened at a point fifty *li* (about sixteen miles) below Samshui. The new Governor-General, Ch'i Kung, received his seal of office at the Hour of the Snake [9 a.m.], at Samshui. He then put out in a canal-boat and joined I-shan and Lung-wen at the point,

[1] II. 66. [2] About twelve miles south-west of Canton.
[3] Twenty-five miles west of Canton. [4] A few miles south-west of Canton.

where they were waiting for the tide. Between the Hours of the Monkey and the Cock [i.e. about 6 p.m.] all three of them changed into a small boat and joined me at Huang-t'ing. Presently they came with me in my boat to Fatshan, to inspect the battery of newly cast guns, after which we all had supper on board. We turned downstream again after a couple of hours and anchored at the Melon Wharf Creek.[1] After the third watch Teng and I set out homeward, leaving the others behind.' March 14th: 'We passed Fati at the Hour of the Dragon [7 a.m.] and at the Hour of the Snake [9 a.m.] entered the City by the Yung-ch'ing Gate, and I went home. I hear that I-shan and Lung-wen both left their boats and entered the City by land, from the Ni-ch'eng[2] direction. They went in by the Great North Gate and are lodging in the Examination Hall. On the other hand the new Governor-General Ch'i Kung went by boat, landed at the T'ien-tzu quay, and went from there to his office.'

We know from an account[3] by Liang T'ing-nan, head of the Academy where Lin had lodged in 1839, for whom Lin had secured a post at Fatshan, that I-shan and Lung-wen had cut across to Canton by land because they were told that, though the English were not interfering with ordinary Chinese shipping, they might very well attack ships whose flags and other trappings denoted that they were carrying high officials. This, says Liang, was the view of both Lin and of Teng. But Liang persuaded Ch'i Kung that such a precaution was quite unnecessary; Ch'i Kung's name, he said, was very well known to the English from former days, and if he crept into Canton by a back entry, they would take offence at his lack of confidence in them.

Here it should be explained that Ch'i Kung was Governor of Kwangtung from 1833 to 1838 and had taken a leading part in the troubles (September 1834) when the frigates *Andromache* and *Imogene* forced the Bogue and came up to

---

[1] Twelve miles upstream.   [2] Three miles west of Canton.
[3] VI. 35. See below, p. 149.

Whampoa. His experience of affairs at Canton had therefore been even longer than Lin's, and according to Mr Liang he thought it rather strange that on meeting Ch'i Kung Lin immediately drew out of his sleeve a pile of his own dispatches about the management of foreigners. 'He surely must know about my having been Governor here', Ch'i Kung said afterwards to Liang. The story is interesting as exemplifying Lin's lack of tact, already shown so often in his handling of Captain Elliot. However, Ch'i Kung seems to have been amused rather than offended, and during the remaining two weeks of Lin's time at Canton he saw Ch'i Kung constantly.

What is probably an authentic glimpse of Ch'i Kung's state of mind at this time and of his character in general may be got from Liang T'ing-nan's account[1] of a conversation he had with Ch'i Kung after the others had left: ' "Who would have thought", said Ch'i Kung with a sigh, "that in the short time which has passed since I left Canton things would have reached such a calamitous state as this?" "We are looking to you to rescue us from this calamity", I said. "Don't expect too much from me", he replied. "By dint of the utmost care and caution I can just get along in peaceful times as Governor of a single province, but I haven't the sort of abilities needed by a Governor-General— still less in times of trouble. You must, I am sure, remember how it was when Teng was away in Kwangsi inspecting troops and I, as well as being Governor of Kwangtung, was left in charge of foreign affairs. If Stone Farmer hadn't been there to keep me up to the mark about everything, just think of all the blunders I should have made!" Stone Farmer was the pen-name of I K'o-chung, from Kao-yang,[2] who acted as his secretary and to whom he had been devotedly attached for several years. At the time Ch'i Kung got his post at the capital (as President of the Board of Punishments, in 1838) I K'o-chung died. That was why he now spoke of him in this reminiscent way.

[1] VI. 35.   [2] About one hundred miles south of Peking.

' "Wouldn't it be the natural thing," I said presently, "in the case of a great gentleman like yourself being so diffident about his capacity for governing, to appoint someone of decided and energetic character to assist him?" "The Supreme Council", he replied, "knew that I had had a lot of experience of foreign affairs, and if I hadn't always managed to find a good excuse, I should have been sent here long ago. This time, heavy though the burden lies on my shoulders, there was no getting out of it, as I was already on my way to the south when I got the Imperial Mandate." '

The last sentence refers to the fact that he had accepted the comparatively minor post of Controller of Commissariat at Canton and was on his way there when he was appointed Governor-General of Kwangtung and Kwangsi.

April 16th: 'I hear that, as the result of Yang Fang's report of the twenty-fifth of the seventh month [March 17th] about our victory at Phoenix Hill, General Ch'ang-ch'un has been accorded the title of Victorious and Valiant Hero, and has according to the usual precedent been given the Peacock Feather decoration. Today the flag-pole of the Customs House was struck by lightning and the guild-merchant Wu Shao-jung of the I-ho firm also met with "lightning disaster".' This expression would normally mean that the merchant, so well known to the English as 'Howqua', was killed. This may in fact have been rumoured; but actually this particular 'Howqua' (there were several of them in succession) did not die till 1843.

April 20th: 'I hear that Yang Fang's dispatch of the thirtieth[1] of the second month [March 22nd] about permitting trade has come back with His Majesty's comments and instructions. Still no sign of disagreement.' The one comment was, in fact, merely a confirmation of Yang Fang's suggestion that the pleas of other nations that trade with the English should be resumed had been engineered by the English themselves. The instructions, as we have seen, left it open to Yang Fang

---

[1] The 'twenty' in IV. 101, line 12, is a misprint for 'thirty'.

to handle the situation as he thought best, pending the arrival at Canton of all the troops from other provinces. A great weight must certainly have been lifted from Yang Fang's mind.

On April 21st Lin had an attack of his usual malady, which I have suggested was perhaps hay-fever, and sent for a Dr Sung. On the 24th Dr Sung came again, but apparently only on a friendly call. On the 27th Lin had another attack, and had to turn visitors away. Next day Dr Sung was replaced by Dr Ku. On the 28th there was a ceremony of sacrificing to battle-banners and a portion of the sacrificial meat was brought to Lin on his sick-bed. On May 1st he was still being attended by Dr Ku and taking medicine. In the afternoon he learnt that on April 16th a decree had been issued ordering him to proceed immediately, post-haste, to Chekiang (that is to say, to Hangchow) and wait there for further instructions. Meanwhile he was to count as an officer of the Fourth Rank. This was a partial reinstatement; but it did not entitle him to communicate direct with the Emperor, and he was obliged to send his letter of thanks through Ch'i Kung and I-liang, Teng being entrusted with the task of composing a draft version of it. On May 2nd, at Ch'i Kung's office, Lin saw the dispatch sent to Peking by Yang Fang and I-liang on April 3rd, containing the proposal that 'Indians' should be allowed to trade. Both the Emperor's comments and his decree accompanying the returned dispatch are, Lin notes, 'very severe, and both Yang Fang and I-liang are to be referred to the Board of Civil Office for strict inquiry into their conduct'. The comments were indeed severe. Against the statement that the Indians, using the Americans and French as their spokesmen, had asked to be allowed to trade, the Emperor wrote in the margin: 'This, and all that follows, deals with matters that, as things are now, should not be discussed at all. For me only the one word "annihilation" exists; moreover, I do not believe anything they say.' And later, apropos of

India: 'But that is where the opium comes from! Whom do you think you are deceiving? It enrages me to read such a dispatch.' And alongside of Yang Fang's statement that he was not following in the footsteps of Ch'i-shan: 'You phrase it differently, but the facts are the same. How you dare try it on, I cannot imagine!' At the end the Emperor adds the note, 'If trade were all that we wanted, why did we mobilize all these troops and transfer them to Canton, and why was it necessary to put Ch'i-shan on trial?'

On May 3rd Lin was seen off by the Governor-General, the Governor and other high officials, as well as by the commanders of the troops brought to Canton from other provinces. He gives minute particulars about the boat that was to take him to Nan-hsiung, where he was to join his wife and two younger sons. This boat was forty-six feet long, and the cabin eleven feet wide. There were three gangway entrances. The crew numbered fourteen, and the price of hire was sixty dollars. He also hired another boat, 'small and old', for thirty-five dollars, in which to put three carrying-chairs and a stock of provisions. When he passed Fati he was met by the poet Chang Wei-p'ing who took him to his famous Eastern Garden. 'The pomegranates and autumn crab-apple were in flower; but the lychee-trees and box-myrtle had already begun to form their fruits.' At Fatshan many friends came to greet him, including his protégé Liang T'ing-nan, who gave him a round fan with a painting and poem on it. He also had a talk with the Manchu General I-k'o-t'an-pu, now stationed at Fatshan with a contingent of Yünnan troops. I-k'o-t'an-pu had been stationed in the summer of 1840 at Ningpo, on the mainland opposite Ting-hai, and gave Lin 'a very precise account' of the fall of Ting-hai.[1]

Henceforward the diary consists of little more than a

[1] He also met Yeh Ming-ch'en (1807–59), destined to play in the Second War a role analogous to that of Lin in the first, but to die in captivity, near Calcutta.

record of places passed through, distances covered, and the names of local people who came to pay their respects. On May 12th Lin's eldest son Lin Ju-chou, who had joined his mother at Nan-hsiung, the point at which travellers disembark and go by land over the Mei-ling Pass, came down the river-to meet him, joining him on his boat a little below Shao-chou. They arrived at Nan-hsiung on May 18th and spent a few nights at the house in Cross Bar Lane where Mrs Lin had been living for the last two months.

At Nan-ch'ang, the capital of Kiangsi, he met (as he had done on February 15, 1839) that great unofficial adviser of statesmen, Pao Shih-ch'en.[1] In a letter[2] written to the aged General Yang Fang on June 11th, Pao says: 'I heard recently that the Chinese marines at the Bogue gave their powder to the English and loaded their cannon with three parts powder and seven parts sand, and that this was why we were defeated. I thought this must be an exaggeration. But last month when His Excellency Lin passed through I pressed him to tell me the facts. What he said was: "The marines at Canton are better paid than any other troops. But only one per cent of their income is derived from their official pay. They get the rest from opium dealers who pay them to keep quiet. If opium trading were to cease, they would lose ninety-nine per cent of their income; so it is hardly surprising that they do not resist the English very vigorously." If that is Lin's opinion of them, then the story about their selling gunpowder may well be true.'

The story is, on the contrary, very improbable. The English had a low opinion of Chinese gunpowder, and would certainly not have accepted it. It is possible that what Lin is alleged to have said on this occasion was meant by him to apply to the marines before he reorganized them in the summer of 1840.

On June 3rd at Yü-shan, near the north-eastern borders of Kiangsi province, he set out by land for Hangchow,

[1] See above, pp. 16 and 137.   [2] IV. 466.

where he arrived on June 7th. But he found that there was not at the moment any high official there through whom he could communicate with Peking. He therefore turned east and went to Chen-hai, where Liu Yün-k'o, the Governor of Chekiang, then was. Here he remained, lodging in a learned Academy, till July 13th. He was waiting, of course, for the 'instructions' from Peking, promised when he was first ordered to proceed to Hangchow.

On June 12th, he hears that on May 21st there was a great victory at Canton. Seven foreign ships were burnt or otherwise destroyed, and seven rebel foreigners were captured alive. Innumerable casualties were inflicted. On June 15th he hears that there has been another engagement and a certain amount of damage inflicted on the enemy. On June 17th he gets a letter from I-liang, the Governor of Kwangtung, dated May 31st, saying that after May 22nd the rebel foreigners had again become violent, but had then once more pleaded for peace. 'I do not know yet what sort of report he [i.e. Ch'i Kung] is sending about this.'

The English accounts tell us only that on May 21st and during the ensuing days the last remaining defences of Canton were destroyed, and that on May 27th the Chinese agreed to pay six million dollars as a bribe to the English to withdraw. Only trifling damage to ships is mentioned and there is, I think, no admission of any casualties. The English account is certainly more credible than that of the Chinese; for if the Chinese had scored a great victory, it is hard to see why they had to bribe off the attackers.

On the evening of July 13th Lin heard that instructions concerning his fate had arrived at the Governor's office, and he hurried round there to receive them. He found that a decree issued on July 1st condemned him to exile at I-li, on the north-west frontier: 'Because Lin Tse-hsü, having been sent to Canton to manage military and foreign affairs, failed to bring either task to a successful conclusion, both he and the former Governor-General Teng, having merited the severest penalty, are to proceed to I-li and there do what they can to expiate their crimes.' He set out early next day and by the time the diary stops, on July 16th, he had reached a point about eighty miles north-west of Ningpo. Towards the end of August he received a decree (dated August 19th) ordering him to break his journey at K'ai-feng in Honan and take charge of river-conservancy works there. After spending nearly a year at K'ai-feng he set out for I-li, arriving at Si-an (the Ch'ang-an of T'ang times) on August 12, 1842. He left his wife at Si-an, and arrived at I-li on December 12th. He kept a diary of the journey from Si-an to I-li; but it is little more than a list of place-names.

This part of my book is an account of Lin's career at Canton, and I am only giving these brief notes on his subsequent life in order not to leave him, so to speak, hanging in mid-air. He was recalled from exile in 1845 and held a number of high posts, down to the time of his death in 1850. In 1847, when Governor-General of Shensi and Shansi, he drew up a document showing how, in the event of his death, he wished his three sons to divide up his property between them. He has always, he says, been too busy with public business to attend to building up the family's fortunes; with the result that he only holds the deeds-of-purchase of ten farmlands, and as to business premises and private houses, he owns no more than twenty-three of them. There were, of course, the normal ways in which officials invested their savings, but we do not often get documentation of this kind. We owe our knowledge in this case to Lin's great-grandson Lin Chi-hsi, who had the will photolithographed and in 1944 presented a copy to the British Museum. In his covering note Lin Chi-hsi said that though there was a good deal of trouble between his great-grandfather and the English, the latter had always had a great respect for him.

I hope that on the whole this study of mine will increase

that respect. Some readers may indeed think I have been too partial to Lin, at the expense of Captain Elliot. But it is the whole purpose of my book to give the Chinese rather than the English point of view.

In some respects Lin and Elliot had much in common. To begin with they were both civil servants, carrying out policies imposed on them from above, and both were cashiered because they failed to do what was expected of them. The difference was that Elliot deliberately ignored his instructions and demanded less from the Chinese than the Government at home had told him to, whereas Lin failed through no fault of his own, but simply because what he had been told to do was, given the military superiority of the English, not humanly possible. Another point of similarity between the two was that they both tended to be wrong in their judgements. Lin, in common with many other Chinese statesmen, believed that the introduction of the death penalty for opium offences would put a stop to opium smoking; he believed that to get rid of the English merchants he had only to make them thoroughly uncomfortable. He believed that the story about the dispatch of an English expeditionary force was mere propaganda and that, even if it came, it could only operate on the high seas. In each case he proved to be wrong.

Elliot, on his side, was deceived by Ch'i-shan's good manners and amiability, and failed to see that in signing the Chuenpi Convention Ch'i-shan was only playing for time— tiding over the interval that must elapse before what he thought to be an overwhelming number of troops could arrive from other provinces, just as Elliot himself had played for time before the arrival of the *Volage* and *Hyacinth*. He also failed to realize that the Emperor and his advisers were completely Peking-minded. Only a threat to Peking and its supplies could have any effect on their policy; to hammer away at Canton was a mere waste of time.

It was, however, at last realized by the English that at Canton nothing could be effected that would dispose the Chinese Government to accept the sort of terms that Palmerston had in mind. In August 1841 the English expeditionary force, now largely increased by reinforcements from India, set out northwards, sacking one coastal town after another on its way. In the latter part of my book I shall translate some documents which show what it felt like to be suddenly subjected to the onslaught of these Early Victorian Vikings. But before doing so I am going to deal with a strange and tragic episode, passed over lightly by English accounts, but of immense importance if one is viewing the war through Chinese eyes—the great Chinese counter-offensive of March 1842.

PART TWO

Songs of Oh dear, Oh dear!

THE English captured Chen-hai, on the mainland opposite Ting-hai, on October 10, 1841; three days later the great city of Ningpo, about twelve miles inland up the Yung River, was also taken. On October 18th I-ching (b. 1793; d. 1853), a cousin of the Emperor, was ordered to go to Chekiang and take the command of a great counter-offensive, the main objective of which was to be the recapture of Chen-hai and Ningpo. As a junior officer he served at Kashgar in the campaign against the Moslem rebel Jehangir in 1826; but he had never held any high military command. He seems to have been chosen on this occasion simply owing to the Emperor's high opinion of his general capacities. The Chinese being unencumbered by notions about 'tempting Providence' or 'counting chickens before they are hatched', the Emperor thought it auspicious to give him as a parting present a cornelian snuff-bottle on the front of which was the inscription 'Sweep away the murk and grime', and on the back was carved the figure of a horseman carrying a red banner, who seemed to be hastening onward to announce a victory. From Peking I-ching (whom I shall henceforward call 'the General') went south to Soochow, where he awaited the arrival of about 12,000 regular troops from other parts of China,[1] to be joined later by 33,000

---

[1] The contingents came from Kansu, Shensi, Honan, Shantung, Hupeh, Kiangsi, Szechwan and Kweichow. There were also 700 aborigines from the Golden River district in the western part of Szechwan.

local militia. At Soochow local officials, merchants and scholars were encouraged to offer their services to the expedition. A hundred and forty-four responded, among whom was a man of about thirty called Pei Ch'ing-ch'iao, whose father urged him to enlist: 'My father was fond of talking about military matters. He had formerly served on the staff of Lu K'un [1772–1835]. But it had not fallen to his lot to accompany Lu either during the campaign [1826–8] against the Moslem leader Jehangir or during that against the Yao aborigines [in Hunan in 1832]. My father mentioned how much it weighed upon his mind that he had missed these campaigns. When the English foreigners began their havoc in Fuhkien and Chekiang I expressed my indignation by writing a set of nine poems. My father read them and said, "If you feel so strongly about it, why don't you join the army?" Upon this I went straight to headquarters and offered my services.' When Pei Ch'ing-ch'iao was starting, his father gave him a sword and at the same time a poem in which he warned his son that unless he used it to cut off the foreign chieftain's head he would not be welcome on his return. But young Pei's services were destined to be achieved with the pen, not with the family sword. When the war was over he wrote a long and detailed account[1] of the campaign as seen through the eyes of a temporary staff-officer. It takes the form of a series of poems linked by long passages of prose. To the Western reader the form seems an odd one for what is in fact an extremely clear and factual account of military staff-work, accountancy, transport and field operations. But this mixed literary form, in which verses (or perhaps more accurately songs) are expanded and explained in passages of prose, has a long history in China. It is usually supposed to be due to the influence of Indian Buddhist scriptures, in which stanzas of song (*gāthās*) alternate with prose developments; but something very like it is found in purely native Taoist works that are long anterior

[1] III. 175 seq.

to the coming of Buddhism into China. The title of Pei Ch'ing-ch'iao's book (*Tu-tu Yin*) means 'Songs of Oh dear, Oh dear!', and is an allusion to the story of Yin Hao, a fourth-century A.D. general, who after he was cashiered did nothing but sit all day tracing with his finger in the air the words 'Oh dear, Oh dear, what an odd business!'

A wooden box, Pei tells us, was set up outside the gate of the General's camp. Those who wished to offer their services as extra members of his headquarters staff put their visiting cards into the box and after three days were interviewed and given jobs according to their capacities. People with special experience in dealing with foreigners were also invited to drop into the box written documents about the best way to handle the present campaign; and no less than four hundred such essays were received. The General had brought with him from Peking a number of officials, qualified as deputies capable of acting in his name. They regarded themselves as Junior Commissioners and insisted on being addressed as Ta-jen (Your Excellency), a title presently also usurped by several of the volunteer staff-members; so that soon the whole camp seemed to be swarming with Excellencies. Later on when the General had moved on to Chia-hsing, about fifty miles south of Soochow, the Excellencies began to be afraid that critics might use the 'box' as a means of exposing their false pretensions, and at their request it was removed. This also brought to an end the recruitment of staff-volunteers.

It was believed that many spies and collaborators with the English were at large, and at the General's camp the most rigid measures were taken to prevent the entry of unauthorized persons and to preserve secrecy. No one was allowed in or out of the camp without showing his pass. No report was allowed to be made verbally, for fear it should be overheard. Instead, everything that had to be communicated was written on an ivory slab and wiped out as soon as read. Believing that dispatches intended for him were being tampered with by Liu Yün-k'o, the Governor of Chekiang, General I-ching ('the General') organized a special postal service of his own. A dispatch of the utmost secrecy, concerning the posting of 'inner-responders' or, as we should say, the Fifth Column, in Ningpo, was entrusted to an orderly to take to the forward camp at Ts'ao-e-chiang, about eighty miles north-west of Ningpo. Not knowing the way there, the orderly asked a regular postal official who thought that Ts'ao-e-chiang (a very small village) was near Wu-sung, far away to the north. By the time the orderly had found out this mistake and returned to the General's camp, the attempt to retake Ningpo had already failed and the attacking armies were in headlong retreat.

Pei Ch'ing-ch'iao's first assignment after joining up was to go to Ningpo to report on the present disposition of the English forces there and also on the various routes by which Ningpo could be approached. The English were handicapped throughout the war by lack of good maps; but so too were the Chinese. After a mild adventure during which he was mistaken for a spy, seized by peasants hired by a rich landlord to protect his property and brought before the local authorities, he was released upon showing the pass concealed under his coat. He was then furnished with guides and brought to the Salt-store Gate of Ningpo. On the wall there dangled a man's head, with underneath it a placard in large letters, saying 'This is the head of the Manchu official Lü T'ai-lai, who came here to obtain military information'. 'I knew', says Pei, 'that Lü T'ai-lai had been sent by the General.' Pei was cross-examined again and again, but at last was let through. He found that in the city there were fewer than three hundred English troops and only two warships anchored in the harbour. 'The senior officer', he reported, 'is the so-called Plenipotentiary Pottinger. Anstruther, Morrison and Ma-kung-t'ai [Malcolm?] are the so-called Grand Commanders by land and sea.'

Major Peter Anstruther was by no means a 'Grand

Commander', but he was well known in Ningpo owing to the fact that he was held prisoner there for about eight months in 1840 and 1841, and gained immense prestige owing to the skill with which he drew the portraits of his captors. He had been seized by local peasants when land-surveying in the neighbourhood of Ting-hai. John Robert Morrison, son of the first Protestant missionary to China, was of course an interpreter, not a military commander. But the expedition owed a great deal not merely to his linguistic powers, but also to his general advice about Chinese affairs, and the Chinese were not wrong in regarding him as one of the outstanding figures on the English side. 'Gutzlaff', Pei continues, 'is the so-called Governor of Ningpo, Robert Thom acts as Prefect of Chen-hai, and Palmerston, otherwise known as Parker, as Prefect of Ting-hai.' Robert Thom was Morrison's fellow-interpreter. The English magistrate at Ting-hai was at this period Captain Dennis; the Palmerston-Parker name is a mystery. 'At no place', Pei continues, 'have the pillage and rapine of the foreigners been worse than at Ningpo. Their main lair is the Ta-ch'eng Hall of the Office of Education. Here Gutzlaff[1] trains the foreign troops every day. Pottinger comes there when he is in Ningpo, which happens only every few days, as he is nervous about leaving his ship. The woman singer of local airs, Yin Chang-yüan, has two daughters, whom she has given to Gutzlaff as his wives. Her adopted son Yü Te-ch'ang has made use of his position to enrich himself and inflate his own importance. He goes about wearing the insignia left behind by Commander Yü Pu-yün [who fled from the British advance in October 1841], cutting a most dashing figure. Everyone refers to him respectfully as "His Honour Yü the Second Uncle". A little white foreigner got drunk and tumbled off a boat into the Ningpo river. A crowd of foreign devils rushed to fish him out, but were too late. They encased his corpse in white sugar. Some say that he was

[1] For further specimens of the Gutzlaff legend, see below, p. 230 seq.

Pottinger's son and that was why they buried him in sugar. People of lower rank are not allowed to be buried in that way.

'In the cloisters of the temple of the Municipal God at Ningpo there are figures of the Black Death and the White Death, both of very savage aspect. When the English foreigners saw them they were overjoyed. ''They are our ancestors'', they cried. ''They ought not to be in this inferior position.'' So they destroyed the figures of the Municipal God and his demon lictor and put the White Death on the central throne, with the Black Death at the side, and they now come morning and evening to worship them.'

One might well imagine that Pei is here merely regaling the general reader with picturesque gossip and that his confidential report to the General, when he returned to camp, was of a more solid and useful nature. However, judging by official reports of Chinese agents sent as spies to other places occupied by the English, it seems likely that what Pei tells us here is not very different from what he told the General on his return. For example,[1] an agent smuggled into occupied Ting-hai in August 1840 to collect military secrets regaled his employers with the information that a Ting-hai literary gentleman called Ch'en Chih-hsien had given his daughter to Colonel Burrell as concubine. The father had taken to dressing in European costume and was escorted wherever he went by a bodyguard of black and white soldiers. Sir James Gordon Bremer 'lives in the Temple of the Municipal God. He stripped off the God's clothes and dressed himself up in them, dressing the God in his own red uniform. That same evening he stabbed himself to death with a dagger. The corpse was wrapped in a large red cloak, three musket volleys were fired, and they then buried him behind the shops at the back of the Brigade-General's office. . . . They carry off young men, shave their heads, paint their bodies with black lacquer, give them a drug which makes them dumb, and so turn them into black

[1] III. 427.

Devils, using them to carry heavy loads.' The only foundation for all these absurdities was that Brigadier-General Oglander, who (as we have seen, p. 113 above) died on the way from Macao, was buried at Ting-hai with full military honours shortly after the occupation.

Pei Ch'ing-ch'iao's next assignment was to superintend the making of five hundred rocket mortars. The model was an ancient specimen supplied by the aged Commander Tuan Yung-fu, and came from Yünnan. Pei was ashamed, he says, that owing to the complete lack of experience of all concerned the best they could produce was a contrivance that looked as though it emanated from the pages of the *Fire-dragon Book*, a seventeenth-century treatise on artillery. These mortars were supposed to be used in setting fire to the sails and rigging of foreign ships, but do not seem ever to have come into action.

The date for the attack was originally fixed for February 9, 1842 (the last day of the Chinese year). Chang Ying-yün, the General's personal representative, was already stationed at the advanced base eighty miles north-west of Ningpo, and every detail of the attack—which units were to be concealed in ambush, which were to advance openly—had been decided. 'At that time', says Pei, 'it seemed only a question of counting the days and waiting till the news of the victory arrived.' On New Year's Day (February 10th) Wang Ch'eng-feng, a skilful painter of landscape and figures whom the General had with him in his camp, presented him with a picture entitled *All Proceeds According to Plan*. 'It had taken him several months to do. It was in a style of great refinement, closely akin to that of the best Academy painters of Northern Sung times. The General regarded it as a great treasure and asked many members of his staff to inscribe poems on it. Later it was carried off by the Assistant Commander Wen-wei [a Manchu; died 1855]. After the disaster at the Ch'ang-ch'i Pass [on March 16th] I don't know what became of it.'

Songs of Oh Dear, Oh Dear!

The General, still far in the rear at Hangchow, went on New Year's Day to the temple of the God of War to pray for victory. He took the omens and drew a slip upon which was the verse:

> If you are not hailed by humans with
> the heads of tigers
> I would not be prepared to vouch for
> your security.

Happily three days later a contingent of aborigines arrived from the Golden River district, all wearing tiger-skin caps. The General believed that this assured him of victory, and he gave handsome largesses to the tiger-men. 'After this tiger-skin caps became the rage in the General's army. There were yellow tiger-head caps, black ones, white ones, winged ones and so on. But when it came to the fighting they did not seem to help much. Someone wrote to the General saying that if a tiger's skull-bone was thrown into the Dragon's Pool this would make the dragon come to the surface and attack and sink the foreign ships. This too was tried, but to no effect. There were a great many literary men on the General's staff, and ten days before the attack commenced (January 31st) he ordered them to compose announcements of victory. Thirty of these were sent in, and the General arranged them in order of merit. The first place went to Miu Chia-ku who had composed a detailed and vivid account of the exploits of the various heroes. Second on the list was Ho Shih-ch'i (a fairly well-known calligrapher) who sent in a vast composition, full of classical tropes and brilliant felicities. Never had such prose been seen since the days when Chang Yüeh (667–730) and Su T'ing (670-727) carried all before them in the literary world!'

Difficulties arose because the General's right-hand man, Chang Ying-yün, now established at the forward base, began to assign the various units to the positions from which they were to advance to the great attack. The commanders of the troops brought in from other provinces were all superior to him in rank and were unwilling to take orders from him. Determined that Chang should be obeyed, the General gave him a special Arrow of Command, and let it be known that anyone who disobeyed him, from Provincial Commanders-in-Chief downward, would be arrested and put on trial. No less than seventy volunteer staff-members were attached to Chang Ying-yün's headquarters; but he was extremely careful not to impart confidential information to any of them except the Deputy Governor Shu Kung-shou and the Prefect Yeh K'un. But both these men were on intimate terms with an exceedingly equivocal character called Lu'Hsin-lan[1] who, having at first worked for Gutzlaff, subsequently announced that he had repented of his treachery, and now undertook to recruit ruffians who were to kidnap the English leaders on the night of the attack. Henceforward all the General's efforts to maintain secrecy were in vain; moreover much of the secret information sent to the General's headquarters (then at Shao-hsing, some ninety miles west of Ningpo) was founded on the concoctions of Lu Hsin-lan. In this way he learnt that 'seventeen brigades had already been secretly infiltrated into Ningpo and eleven into Chen-hai'. There was not a word of truth in this; but it naturally seemed to the General that the recapture of the two towns was going to be 'as easy as turning over one's hand'. 'When the advance started', says Pei Ch'ing-ch'iao, 'I was at the Camel Bridge at Ningpo [seven miles north-east of the town]. Imagine my astonishment when afterwards at the General's camp I found a secret dispatch saying that I and a Chen-hai man called Pao Tsu-ts'ai had lain in ambush with five hundred southern irregulars on the Chao-pao Hill [a mile or so north-east of Chen-hai] and had there fallen upon and captured an enemy battery!'

The unfortunate Golden River aborigines, who suffered so heavily during the campaign, were in trouble from the start. Soon after their arrival ten of them were sent out on

[1] See below, p. 174.

patrol. They lost their way and stumbled into the camp of an officer who, misled by their unfamiliar language and costume and thinking that he saw in the writing on the tablets they wore at their waists some resemblance to European script, fell upon them at once. Three were badly wounded, flung themselves into the water and were drowned. The rest were trussed up and brought in triumph to Chang Ying-yün's camp. An indignant riot broke out among the main body of aborigines, which only subsided when the officer who had made the mistake was carried off to prison and thirty of his men were publicly scourged.

Ts'ao-e-chiang, where Chang Ying-yün had made his headquarters, was only a hamlet of a few hundred houses. Prices soon began to soar. Moreover peasants would only take copper-cash and the soldiers, who were paid in silver, could only get it changed at very disadvantageous rates. In the end the General set up four exchange officers, one for each of the principal bases, where silver was changed for cash at the normal rate. Characteristically he named the offices 'First Victory', 'Second Victory' and so on, numbering them, however, not with ordinary numerals, but with the first four characters of an ancient classic, the *Book of Changes*.

In order to follow up the 'tiger' omen (see above, p. 165) the General finally decided to attack on the twenty-eighth day of the first month (March 10th), at the Hour of the Tiger (3 to 5 a.m.), 1842 being a 'tiger' year, the first month a 'tiger' month and the 28th a 'tiger' day. This decision was not a whim of the General's, based on some personal superstition. The selection of a 'tiger' date for attack belonged to traditional Chinese war-magic. An example with which I happen to be familiar (and there are doubtless many others) is the battle in which the legendary boy-hero Han Ch'in-hu defeated the ruler of Ch'en, and so secured (A.D. 589) the unification of China under the Sui dynasty. 'What was the hour and what the season', asks the legend,[1] 'when he drew

[1] 'The story of Han Ch'in-hu.' Stein MSS. 2144.

up his troops in this formation? It was a tiger year, a tiger month, a tiger day, a tiger hour.'

The secret of the day and hour, says Pei, was not well kept, and when the English heard of it they put up notices warning the inhabitants to flee and stuck up handbills inside and outside the walls bearing the words 'The Four Tigers'. The evidence of the English accounts seems, however, to be that, though an attack had been expected week after week, the day and still less the hour were quite unknown to the English command, and no particular precautions were taken on the night of the 9th to 10th. Gutzlaff, who besides being magistrate of Ningpo and official translator was also director of intelligence, had heard that an attack was imminent; but it appears, says Lieutenant Ouchterlony (*The Chinese War*, p. 229), 'that he did not express himself to the military authorities in a manner sufficiently marked to lead them to suppose that he himself attached credence to the report'.

The advance from the forward base at Ts'ao-e-chiang began on March 5th. As it was through well-populated country, it was assumed that the troops would be able to cater for themselves on the way, and they were not burdened with any rations. But the villagers, convinced that the soldiers would pillage their stocks without giving any pay, fled when the army approached, carrying all their foodstuffs with them. The famished troops threatened to disband unless supplies were brought up. Orders for food were rushed to the base camp; but the officials at the accountancy office made difficulties about producing the necessary funds, and were dilatory in arranging for transport; so that the sufferings of the troops, Pei says, 'were unendurable'.

The guns and baggage were transported by water, along the Yao river. But its upper reaches are only navigable by very small boats, and a sufficient number of these could not be collected. It was decided to hire porters to take the stuff by land. 'We hired 2,400 men, half of whom were beggars of very poor physique and incapable of covering much more than ten miles a day. The winter ice was beginning to melt, moreover for several days it had been raining in torrents, so that the roads and paths were deep in mud. Half and more than half of our porters decamped before their task was over.'

The original plan had been that 17,000 troops should attack the western gate of Ningpo, 19,000 the south gate, while 15,000 attacked the neighbouring town of Chen-hai. Large numbers of troops were also to be held in reserve, for example at Camel Bridge, seven miles north-east of Ningpo, where Chang Ying-yün and with him Pei Ch'ing-ch'iao, our author, were to be stationed. But according to Pei,[1] at the time when the attack began large numbers of the troops expected from other provinces had not yet arrived and could not any longer be waited for. Moreover 'six out of ten' of those who had come were kept back as bodyguards for the General and his host of attendant 'minor Commissioners'. The actual number of those taking part in the attack on Ningpo and Chen-hai, says Pei, was not as much as 3,000. I wonder if this is not a rhetorical understatement, flung out in a moment of bitterness. Captain Bingham (*Narrative of the Expedition. . .* , II. 369) says: 'About ten or twelve thousand men advanced upon the south and western gates', at Ningpo alone. However Bernard in *The Nemesis* (p. 291) gives a very different figure: 'The force they brought against us is supposed to have exceeded 5,000 men.' Probably Pei's estimate is somewhat too low, and Bingham's far too high.

The signal for the general attack was to be the setting alight of the fire-rafts which were to be let loose upon the English ships and, drifting against them, would set fire to them before they could weigh anchor. All previous attempts of this kind at Canton had completely failed. So many favourable factors of wind, tide, complete surprise and so on were required if there were to be any chance of success that the odds were always heavily weighted in favour of the

[1] III. 229.

attacked. Above all, it was essential that the fire-rafts should be towed, undetected, to within a very short distance of the target. But upon this as upon previous occasions the attackers became nervous when they thought they were within range of the warships' guns and ignited the rafts when still some three miles away from their targets. The English ships' boats put out long before the blazing rafts arrived, took them in tow—a ticklish operation during which several sailors were badly burnt—and beached them. A second contingent of fire-rafts at a point some miles away was also prematurely ignited as soon as the flames were seen rising from the other rafts; but when less than half of this second contingent had been launched the Chinese irregulars in charge were attacked by boats put out from English warships, and fled.

Someone suggested that fire-crackers should be tied to the backs of a number of monkeys, who would then be flung on board the English ships. The flames would spread rapidly in every direction and might with luck reach the powder-magazine, in which case the whole ship would blow up. Nineteen monkeys were bought, and at the time of the advance were brought in litters to the advanced base. After the failure of the Chinese attack they accompanied the retreating armies to Tz'u-ch'i.[1] 'The fact is', says Pei, 'that no one ever dared go near enough to the foreign ships to fling them on board, so that the plan was never put into effect.' During the panic that ensued after the defeat of the remaining Chinese troops on the heights behind Tz'u-ch'i, the people fled from the town, including a Mr Feng in whose charge the monkeys had been put. There was no one to care for them, and they eventually died of starvation in Mr Feng's deserted front lodge.

The attack on the western gate of Ningpo was led by a band of Golden River aborigines. At about 4 a.m., March 10th, a sentry on the ramparts saw a figure advancing towards

[1] Eighteen miles north of Ningpo.

the gate. He called out to him '*Wei lo!*'[1] (Go away!), but the challenger continued to advance, holding in his hand a small lighted torch. The sentry repeated '*Wei lo!*', but the challenger, without halting, replied in a firm voice '*Wei lo moa*', (Will not go!). The sentry levelled his musket and the solitary challenger fell dead.

The Golden River aborigines were excellent shots; but the General, acting on the advice of Liu Yün-k'o, the Governor of the province, had given orders that, to avoid so far as possible causing casualties to the inhabitants of Ningpo, artillery should be used very sparingly. The aborigines, misunderstanding this order, thought that it applied to matchlocks as well as to cannon—the word *pao* being often used in both senses—and on the night of the attack discarded their matchlocks and advanced to the west gate armed only with knives. The English, Pei says, had mined the space between the crescent-shaped bulwark masking the gate and the gate itself, and had left the gate wide open, in order to give the impression that they did not mean to defend it. The Chinese commander, Colonel Tuan Yung-fu, thought that they had fled, and ordered his troops to press straight on through the gates. 'As soon as they reached the outer wall the mine went off and our soldiers fled precipitately. But the streets and lanes [outside the gates] were so narrow and soggy that they could not get away, and our losses were very heavy. The brunt of the disaster fell upon the aborigines, who lost a hundred men, including their leader, A-mu-jang.'

The author had been put in charge of some local militia who were proving very intractable. No part in the attack had been assigned to them, but it seemed to Pei and his superior officer a pity, after all that had been spent in training them, not to put them to any use; so they were marched to the west gate, arriving just when Tuan Yung-fu

[1] I reproduce the words as they are given by Ouchterlony, *The Chinese War*, p. 231. I do not know what dialect they are meant to represent.

was trying to push his men into the city. Tuan said that militia had better not be in the vanguard, and herded them back into the rear. But when the mines went off and flames were leaping up on all sides the English flung open the north gate of the city and, working round by a small path just outside the walls, arrived in dense throngs outside the west gate, so that it was the militia in the rearguard that bore the brunt of their attack. Six of the leaders of the militia fell, and their followers soon broke up and scattered.

About the assault on the south gate, which the Chinese succeeded in entering, Pei has less to say, not having been present. We know from the English accounts that the Chinese, having advanced almost to the heart of the city, were met by English troops sent to reinforce the guard at the south gate and were driven back again to the gate with heavy loss. Pei contents himself by recounting the heroism of Captain Hsü Huan who, even after receiving a bayonet thrust in his side, slew over ten Englishmen and took one prisoner before he died. 'On our side not a single man was killed', says Ouchterlony; and as Pei is here only speaking on hearsay his story about Captain Hsü may well be apocryphal.

The attack on Chen-hai, some thirteen miles to the northeast of Ningpo, down the River Yung, was a fiasco. According to Pei none of the troops taking part in it were armed with anything but spears and knives. Moreover Colonel Chu Kuei, with his contingent of troops from far away Kansu, got lost in the darkness and did not even arrive at Camel Bridge, seven miles from Chen-hai, till noon next day, long after the attempt to storm the town had been abandoned.

Even more abortive was the attempt to retake Ting-hai; as might have been expected, seeing that the place is on the island of Chusan, separated from the mainland by a strait which is some thirty-six miles wide at the usual point of crossing and the English were in complete command of the sea. The attack was to have been simultaneous with those on Ningpo and Chen-hai. The original plan was to make it with troops from North China; but these turned out to suffer so much from sea-sickness that there could be no question of using them in a naval battle. Fishermen from the Yangtze mouth area were then mobilized as 'water-braves' and expected to navigate the 276 small craft that were collected for them from all along the Chinese coast. But it turned out that the 'water-braves', though familiar with every shoal and sandbank of the Kiangsu coast, farther north, were quite unable to pilot themselves successfully amid the reefs and rocks that surround the island of Chusan; moreover at the appointed hour (4 a.m. on March 10th) the tide was against them and, by the time it had turned, the news of the double disaster at Ningpo and Chen-hai had already reached them. 'They lost all heart for the fray', says Pei, 'and putting out again to sea cruised about aimlessly for more than a month without the courage to commence an assault.'

The leader of the flotilla, Cheng T'ing-ch'en, had been entrusted with 220,000 dollars to meet the expenses of maintaining it, and when weeks went by without it going into action, the General was on the point of summoning Cheng to his camp and court-martialling him. Suddenly Cheng reported that on April 13th officers under his command had launched a brilliantly successful fire-raft attack, destroying one large English warship and twenty-one smaller boats, at the cost of only three casualties on the Chinese side, whereas over two hundred English had been drowned and 'more than could be counted' burnt to death. A wrangle as to the authenticity of the report followed, a committee of inquiry was instituted and finally two local officials produced some charred wreckage which was supposed to support Cheng's claim. Cheng also resolutely stuck to his story and offered to pay for it with his life if a word of falsehood could be found in his report. The General at last decided to accept the report, and passed on its contents to Peking; with the result that Cheng was promoted to the Fourth Rank and accorded the Peacock Feather. This led to a whole series of

similar claims, the last of which was that of a certain Wang
Yüeh-yü, to whom the General had given two thousand
dollars and about 270 pounds of saltpetre and sulphur for
use on the great day, in a subsidiary fire-raft attack. On
receiving the money Wang disappeared and no more was
heard of him till April, when he appeared at the General's
camp, announcing that he had secured a great victory. The
General did not believe the story, and was about to demand
the return of the money and condemn Wang to heavy
penalties when Wang once more disappeared. 'After that',
says Pei, 'there was no more talk about fire-attacks.'

The Chinese seem to have regarded the attempt to
infiltrate a secret Fifth Column into Ningpo as having been
carried out in so cursory a manner as to wreck the whole
plan for the recovery of the city. But Bernard (*The Nemesis in
China*, p. 289) says: 'There is reason to believe that a good
number of Chinese soldiers must have previously come into
the town in disguise, for the gates were attacked simul-
taneously both from within and without.' It is clear at any
rate that the Fifth Column gave nothing like as much help as
had been hoped. I have already mentioned (p. 166) that a
certain Lu Hsin-lan, who had previously been working for
Gutzlaff, subsequently declared that he had broken with him
and undertook to assist the grand attack by kidnapping the
English leaders at the moment when it commenced. However a few days before the attack, when the General was
'waiting for news of victory' at Tung-kuan, about ninety
miles north-east of Ningpo, Lu Hsin-lan suddenly turned up,
saying that news about the date of the attack had leaked out
beforehand, and the English had taken such strict precautions
that it had been impossible to kidnap 'the foreign leaders,
Gutzlaff and the rest'. The General, now convinced that Lu
Hsin-lan was still in the pay of the English, had him flung
into the military goal; but in the confusion of the great
retreat he escaped and was never re-arrested. A relative of
Lu Hsin-lan told Pei that Gutzlaff had been in the habit of

sending Lu out into the neighbouring towns and villages to change copper-cash into silver. A few days before the attack Lu invented the story that he could get a better rate of exchange farther afield, at Shao-hsing or Hangchow. Gutzlaff consequently gave him 60,000 strings of cash to change into silver, after which the English saw no more of him!

The Chinese armies that retreated from Ningpo entrenched themselves on the heights of the north of the town of Tz'u-ch'i, eighteen miles north of Ningpo. Here, on March 15th, they were again routed, but put up a strong resistance and the English suffered twenty-three casualties, of which three were fatal. This was, I think, the heaviest loss that they had sustained in any action during the war. The English wounded were attended by admirable surgeons and had a good chance of recovery. On the Chinese side those who were seriously wounded and could not join the retreat fared better than those who managed to drag themselves to Tz'u-ch'i. The Chinese doctors were able to extract bullets and shrapnel, but had no efficient dressings, so that the great majority, even of the slightly wounded, died from blood poisoning. Liu T'ien-pao, the leader of the troops from Honan, had with him a 'metal-wound drug'. He told our author and some other officers to mix it with wine and apply it to the wounds. But there was no wine to be found in the camp, 'moreover there was not nearly enough of the drug to go round, and not as many as even two or three out of every ten survived. We sat by helpless, watching the others expire. Even now the thought of it agonizes me.' On the other hand the Chinese wounded who remained on the battlefield were cared for by the English in exactly the same way as their own men. This is attributed by Pei not to general principles of humane conduct, but to the belief that the grateful patients, when sent back to their compatriots, would belaud the kindness of their captors, and so weaken the hostile spirit of the Chinese troops.

Camel Bridge, being about equidistant from Ningpo and

Chen-hai, was the obvious place to station reserves who could be brought up to either place as needed. The General's favourite officer Chang Ying-yün was stationed here, and at dawn on March 10th, when the firing of heavy guns was heard, someone pointed out to him that, as the Chinese were not using artillery for fear of damaging the city, the guns they had just heard must be English ones. In that case the attackers might be in difficulties, and it would be as well to move up reinforcements at once. But Chang Ying-yün was an opium addict, the 'craving' was at that moment upon him, and he was incapable of attending to his duties. Rumours of the double disaster at Ningpo and Chen-hai began to come in during the morning, and at noon the defeated remnants of the army that had attacked Chen-hai began to straggle in. The survivors of the attack on Ningpo had retired to the Ta-yin hills, to the west of the city. Chang Ying-yün's officers were still debating whether to advance or retreat when, through the dusk, the sound of cannon and musketry-fire drew closer and closer. Panic seized his troops and with one accord they fled towards Tz'u-ch'i. Chang himself was still puffing away at his opium pipe. At last he staggered into a litter and was carried away. It is well known, says Pei Ch'ing-ch'iao, that the English have a tenderness for opium smokers and never put one to death. At the time of the second capture of Ting-hai (October 1, 1841) the Deputy Governor Shu Kung-shou was taken prisoner. Some well-disposed person had slipped a ball of opium into his pocket. 'The English foreigners searched him and, finding the opium, credited him with being a smoker, and at once released him and sent him back to the mainland.'

It was at Camel Bridge, presumably on this occasion, that the author narrowly escaped with his life, a rocket passing through the sleeve of his coat.[1]

The General, having failed to get the English out of Ningpo by force of arms, was determined to make the place

[1] III. 213.

so uncomfortable for them that they would leave of their own accord. A band of 362 ruffians were recruited from farther down the coast (so Pei tells us). They were called the Rafters Militia, their task being to get on to the roofs of the places where the foreign leaders were lodging, creep along the beams and drop down upon them while they slept, snatching away their fire-arms or other weapons, and then cutting off their heads. Gutzlaff and the rest became so jumpy, Pei says, that they constantly woke with a start in the middle of the night, even when nothing was happening, and attacked one another. 'Finally the foreign leader Pottinger's personal follower Hsien-ch'en-ku was stabbed by the rafter-men. His friends began to realize that life in Ningpo had become too unsafe, and on the twenty-seventh of the third month they weighed anchor and went elsewhere.' Hsien-ch'en-ku is certainly the transcription of a foreign name, but is impossible to identify. The English accounts know of no such incident. But they do mention that at this period a number of abductions, about forty in all, occurred at Ningpo. In most cases the victims were decoyed into low haunts, liberally plied with drink and, when unconscious, carried off to Hangchow, where they were released later in the year. Pei gives the names (unidentifiable, except perhaps for the sailor Norris) of eleven Englishmen and seven Bengalese who were held at Hangchow; but he represents them as having been captured in battle. He says he got the names from the *ma-chan's* list, *ma-chan*[1] being what the English foreigners call a translator'.

Someone, soon before the grand attack, said that the English at Canton were terrified of catching the smallpox. Would it not be a good plan to infect cattle and sheep with the disease according to the Chinese method of inoculation, and give them these animals next time they came foraging? Within ten days the poison would take, and they could then, when prostrate with the smallpox, easily be rounded up and

[1] I hope some reader will be able to throw light on this word.

slaughtered. But the General thought the plan discreditable, and it was not carried out.

It seems, then, that it was the Chinese who invented germ-warfare, though they can claim the credit of having refused to make use of the invention. But the idea of a 'Chinese method' of vaccination is a myth; the Chinese learnt the art from Dr Alexander Pearson,[1] the chief surgeon of the East India Company, at Canton in the early years of the nineteenth century.

In June Soochow, the author's home town, seemed to be threatened. He heard that many of the inhabitants were already fleeing and that their homes were being ransacked by native looters. Leaving the General's camp, which was now at Shao-hsing, over a hundred miles south of Soochow, he hurried home. 'I could not', he says, 'help being very worried about what was happening to my family. I found, indeed, that they had already packed, and were on the verge of departure. I persuaded them that the foreign ships were so large that they could not possibly get into the Inner River. However, I found that quite half my relations and friends were on the move, and it was small wonder that my argument about the size of the ships did not carry conviction, when they could see with their own eyes that all the high officials, from the Governor-General downwards, were sending their families away.' But the old father's 'martial spirit' was unquelled. His only welcome was to tell his son to go back and do some more fighting; and after ten days Pei Ch'ing-ch'iao returned to the camp.

Soochow was in fact never attacked; but Wu-sung fell on June 16th, Shanghai on June 19th and Chinkiang, about 150 miles up the Yangtze, on July 21st.

On August 29th, as everyone knows, the Treaty of Nanking was signed, and for the moment the war was over. Pei carries on his narrative till the end of the year; but it did not fall to his lot to take part in further fighting, and he is

[1] Or possibly a year or two before from Spaniards?

not able to tell us any more than may be found in numerous other books of history. The latter part of his book deals largely with the financing of the campaign. At the outset of the campaign the General set up four Quartermasters' Offices: one at Hangchow, one in the rear at Soochow, one at Shao-hsing and one that was to move forward with the advancing armies. Remittances from Peking were sometimes sent separately to each office and sometimes in a lump sum to one office, to be divided into four and distributed. They never informed the General what they had received, nor did they notify one another. The paymasters sometimes notified the General of their disbursements, but sometimes only informed his assistant Wen-wei, or else simply sent the receipts to the head Quartermaster without notifying either the General or Wen-wei. By the time this had been going on for six months it was practically impossible to discover what had been paid out. Consequently when the Governor of Chekiang, Liu Yün-k'o, sent in a memorial accusing the General of reckless expenditure and demanding an inquiry, the General had no idea of what the expenditure had actually been. He ordered the four Quartermasters' Offices each to make out separate accounts; but when these were added up the total never tallied with what had been received. This was partly due to the complications involved in constantly converting copper-cash into silver and silver into cash; as also to the fluctuating value of foreign money (Mexican dollars). The General accordingly set up a committee of six to inquire into the expenses of the campaign, one of the six being Pei Ch'ing-ch'iao. The total they arrived at was 1,645,000 dollars, corresponding to between £500,000 and £600,000.

This latter part of Pei's book is indeed to a large extent a recital of sordid army scandals—bribery to get mentioned in dispatches, pay drawn several times over, claims for reward of services never rendered, and so on. I will not follow up in detail all these shady machinations. The story of the Eight Boxes, however, sheds so much light on the office work of the campaign that it is worth telling.

The General relied for reference solely on his own personal files. All communications, instructions, notifications and replies to reports from subordinates were summarized, and the summaries attached to the dossiers, which were brought to him every evening in files so high that two men had to carry them. When he had been through them, he filled in the date and under it signed them with his rebus. Afterwards his seal was imprinted on the sewn binding, so that no page could be removed without detection. But there were every day many communications that he handed over to his secretariat to answer without keeping any record of them, and the officials of the secretariat flung them into an attic cupboard. In fact, only two or three out of every ten papers were in the General's own file; the rest lay higgledy-piggledy in the attic, piling up till there were eight boxes of them. No check was kept on them, and many disappeared altogether; the rest were entirely out of their proper chronological order. Finally when the General heard that he was to return to the capital (December 11, 1842) some people said that all the loose papers ought to go to the Board of War, others were for sending them to the Governor of Chekiang or to the four Quartermasters' Offices. But the members of the General's secretarial staff feared that the papers, in their present condition, would create a bad impression, and they persuaded the General to send only his own files to Hangchow to serve as a basis for the official report on the expenses of the campaign. The Eight Boxes were carried off by the General's friend Shih Chien, who was glad to acquire so fine a supply of scribbling-paper. When the General's personal files reached Hangchow, the Governor-General Liu Yün-k'o was surprised to find appended to them a number of papers concerned with the raising of local militia by members of the General's staff. The originals of these had found their way into the Eight Boxes and disappeared; but the officers concerned had persuaded the General to add records of their services in connection with the militia to his personal files. As these files were sealed across the stitching at the back, it was impossible to insert these papers where they belonged, that is to say, to the winter of 1841, so they were appended to the files of October 1842. The Governor-General felt sure that the claims were fraudulent, and ordered an inquiry. The officers concerned knew that somewhere in the Eight Boxes the original records of their having raised militia could still probably be found and managed to get the boxes back from Shih Chien's house. But in the course of rummaging through the papers they found so much that was compromising to them that in the end they extracted more than half, and only two boxfuls were sent to Hangchow. Meanwhile Liu Yün-k'o had moved on to another post. His successor Pien Shih-yün had been one of the four Quartermasters, and knew that much of what had really been going on could not possibly be reported to the Throne. He therefore threw away all the original documents and made everyone concerned draw up a fictitious account of expenses, founded on the normal and accepted needs of an army in the field.

Unlike many 'exposures' of the period Pei Ch'ing-ch'ao's account of the Eight Boxes is written calmly and objectively, without (at least on the surface) any touch of malice against erring colleagues. Towards the General himself Pei's attitude is one of just appraisal, certainly admirative, but never verging on hero-worship.

'When the General heard rumours about himself—for example, that he spent his time with singing-girls, or that he took bribes—he was depressed all day. "I exercise the greatest self-restraint", he would say. "I cannot understand why I am slandered like this." When any of his officers behaved in an insolent or swaggering way under cover of his name, the General never inquired into complaints about it; but if he chanced to know who it was, he reproved him ever so gently. After the armies moved south he refused all presents. The only exception was when at Chia-hsing the Governor sent him four tubs of orchids. They delighted him so much that he could not bring himself to refuse. He once said that when the war was over and the troops disbanded, apart from his personal belongings these flowers would be his only luggage. When he was put on trial, they had to be left behind, and I do not know who got hold of them.'

According to Pei the reason why the General had the reputation at Soochow of being a great frequenter of brothels was a very trivial one. One of his junior officers, a certain Yang Hsi, spent a lot of his time with prostitutes. One feature of the slang used by these girls was the adding of an extra syllable to surnames. They called people with the surname Yang 'Yang-wei'. 'Yang-wei', pronounced in just the same way, though written differently, happened to be the General's honorific title. The girls constantly chattered about 'Yang-wei's' visits, and so it got about that the General was a frequenter of these haunts. The rumour spread to the English, and we find Sir John Davis (*The Chinese War*, p. 226) speaking of 'the dissolute Yihking', i.e. I-ching.

'The General was extremely frugal. When he was about to leave Peking he said to his staff, "We must all live very simply in the south; otherwise the general public is sure to say hard things about us." After he crossed the Yangtze presents of food were being continually made to his head-quarters, and most of his people stuffed themselves almost to death. But the General never had more than four dishes laid, and even then felt he was being very luxurious.' His bosom friend Tsang Yü-ch'ing gave him an inscription to put up on the pillar at his quarters, containing the words: 'The heart of a Bodhisattva; the face of Vajrapani.' Vajrapani is a scowling and ferocious divinity; Bodhisattvas are the embodiment of compassion. But Tsang did not mean by this that he approved of the General's clemency; he was an out-and-out die-hard, and in the winter of 1841 he had persuaded the General that commanders who had deserted their posts, for example Yü Pu-yün at Chen-hai in October, ought to be beheaded. But after he had actually written a petition demanding their execution, the General reflected that he might one day find himself open to a similar charge, and rather than set a dangerous precedent he withdrew the petition. Moreover, before his appointment to lead the expedition to the south the General had belonged to the party at Court that was in favour of a policy of appeasement, and Tsang Yü-ch'ing had only with difficulty persuaded him that this policy had no better chance of success now than in the hands of Ch'i-shan before, and would only lead to further loss of prestige.

Continuing his retrospective remarks on the General's tastes and character, Pei tells us that he was a skilful painter, particularly in the ink-blob style associated with the name of Mi Fei (eleventh century A.D.). While the campaign was still in progress he was too busy to give a thought to painting. But in August, while the peace negotiations, concerning which he was not kept informed, were in progress at Nanking, he occupied himself with calligraphy. There was a rush for his productions and 'the day was hardly long enough to meet the demand'.

'At the Tiger Hill at Soochow there was a sculptor called Hsiang who made small portrait-figures in clay. He managed to get introduced into the camp, and the Guards Officer Jung-chao recommended him to the General. He made figures of the General himself and of all his Staff, and they were considered excellent likenesses.'

On December 11, 1842, the General received instructions to come to Peking. On the 24th a rumour went round the camp that he had now been told instead to go south, to Chekiang, and take charge of drawing up the report about the expenses of the campaign. This sounded less sinister than an order to go to Peking, and there was general rejoicing, but no one knew how the rumour started. It was not till nine at night that the General's secretariat produced an express message from the Board of War which did in fact cancel the first order, and commanded him to go south. The delay had happened because all communications arriving through the official relay-post were first opened by the secretariat and then handed on to the General. On this occasion all the members of the secretariat were busy packing up, and had no spare thoughts to give to office work, which accounted for the delay of almost a whole day. The origin of the rumour was that the postmaster at Wu-hsi Hill had taken it upon himself to open the letter. The General accordingly set out from Wu-hsi,[1] but when almost at Soochow he received another order, saying that he was to be arrested, brought to Peking and there tried on a charge of wasting the resources in men and money that had been entrusted to him. Pending trial he was to be confined in the gaol of the Court of Imperial Clansmen. The members of his Staff, frightened of becoming involved in the case, all quietly disappeared. 'No one saw the General off except some of the scholars attached to his Staff, who went with him as far as Chinkiang.'

The General was sentenced to death, but at this period such sentences were seldom carried out, and in April 1843 he was appointed to a post at Yarkand, in Turkestan. There were protests from the die-hard party against this lenience, and to those protests the Emperor replied in a remarkable Edict, issued on May 3, 1843. He now realized, he said, that the Chinese defeats at the hands of the English were due to his own failure to use the right men. I-ching and the rest had not sufficient military experience, and it was this that had led to their failure. But they had great abilities and were still in their prime, so that it was right to give them another chance, in some more suitable capacity. However, as a compromise, he had now cancelled their appointments and ordered them to 'meditate on their shortcomings behind closed doors'.

[1] About fifty miles north-west of Soochow.

Songs of Oh Dear, Oh Dear!

In November 1843 the General was ordered to proceed after all to his post at Yarkand; in 1844 he was given a similar post at I-li. In 1853 he died of malaria while defending Hsü-chou (in northern Kiangsu) against the Taiping rebels.

During the war the Emperor had consistently laid the blame for everything that went wrong upon other people. Humanly commendable though his present change of heart may have been, he was quite wrong in thinking that China's defeat was due to the inexperience of her military leaders. Superiority of fire-power and command of the sea and of the major waterways were what made the English invincible. No generalship, however talented or experienced, could have made the course of events go differently. But the Manchus were a conquering race and were reluctant to accept the fact that the weapons with which they had conquered China two hundred years ago were now out of date.

PART THREE

Shanghai

THE English had never intended to occupy Ningpo except as winter quarters, and on May 7th they moved out and sailed north. The Chinese, of course, attributed their departure to the activities of the 'rafter-assassins' (see above, p. 177) who were supposed to have made things so uncomfortable for the invaders that they were obliged to clear out.

Chapu, on the northern arm of the Bay of Hangchow, was (as I have already mentioned) captured after heavy fighting on May 18th; Pao-shan and the Wu-sung forts (fourteen miles north of Shanghai) on June 16th. The expedition then turned south and attacked Shanghai, already at that date a port of considerable importance. We possess a diary[1] recording thirteen days of foreign invasion (June 16th–28th) by a Shanghai man called Ts'ao Sheng, who describes himself as 'an impractical old book-worm', but was a Warden of his district and took an active part in organizing a sort of Home Guard during the crisis. He was a member of a fairly well-to-do family, and lived surrounded by numerous relatives in a large patriarchal compound, consisting of pavilions with separate entrances.

After the capture of Wu-sung Shanghai seethed with rumours, often of the most improbable kind. June 16th: 'In the afternoon the news was good. His Excellency Ch'en, it was said, dived into the sea and swimming under water made holes in the bottoms of the foreign ships, sinking two of them. The foreign troops have run out of ammunition and retreated in terror. Deputies from His Excellency have just arrived bringing a present of several loads of sugar-loaves.' In the last story at any rate there seemed to be some element of truth; for going to the Prefecture Ts'ao saw a number of orderlies dashing about amid mountainous piles of sugar. But the story about His Excellency Ch'en's sub-marine feat was modified next day (June 17th). It now appeared that though Ch'en had sunk an enemy ship, there were no men on board it; only wooden figures. Actually Ch'en Hua-ch'eng, a veteran General who did all that was humanly possible to defend the Wu-sung ports, had been killed during the bombardment of June 16th. He is still reverenced by the Chinese as one of the chief heroes of the Opium War.

The author of this diary took, as I have said, a prominent part in organizing the civic guard; but by June 18th almost all its members had fled from Shanghai, as had practically all the local officials. The markets inside and outside the walls had closed down. 'I made up my mind', says Ts'ao, 'to send one of my children away from the city, but could not decide which. It happened to be Little Juniper's tenth birthday. I said to myself, ''There's no certainty that those who go will be any safer than those who stay. But on the whole those who leave stand a better chance, and as it happens to be his birthday Juniper had better be the one to go.'' So I fetched the wooden spirit-tablets of my father and mother and the chronicles of our family and gave them to him, telling him to go with them to Uncle Tieh-yüan at the Southern Tombs. It occurred to me that my late father-in-law had no son and though my mother-in-law had been evacuated, my father-in-law's coffin was still in the house. The thought that it might be burnt if the house were set fire to was unendurable, and I collected some men to help me carry the coffin, meaning to keep it for the time being at the back of the mortuary at our family burial-place. We had fetched the coffin and were on the way to the mortuary when we were held up by brigands. But when I assured them it really was a coffin and that we were not using it to smuggle out valuables, they let us go on.'

After a strenuous time spent in trying to rally the few remaining members of the guard and spread them out over the various guard-sections, at about three in the morning Ts'ao Sheng reached the city gate, and heard someone outside shouting to be let in. 'I asked him who he was, and he said he was the sentry! I asked what he was doing outside the gate. "Well," said the sentry, "I got nervy, all alone in the middle of the night; I had the feeling something might suddenly happen, so I went and slept with friends outside the wall. But when it began to get light I was afraid Great Old Daddy [honorific term for his commanding officer] might want to know what had become of me; so I thought I had better come inside." I let him in, but took charge of the key.'

On going back to make sure that the watchers were at their posts, he found that not one was on duty. 'I went from house to house knocking them up; but they all said: "We're giving a bit of a rest to our legs. In the morning there may be trouble, and if we are to be on guard all the time then, we can't be expected to be up all night as well!"'

'I was looking up at the Milky Way which was glittering brightly, when I heard a burble of voices outside the city wall. People down by and along the bay seemed to be calling for help. They were presumably being attacked by brigands who, taking advantage of the general breakdown of law and order, had poured in from the neighbouring countryside. Choked with tears I went home, and utterly overwhelmed by my misery I opened a jar and drank and drank until I was completely intoxicated. I had had no sleep for several nights, but last night I slept like a veritable Liu Hsüan-shih.' The allusion is to a man who got so drunk that his relatives buried him, thinking he was dead. He did not wake up for a thousand days.

A rumour began to spread that orders had been given to the troops to massacre everyone in the town, the reason being supposed to be that mobs had attacked and damaged Government offices. On the afternoon of the next day (June 19th) 'news came that the General Chi Lun was advancing upon the western gate. Terrified voices came from every door down the street, screaming "He's come to massacre us all!" The panic had not subsided when the sound of a long and continuous cannonade began. Again the cry went up, "He's massacring the city!" As a matter of fact Chi Lun had gone away again; the guns that were being fired were those of the foreigners! I knew now that the worst was at hand. I hid my wife, and blocked up the gate and doors. My fourth nephew Autumn Boat had still not yet gone, and I urged him to do so. I then climbed over the garden-wall and went to have a word with such of my neighbours as had not fled, trying to make them join with me in promising that, come what might, we would all stick together. Some promised, but others would not. Suddenly fire rose from the Prefecture, and at the same time the foreign soldiers arrived in force, both by land and from their ships. When they first came there were six ships, two of them what are called firewheel ships [steamers]. These anchored at the southern quay of the main bay. I for my part did not go and see what kind of cannon they had nor how many soldiers there were, and so am not going to venture on any rash statements on the subject. But a certain class of person, appearing one at a time and all alone from different directions, formed into a solid band and went down to the shore to see what was to be seen. What they had in mind I do not know. Some people said they had certain expectations; but what these expectations may have been, I have no idea.'

The implication, of course, is that they were traitors, with whom the English had been in touch before, and who now expected to be given fat jobs in the occupied city. At 5 p.m. 'about a hundred foreigners came to the main southern gate and, squatting among the parapets, looked round in every direction through telescopes'.

'Strictly speaking,' Ts'ao reflects, 'when a city falls one ought to die fighting. But to sacrifice oneself alone and unaided, to die to no purpose, is to perish like a weed. Moreover as all the officials fled long ago, even if I were to seek death at the hands of the enemy, there would be no one to report upon it. So I went on reproaching myself and finding excuses for myself, scribbling "Oh dear, Oh dear!" in the air [see above, p. 160], hardly knowing whether I belonged to the world of the living or the realm of the dead. After midnight I saw flames rising in the north-west and thought that perhaps an army had come to drive the enemy away. But when morning came I learnt that the flames were at Mr Chu's house, which the foreigners had set on fire.'

June 20th: 'I went home by the small path and when I got to my gate I found several foreigners there, beating it down with their muskets. I thought of my wife still hidden within and determined that if death was to be her fate, I would share it. I rushed up and attempted to thrust myself between them and the gate, but was seized and held. They then went into the house and ransacked all the chests and boxes, taking money, headdresses, trinkets—everything they could lay hands on. When this plundering was over they held a knife to my throat, threatening to kill me unless I showed them where I had hidden my other valuables, and continually repeating the words, *"Fan-ping, fan-ping"* ['foreign cakes', i.e. foreign dollars]. I did my best to make clear to them by gestures that we were not rich people, and at last they let me go. They then went to my nephew's place and I received them there. The foreigners made a hasty search, but found nothing except books, so they went away. They then went to Cousin Shao-yüan's gate, which I also opened to them, and they searched as before; after which they knocked at Brother Sha-yü's place, and when I came to the door and received them, they all pointed at me laughing and went away without going in. During the day several large bands of them came, and the same performance was repeated. None of them, thank Heaven, ever got to the place where my wife was hiding.' A neighbour looked in saying that the foreigners had put up proclamations, 'only a few words, but all written in Chinese, so that it must be the work of traitors'. Another neighbour reported that at the Temple of the Municipal God the foreigners were giving placards guaranteeing from molestation and plunder anyone who brought a chicken. In some cases, he said, these had been given to people in exchange for all sorts of things other than chickens that were eatable or useful. 'I had heard', says Ts'ao, 'that they did the same thing previously in Chekiang, and hoped to go next day and see if I could get one. Towards dusk I heard a knock at the door. I went and opened it, and saw a black devil [i.e. an Indian soldier] carrying a chicken and a great sack full of other things. I asked him what he wanted and he answered, in Chekiang pronunciation: "Somewhere to lodge." I did not answer; but by that time he was already inside, and there was nothing I could do. When he came to the central hall, he saw a wet patch, some oil perhaps, on the ground; upon which he said "No good, no good", repeating it several times, picked up his belongings and went away.

'At midnight when I was with my wife in her hiding-place we heard a sound of footsteps on the roof-tiles. We were afraid it was the foreigners coming at night. I ran out to look, and found it was two thieves, about to let themselves down into the house. I shooed at them, and they retreated. After that I felt less than ever able to go to sleep. Today the local bandits have been pillaging on a grand scale, the foreigners having made things easy for them by beating down so many people's gates and doors.'

June 21st: 'Before dawn I heard a loud and insistent

banging on the gate. I undid the bolt and found it was a foreigner. He rummaged round as the others had done, and also clamoured for *kuo-kuo* [baby-language for 'things to eat'?].' Presently the author was again pursued, apparently by the same foreigner. 'He broke down the front gate, came in and bound me with a rope, making as though to kill me; but after a time he let me go. He then searched the house again; but found nothing, and went away.' Shortly afterwards four neighbours came and talked about the 'protection placards'. Ts'ao told them he had no chickens; but one of them, a Mr Wang, said that he had four, and offered one to Ts'ao. Ts'ao did not feel that he could safely leave the house, but asked Wang to obtain a placard for him by proxy, if that were possible. 'In a few minutes', says Ts'ao, 'he came back with one of the so-called "protection placards" and fastened it to my gate. . . . My wife had had nothing to eat for three days, and now that I had my protection placard I thought I might venture to leave the house and arrange for her to go outside the city walls. For two dollars I hired two porters to carry her belongings, and sent her to join the others at the Southern Tombs. . . . At the Hour of the Sheep [1 p.m.] a crowd of foreigners came; but when I pointed at the placard they nodded and went away. Presently my son Little Pine-tree arrived. I asked him why he had come back. "I couldn't bear to think of you and my brother still living in danger inside the walls," he said, "so I have come back to be with you." I was deeply touched, and found myself wiping away a tear. But I reflected that my wife was now out of the city—in no Paradise, to be sure, but at any rate in less danger than here; and though I still had Little Pine-tree, Little Yün-tree[1] and three of the neighbours' girls in the house, I felt as though half of the heavy burden had been taken from my shoulders, and was a little less depressed. . . . Presently Neighbour Wang came through the rain, bringing me half a roast chicken. This was splendid,

[1] I do not know what sort of tree it is.

and in return I gave him a bottle of wine, with which he too was very pleased. After the fall of the city it was impossible to buy anything in the market, and we had lived on cold scraps. The heat was terrific and food went bad almost at once. Most people were getting nothing to eat at all, much less chicken or wine. At supper that night, chicken-bone in hand and cup between my lips, glancing back at my two sons who were waiting upon me just as usual I stretched out my hand and stroked their heads. There was no doubt that they were "the old article". But then I thought of the people out at the tombs, and that gave me a nasty feeling in the stomach. In fact, one way and another, I did not know whether to laugh or weep.

'At about the Second Drum-beat [9 p.m.] the rain at last stopped and the moon shone fitfully. A band of local brigands now arrived, having got in by pushing down part of the wall. They said they had only come to shelter from the rain; but there were twenty or thirty of them, and they soon began a search even more thorough than that of the enemy. In fact everything that the foreigners had not taken they made a bundle of and took away. As I was single-handed[1] there was nothing for it but to stand by and let them do as they pleased. A check-up after they had gone showed that they had not left a single farthing or a single grain of rice. Coverlets, trousers, coats, shoes—everything that could be eaten or used—had practically all disappeared. This really was, as they say, the calamity of calamities!'

Early next day he went out with a basket, 'like a monk with his begging-bowl', and managed by going from house to house to collect two pecks of rice. 'Today', he says, 'there are beginning to be more people about the streets. Actually the foreigners have contented themselves with loot and rape, but as the city fell without resistance, there has been no general slaughter, and on the thirteenth [June 21st], after the Hour of the Sheep [1 p.m.], their officers disarmed them.

[1] The two boys were little more than children.

'The black devils have all put on white caps. Someone
who was captured by them and afterwards escaped, told us
that they did this because white is their auspicious colour:
as long as they are dressed like that they won't kill. So he
told us, and it is a fact that during the three days that they
have been here they have not put to death more than a very
small number of people. . . . But they are pressing the
people into their service to do all their heavy work, such
as shifting gun-emplacements and gunpowder, and utensils
of all sorts. They take anyone they come across—Buddhist
monks, Taoist monks, notables and well-to-do people, and
keep them all day and all night. Others they detain in their
ships, and do not let come back. . . . I heard that the
foreigners were looking everywhere for Commander Ch'en's
body, and had offered a reward of fifty dollars to anyone
producing it. I trembled at the thought of what they meant
to do with it; but later someone from the coast said to me:
"They want to give it a decent burial; it's not in order to
revenge themselves on him." But they never got it, which
was a source of great grief to them.'

In the afternoon a drunken capering 'black devil' arrived,
asking as usual for dollars. When Ts'ao failed to produce
them, the 'devil' belaboured him with an umbrella. To get
rid of him Ts'ao pretended to go off to the English headquarters 'to fetch the whites'. This was a device by which
many people had got rid of their Indian visitors. 'I did not,
of course, really go,' says Ts'ao, 'but only hid for a while.
When I came back the devil had gone; but a teapot and some
cups and other things were lying in pieces. I asked Little
Pine-tree what had happened. "After you went", he said,
"he came into the house and after twice falling flat on the
ground he got to the central hall, flung the crockery and
things on to the floor, and went away. That was all." I
said, "This security placard is no use. It is hardly two days
since we got it, and already they're up to their mad pranks.
Where is it going to stop? I can't let you stay here. To-

morrow you and your brother must go. I will look after the house alone. I shall be all right, you needn't worry about me." He didn't want to go and began to sob and weep.'

At dusk some neighbours into whose house foreigners had burst took refuge in Ts'ao's house. He tried to persuade them to slip out by the back door; but they were too frightened to stir. Fortunately as there was no light in the house the foreigners, after a whispered discussion, decided to move on. 'After that', says Ts'ao, 'Little Pine-tree really was afraid. Since he was quite small he had practised the Purification of the Three Spiritual Elements[1] and recited Taoist scriptures in season and out. Tonight he burnt incense and then kneeling on the floor began chanting ceaselessly. I was amused and at the same time touched. At last, at about the Fourth Drum [1 a.m.], he suddenly said: "Father, there's no need to worry. The foreigners are soon going. The Spirit [*shen*] told me so." I questioned him more than once, but that was all he could tell me. I scolded him for being so superstitious and urged him to go to bed; which he did.'

June 23rd: 'Before it was quite light I heard a continuous rustling sound coming from up on the city walls. I peeped through a hole in the shutter and saw countless foreigners moving along in single file like an army of ants, *all carrying their muskets*. They were going along the wall from west to east. The noise I had heard was made by their feet shuffling through long grass. How many had already passed when I first looked, I don't know. But I was in time to see between one and two thousand of them, and it was full daylight before they had all gone by. I hastened to wake Little Pine-tree. "The prospects for today are none of the brightest", I said to him. "Have breakfast quickly and then take your younger

---

1 Heaven, Earth and Water. This Taoist Cult was very popular in the nineteenth century, as is shown by the large number of copies of the *Book of the Three Elements (San-yüan Ching)* that were brought back by missionaries.

brother away from here. There's no sense in everyone staying to be slaughtered".' At this point a neighbour came and announced that according to someone he had met in the street all the foreigners had already left the town. But Ts'ao could not get it out of his head that the English he had seen passing along the city wall, all armed to the teeth, were intending to carry out a general slaughter of the inhabitants. He went to the Small South Gate, which was nearer than the large one, and what he saw proved that the report was over-optimistic. *All* the foreigners had certainly not gone; for at the entry to the gate he saw, as he approached it, six foreigners, scantily dressed, lying huddled one upon another, fast asleep. He withdrew hastily and ran home. 'Presently neighbour Huang arrived saying "The devils have gone!" I told him I had seen them going fully armed along the walls and had also seen a number of them still at the Small South Gate. "I didn't believe the news myself", said neighbour Huang, "and went to look. I was just in time to see six devils pick themselves up and make off as fast as they could go. Someone who lives alongside the wall told me that they were drunken devils. When the other devils left the city, he said, they kicked them, but they didn't move. So they left them behind. They have just woken, and have scampered off in the hope of catching up with the rest." That seemed unanswerable; but I knew nothing about the person from whom the story came, so I told Little Pine-tree to stay where he was for the time being, and went to see for myself. It was true; there was no trace of them.'

The remaining entries in the diary which, as I have said, goes down to June 28th, deal largely with the restoration of law and order in the city after the departure of the invaders and are, for our purposes, of relatively little interest.

PART FOUR

Chinkiang

A FTER sailing and marching north again to Wu-sung
the English turned west and, going up the Yangtze
estuary, made for Chinkiang and Nanking. The
resistance at Chinkiang was the most formidable they had
encountered, except perhaps at Chapu, and the British
casualties were 168[1] out of a force of 9,000. We possess
several diaries written during the occupation of the town.
I shall here quote some passages from one by the poet
Chu Shih-yün, who lived outside the walls, on the bank of
the Grand Canal.

July 9th: 'The foreign ships have entered Fu-shan creek
[ninety-one miles down the Yangtze from Chinkiang].
There are a lot of conflicting rumours and the people inside
and outside the walls are all in a state of unrest. However,
one rumour is that they are only merchant-ships, and that
has calmed people down a little. But from the first week
of the fifth month [about June 14th] rich people had already
begun to move out of the town (this was by order of
Lieutenant-General Hai-lin[2]) and the number of those
leaving grew daily. The Lieutenant-General was in a very
excited state. All over the town he arrested harmless people
on the ground that they were in league with the enemy.
He handed them over to the Prefect [Ch'ien Yen-kuei] to

---

[1] Bernard, *Nemesis*, p. 432 (1st edition).

[2] In command of the Manchu garrison, and himself of course a Manchu.
Sometimes called Hai-ling. The round-bracketed sentence is the author's note.

imprison and flog, allowing no distinction in the treatment of them. Some of the Manchu troops took advantage of this to go about plundering and pillaging. Fortunately the Prefect had sense enough to see that great injustice was being done, and released many of those arrested. But Hai-lin, furious at being thwarted, was even on the point of sending soldiers to arrest the Prefect, calling him "the traitors' great stand-by"; fortunately, however, some of his subordinates told him that this would be folly, and he desisted. After that he removed all the troops from Ch'ing-chou [Shantung province] who had been posted outside the northern gate to defend the river approaches, and brought them into the city, where he stationed them at the four gates, his strategy now being, when the enemy came, to defend the city from within closed gates. The city gates were kept shut except from the Hour of the Dragon to that of the Monkey [7 a.m. to 3 p.m.], and the western small gate was never open at all. He explained that this was to prevent traitors from going in and out. This was early in the fifth month when the foreign ships were far away at Shanghai and when there was still no news of their coming up the Yangtze. But these measures naturally alarmed the inhabitants and resulted in a general migration. It was said that Hai-lin had received a letter from the Governor-General [Niu Chien] blaming him for scaring the people by his alarmist attitude, and that it was in consequence of this that he opened the small gate and issued a reassuring proclamation, in which he dwelt upon the impregnability of Ch'ung-ming island [at the mouth of the Yangtze], Fu-shan [ninety-one miles downstream from Chinkiang], Goose-nose Point and Sui-shan [about twenty miles below Chin-kiang]. It was quite impossible, he said, that the foreign ships should get past these strongholds; and even if they did he would at once lead out his troops and drive them back. "A brilliant plan has been made", he said, "which assures us of complete victory; so there is no reason to panic and stampede." At this time, although he had disposed his forces so as to defend the city against assault, it was only at the four gates that he had cannon pointing outwards. Inside the city his whole activity consisted in arresting passers-by day and night, on suspicion of their being traitors. Whenever women or children saw Manchu soldiers, they fled in terror; upon which the soldiers ran after them and slew them, announcing to Hai-lin that they had disposed of traitors; for which he gave them rewards.'

July 10th: 'The foreign ships have reached Kiangyin [sixty-six miles away]. The Governor-General has issued a proclamation, reassuring the population.

'When the foreign ships anchored off Kiangyin they did not do any harm to the people and even insisted on their keeping out of the line of fire, in case they should be hit by accident. A gentleman of this place has had secret news of a kind that has stepped up the number of those moving out. The cost of a passage on the river has gone up tenfold. But there is a ring of swindlers, operating both in the city and without, who have to be squared before one can start, and in some cases people who had already got their whole families and all their household effects on board have still failed to get away. The proclamation of the Governor-General ran: "Misleading reports have been spread by a certain captain, who has already been cashiered. The ships in question are merchantmen; moreover it is not considered possible that they will venture far up the river. You can go to your beds and sleep in perfect security".' This proclamation, the diarist adds, was still pasted on every wall even as late as July 15th, when the ships were already at the Sui-shan, only some twenty miles away.

July 11th: 'The foreign ships are still anchored at Kiangyin. The Intendant-Marshal Chou Hsü and an Adjutant whose name I don't know have one after another moved up their troops to defend Goose-nose Point, and at Chinkiang militia have been concentrated to guard the harbour and river-mouth. But Hai-lin still sits tight in the city, amusing himself with wine and women, and never even asks what is going on outside. The Assistant Commissioner Ch'i-shen[1] [he had recently arrived from the south] and the Governor-General Niu Chien have, in succession, been at Chinkiang, and the number of troops that has been concentrated is nearly 10,000; but nothing can be found out about how they are going to be used for the defence of the town. Niu Chien was at Chinkiang for only one night, and then went back to Nanking. I don't know what his business here was.'

July 12th: 'The foreign ships have passed Goose-nose Point. The Intendant-Marshal Chou Hsü and the Adjutant have fled back to Chinkiang. Chou Hsü went on to Yangchow. Meanwhile Hai-lin still sits quietly in his quarters, as though nothing were happening. But I hear that the Governor [Hsiang-lin] collected spare grain-transport ships, which were to be loaded with earth and stones and used to block the narrow channel under the Sui-shan hill. In one night he got as many as fifty of them; but in the end the plan was not carried out.'

July 13th: 'Heavy cannon-fire at the Sui-shan.

'Two of the approaching ships were destroyed. The red flag was hoisted to announce a victory. I have asked everywhere what sort of ships they were. Some people said "foreign ships", others said "merchantmen". I could not find out for certain. However the soldiers who fired have already been awarded the golden hat-button.' (Diarist's note: 'It afterwards transpired that no ship was destroyed.')

July 14th: 'Tonight at the Second Watch [9 p.m.] the street was blocked with fugitives. I opened my gate and questioned some of them. They said, "Now that the narrows under the Sui-shan have been forced and the militia posted there have fled back to the city, we are clearing out as fast as we can". What happened was that when the foreign ships

[1] Not to be confused with the famous Ch'i-shan.

reached the Sui-shan they fired a large gun and knocked out the Sui-shan battery. Our troops were scattered in every direction by the explosion and fled back to the city. After that the Sui-shan position was left undefended.' (Diarist's note: 'There were some thirty or forty gunners at the battery, but they had no gunpowder. When the attack began they sent a runner to the city to ask for some, but Hai-lin sent none. That was why they fled.') . . . 'In the last few days Hai-lin, the Governor and the Prefect have all sent their families out of the city.'

July 15th: 'Early today the foreign ships were still under the Sui-shan, sixty leagues away; but here the four city gates were all shut and the people were so alarmed that the markets closed down. The Assistant Commissioner Ch'i-shen had at first camped outside the north gate, to defend the riverside. But when he heard the disquieting news from the Sui-shan, he moved his men towards the city and posted them just outside the west gate, at the club-house for Shansi residents. The reason he did so is that this point is well covered by rising ground, and he made sure that the foreigners' fiercest fire could not reach it. Hai-lin posted his soldiers on the walls, and after a brief tour of inspection came home and wept till his eyes were swollen. Everyone inside the city and out was still expecting him to make a sortie. But he stuck to what he had said before, and merely from time to time fired a few random shots of cannon- or rocket-fire. The night before last he collected from the sheds along the up-river shore several thousand bundles of reeds stored for firing, as also a large quantity of dryandra-tree oil and so on and loaded it on empty ships, the idea being that they were to be ignited and then allowed to drift downstream and set fire to the foreign ships. I suppose this was the "brilliant plan" of which he spoke in his proclamation. But when it was tried out up-river the smoke and flames all went straight up into the sky and had no effect at a lower level; so the idea was given up.'

The author then describes the usual scenes of plunder by roughs and bandits, consequent upon the breakdown of law and order in the city. 'Today,' he continues, 'between the Hours of the Snake and the Horse [9 a.m. to 1 p.m.], the gates were temporarily opened and the people streamed out of the city like a swarm of ants. As my house is outside the walls, many friends stopped there for a short rest. Boxes, baskets, bags and sacks covered the floors, so that there was not an inch of free space. They were mostly waiting for missing members of the family to join them, when they would set out upon their flight either on board ship or in carts. But when the city gates were suddenly shut, there were some who were already outside and wanted to get back, others who wanted to get out but could not, others belonging to families of which one or two members had managed to get out while the rest were still shut in. All these gazed at one another in speechless despair. In my house alone there were twenty or thirty of them, so it may be imagined what the total number was. At the Hour of the Dragon [7 a.m.] a boat happened to come from the north side of the river and I hastily embarked more than twenty members of my household, so that they might be taken back in it across the river and take refuge on the other side [in the direction of Yangchow]; I and my younger brother staying to look after the house. . . .

'The Governor entreated Hai-lin to go to the Sui-shan and organize the defences there; but he refused. The Governor then went there all alone; but after a cursory inspection, he came back. Tonight there was some occasional rocket and matchlock fire from on top of the city walls. The inhabitants were naturally very agitated, and did not dare to go to bed. . . .'

July 17th: 'Five foreign ships have reached the riverside, and a thunderous cannonade is going on. Since this started the city gates have been closed for good and all. Hai-lin does nothing except make his Manchu troops search everywhere for traitors; anyone walking in the street at night whom they don't know by sight they kill on the spot. Having said that the town contains nothing but traitors and threatened to exterminate everyone in it, he moved a big gun and mounted it at the Red Flag Creek, apparently meaning to open fire on the city. The people were in terror; but when they tried to escape they found all four gates closed; and against the south and east gates earth had been piled. There was no possibility of escape and they could only fold their hands and await destruction. Afterwards [the diarist adds retrospectively] someone who had escaped earlier by the north gate told me that the foreigners, having stationed several hundred men on the Pei-ku-shan [hill-· promontory just to the north of Chinkiang] had originally intended to attack the city on the fifteenth day [July 22nd]. But when their Commander-in-Chief heard the news that Hai-lin was about to slaughter the inhabitants, he ordered an immediate attack, forbidding however the use of cannon, for fear of inflicting heavy casualties on the inhabitants; only rockets were to be used. It was not till our troops fired cannon that the foreigners did so, contenting themselves, however, with destroying the Shih-san Gate (western outer gate) behind the Governor's office.[1] When they entered the city in strength, they did not wantonly kill a single person, and let anyone who wanted to, man or woman, leave the city. Those who were killed had all carelessly put themselves in the line of fire, or taken their own lives out of fright. . . .

'My house opens on to the Grand Canal, and all day I saw soldiers passing along its banks in an endless stream. They all said they had had nothing to eat, owing to the city gates being closed. They murmured incessantly against Hai-lin, angrily charging him with having prevented the Prefect from coming into the city on business, saying he was not

---

[1] Actually, no big guns were used. The gates were blown in by exploding a charge of powder.

going to have that arch-traitor in the town. The Prefect and Intendant of Circuit were both at the time stationed at the temple of the God of Pestilence [on an island in the river], in charge of the commissariat.'

During the afternoon of July 19th there was a false rumour that the foreigners had landed. This at any rate relieved the author of the friends and relations who had quartered themselves on him: 'Since the gates were shut on the eighth day [July 15th] I had had more than thirty friends and relations, both men and women, staying in my house. They spent the day with nothing to do but sit face to face sipping gruel; at night, as there were not enough beds to go round, they had to take turns with them. On the eleventh day [July 18th] the women, more than twenty of them, moved out into the countryside; today the whole lot, men and women, have departed. Things look so precarious that the three or four men-servants and maid-servants, who had stayed till now, have all fled. The two relatives who are helping us to mind the house both urged me and my younger brother to flee at once; and we had got as far as dividing between us several bags of dried provisions that we had prepared beforehand.' However, the news about the landing of the English turned out to be premature, and the brothers stayed where they were.

July 20th: 'From the eighth to the twelfth day [July 15th–19th] the foreign ships cruising about on the river did not interfere with Chinese boats that were crossing; but now they dare not go across. Early this morning a rice-transport boat tried to cross. It was challenged by the foreigners, but did not reply. They fired, and wounded one of the crew. Afterwards I saw a man with a piece of blue cloth tied round his head, looking more dead than alive. Another man had his arm round his waist and was helping him along. Someone pointed to him and said, ''That is the man who was wounded by the gun''. . . . When he saw the foreign ships arriving in force the Assistant Commissioner

Ch'i-shen moved his troops to a deep and secluded fold in the hills, known as Ma-wang Temple, while Commander Liu Yün-hsiao[1] retreated to the Chang-wang Temple. Some people said this was a stratagem well-known to the handbooks on the art of war; the idea being that when the foreigners landed and saw no opponents anywhere, they would advance boldly inland. Then our forces would fall upon them unawares, and the whole ugly tribe would be annihilated. I, too, thought that this must be the intention.

'At the Hour of the Monkey [3 p.m.] I heard the sound of a large force of our troops coming along the road. I hastened to the gate to look at them and saw that they were marching with war banners flying, in excellent formation, creating indeed a most formidable impression. One of them told me that, as the foreign ships had now arrived in force, these troops had been sent on parade, in order to make a demonstration of strength, and also to search for traitors.'

But owing to the city gates being closed and the markets not working many of the troops had not had a solid meal for five days, and could be seen holding raw egg-plants, at which they nibbled while they marched. 'Tonight', Chu says in his diary, 'Commander Liu's troops, owing to the gate being shut and there being nowhere they could buy food, have collected under the walls, threatening to open fire, storm the city, capture General Hai-lin and eat him raw!'

July 21st: 'Today at the Hour of the Snake [9 a.m.] the foreigners disembarked. The Assistant Commissioner Ch'i-shen and the Commander-in-Chief Liu Yün-hsiao hastily marshalled the troops whom they had secluded in a fold of the hills, and directed operations sitting in carrying-chairs. Our troops fired several rounds; but the foreigners continued to advance. The two generals then left their chairs and fled on horseback; whereupon all their men broke into a

---

[1] Commander-in-Chief of all the forces 'South of the River', with his headquarters at Nanking. Our author writes the name incorrectly. Liu died in September 1842, aged sixty-six.

general stampede up hill and down dale, in the direction of the Tan-yang high road [i.e. to the south], to the great amusement of the foreigners.'

The Assistant Commissioner's official report on this engagement (iv. 146), dated July 27th, gives a very different account of it. He represents himself as having fought continuously from July 15th to July 21st, killing more than three hundred foreigners, including a foreign chieftain dressed in red, and as having only retired down the Tan-yang road to prevent an overland incursion of the English in this direction. Nothing, of course, about carrying-chairs. He was riding on horseback at the head of his men, he says, when his horse was shot under him, and he was obliged to find another.

'A villager who had been impressed into service by the foreigners and who had managed to escape from them told me afterwards that a lot of them gathered together in Mr Li's flower-garden, and did an imitation of our men firing. They ducked their heads and bent double, making a popping sound like guns going off. Then all of a sudden they flung down their muskets, turned and fled. The performance was greeted with clapping and loud laughter. . . .

'I and my brother had our provisions ready and had decided that the time had come for flight. But my brother was not in favour of starting at once. However, he urged me to go and, reluctantly, I left by the back gate and went up the hill, to wait for him there. I looked towards the northern gate. Under the wall a fierce cross-fire of guns and rockets was in progress. Spurt after spurt of white smoke darted out in quick succession, till everything was covered in a thick, coiling cloud; underneath which, I well knew, the dead must be piled corpse on corpse. I consoled myself by thinking that our men evidently still "had some wind in their sails" and hoped they might perhaps after all be victorious. I had, however, no idea what troops these might be who were putting up such a stiff resistance. Presently I learnt from a peasant that they were the men from Ch'ing-chou [in Shantung]. If reinforcements had come to their help, it is possible that the north gate would not have been forced.

'Suddenly the firing ceased, and at that moment flames shot up from the watch-tower at the northern gate. There was a fierce south-east wind blowing and the purple flames under the double eaves flounced out as though there were some demon in their midst, plying a bellows. Yet all the while a pall of blue smoke hung above, so dense that it did not budge. . . . My thoughts turned to the hundreds of thousands of souls, shut into this seething cauldron without chance of escape. What was happening at this moment to this or that life-long friend or near kinsman? I struggled in vain to keep back my tears.

'When the fire at the north gate watch-tower was still only beginning, the rocket attack spread to the whole line of parapets towards the east, and was replied to by our men. After a while there was an extremely concentrated attack by rockets on the part near the watch-tower on the eastern wall, and now when I cast my eye round the whole circuit of the walls I could not see a single defender, except at the point where the foreigners were actually trying to scale them; here twenty or thirty of our men were still crouching between the parapets.

'All this was watched by thousands of spectators who had crowded on to the hill. "The people in the city must be wondering why no help comes to them from outside", they murmured to each other with a sigh, little suspecting that by this time the Assistant Commissioner Ch'i-shen and Commander Liu Yün-hsiao were already comfortably installed at Tan-yang, jackets off and well sheltered from the summer heat.

'Suddenly everyone pointed at the watch-tower on the western wall. "It's ablaze again", they said. I was sure now that the city would not hold, and hastened to send someone to fetch my brother, while I myself rested for a time in a small grotto at the foot of the hill. But soon the news became more and more desperate, and I hurried towards the southern hills. I was holding an umbrella and making my way through the blazing sun, yet in no part of my body did I sweat—a most strange thing. I reached a hill-top and sat down on a rock. Looking round the walls I saw that the men between the parapets on the eastern wall were still firing guns and rockets, and knew that the city had not yet fallen. Suddenly three large cannon fired from the eastern wall, one after another. But they were a long way off from where the foreigners were making their assault, and may well not have reached them. In a moment I saw the foreigners spread out over the road and march straight through the southern gate. My brother and I then took a track that went down the hill and reached the house of a certain Mr Chang, who received us very hospitably, giving us millet and meat. After we had eaten, someone came from close outside the walls, saying, "The city has fallen, but I don't know by which gate they got in". Afterwards I learnt from someone who had escaped from inside that the Manchu troops had fired a large cannon and killed one foreign devil on the Pei-ku-shan. It was only then that the foreign devils began firing all their big cannon. They hit the Shih-san gate behind the Governor's office and then rushed it in one solid mass.

'After firing their cannon the Manchu troops hoisted the red flag of victory and the whole camp cheered vociferously. Hai-lin relieved the troops who had secured this triumph, and they came back to their quarters dancing and drumming, to celebrate the occasion with a wine-feast. But no other Manchu contingent was sent up to take their place, with the result that there were only twenty or thirty Shantung troops on the walls; and that was why they could not be held. But the wine had scarcely wetted the Manchu Banner-men's lips when the sword was already at their throats.' The author also repeats a story to the effect that the ladders by which the English scaled the walls were some that were 'kept at the Academy for use in repairing the city walls'. It is, however, clear from the English accounts that they were special scaling-ladders brought by the English for this purpose. The author's animus, all through the account, is against the Manchus and in particular against their leader, Hai-lin, rather than against the English. So far from leaving the fighting to the Chinese the Manchus, as all English accounts make clear, fought for some three hours with extreme gallantry against assailants more than three times as many in number and infinitely better armed and equipped.

'When Hai-lin saw that the north gate had fallen, he hurried to the south gate, making pretence of having won a victory, and calling on his men to pursue the enemy. He hoped in this way to have a chance to slip out of the south gate and escape from the city. But earth had been piled against it and it could not be opened. He then got into a small litter and had himself carried to the Lesser Drill Ground. What happened to him after that I do not know.'

That Hai-lin did not survive seems certain; but there are many different accounts of how he died. The story generally believed both by the Chinese and in the West is that he burnt himself to death in his office on a pyre of official papers. Other versions are that he fled to Chin-tan, some forty miles to the south; or again that he was assassinated by the inhabitants of Chinkiang, or alternatively that he was killed in battle. The interpreter J. R. Morrison believed that he had seen Hai-lin's charred remains in his office. 'Mr Morrison found, among some heaps of ashes and half-consumed wood, evidences of the awful sacrifice which had been so determinedly consummated . . . the skull of the general was yet unconsumed', and so on.[1] But how Morrison recognized the skull, when he did not even know Hai-lin by sight, we are not told.

'Chou Hsü, the Intendant-Marshal,' the diary continues, 'the Governor of Chinkiang, the Prefect of Tan-t'u and all

[1] Ouchterlony, p. 405.

the other officials in the city fled. Tonight I and my brother stayed at Mr Chang's house. The heat was intense, and during the night I got up and sat in the open; but I was very tired, and soon lay down again. I felt at that moment that I had no more connection with the world of men than has a gnat on a dung-heap.

'When Hai-lin was fleeing to the south gate, a Manchu soldier called down to him from on top of the walls, "No, no, Your Excellency! This ill becomes one who has received such favours from His Majesty the Emperor. You should be mustering the troops you command, to fight to the last in the streets and sacrifice their lives, if need be, as their duty to the State demands." But Hai-lin passed on, pretending not to hear.'

July 22nd: 'I and my brother are at T'ang village [about a mile and a half south of Chinkiang]. We got up early and went for a walk in front of the village. Jutting hills clasped the scene before us with a ring of hazy blue. In the middle distance green fields interlaced, water-channels criss-crossed and interlocked. Warmth was beginning to come into the morning light. Far villages and near villages showed dimly between the heavy green of the misty woods. The young women of the villages were busy drawing their morning supplies of water, or were going off to work in the fields. Chickens, dogs, mulberries, hemp—all the sights that speak of an untroubled life, and this only three or four leagues[1] from the city! Indeed no one here seemed to have any inkling that a deadly conflict was raging.

'We walked slowly through thickets that were fresh with the breath of the night-dew. All around us birds were singing and insects chirping. . . . It was hard to remember that only last night we extricated ourselves from the scene of battle. The Mr Chang in whose house we had slept, fearing that we should lose our way, now came hastening to meet us, and in his company we crossed the foot-hills

---

[1] A mile or so.

and visited an old friend who had also fled into the country. When we had chatted for some time, he gave us breakfast, and then went back with us, a very civil thing to do, as far as the main path to T'ang village. When I had got half-way to the village my feet began to hurt, and I could walk no farther. A villager came with a cart and I and my brother drove to another village, where the family of one of our servants lived. It was a mud hovel, cramped and tumble-down, entirely pervaded by the smell of manure. I spent the night in a small loft, where the heat was scorching, and could not get a wink of sleep. I kept on thinking of my wife and family whom I had sent far away to the north of the river. Having heard of the fall of the city they must be desperately anxious about what has happened to myself and my brother. I went on and on worrying about this.'

July 23rd: 'At T'ang village. . . . A villager who has come back from the city told us: "They are letting people go in and out by the north gate. The foreign devils are going round from house to house, seizing gold and silver and women's headdresses. The clothes they toss to the poor. Rogues from far and near got wind of this, and crowds of them have come to guide the foreigners to likely houses. When the foreigners have smashed in the gates and taken what they want, these scoundrels take advantage of the confusion to make off with everything that is left, even loading on to carts what they cannot carry on their shoulders." Today my brother went back to our home to see how things are. The few relations whom we left behind there are all right so far. This evening my brother came back.'

Under this date the diarist also tells how the villages of the neighbourhood where he was have organized themselves into a defence corps to protect their homes against looters and robbers. Every family was pledged to supply one member, whether male or female. They were armed only with rakes, hoes and thornwood pikes, but were able to drive away the intruders, meeting out summary justice to any of them whom they overtook and captured.

July 24th: 'At T'ang village. . . . The foreigners have executed two black devils and two Chinese looters, and exposed their bodies in the market-place. They have issued a proclamation forbidding rape and pillage. My servant has been to our house and brought back some rice, books and various odds and ends.'

July 25th: 'Still at T'ang village. Our house has been pillaged. My brother has come back. It appears that local roughs, knowing that the house was empty, hacked down the back gate and made off with everything. When my brother left the house to come back here, the few people remaining there also fled.'

July 26th: 'At T'ang village. Lately I have been feeling more and more depressed. To begin with I was very anxious about my brother when he was in the danger-zone; and then equally worried all the time about my wife and others who have taken refuge north of the river, and who have no news of what is happening to myself and my brother. One villager after another comes back from the city saying: "Such and such a place has been burnt to the ground", "Such and such a family has been robbed of almost all it possessed", "The town is littered with corpses, young women are wandering homeless; the state of affairs is absolutely indescribable". At every moment one hears some fresh tale of horror. Is it ever going to end? Will the family ever be reunited? I find myself pushing away my food before I have eaten anything, and having to lie down without really being tired. Sometimes I try to distract myself for a moment by gossiping with one of the villagers, but all that I get from him is the same chapter of horrors in a thousand different forms, almost equally upsetting whether one believes in every detail or not, so that one is driven to absolute distraction. Looking back on the time, only a few days ago, when all was peaceful and one could wander down any back street that took one's fancy, it seems to me now like some tale of fairyland.'

July 27th: 'At T'ang village. This evening someone came from north of the river and said that Yangchow has not been attacked, which made me feel easier about my wife and family. I also hear that large numbers of the foreign devils are embarking on their ships, having impressed Chinese to carry their spare clothing and other goods. It looks as though they were detaching part of their forces to go to Nanking.'

July 28th: 'At T'ang village. . . . The foreign devils, both inside and outside the city, are seizing people, cutting off their pigtails and turning them into soldiers. Early in the morning I went to various villages to visit friends. I was very tired when I got back, and my servant prepared a meat-dish for me. But my thoughts kept on going back to old days and I was in such misery that I could not restrain my tears. In the evening, I sat out in the open under some trees in the Poppy Woods and at a low desk wrote a letter to send north of the river.'

July 29th: 'I hear that a boat crossing the river below Chiao-shan Island [three miles east of Chinkiang] was stopped by the foreign devils, who demanded foreign dollars. Those on board said they had none, but offered two strings of copper-cash. The black devils were furious, and after rummaging about everywhere found thirty or more silver pieces, wounding four men with their knives in the course of doing so. At this point some white foreigners came up, drove the black devils away and ordered the boat to go back.

'For days on end great numbers of women in the city have been raped or carried off. Their names are well known, but I forbear to mention them. Two sons of well-to-do families have had their queues cut off and have been carried away; so it may well be imagined how others have fared. My servant has come back with a letter from my brother saying that south of the city the foreign devils' tents have all disappeared.

They have also quitted the city itself and are now for the most part only stationed in the quarter outside the north gate; but there are still forty-five ships along the shore. He also said that black devils came again yesterday to our house and took several things away.'

On July 31st he left T'ang village and returned to his house on the banks of the Grand Canal. The entry for this day is largely concerned with looting by local roughs, which was still going on night and day. The entry for August 1st deals with the exploits of the beadle of Tan-t'u Chen, five miles south-east of the city walls, who displayed the greatest energy in raising volunteer forces to put down looting, sold rice to the poor at normal prices, persuaded the people not to slaughter their cattle and finally 'burnt incense and prayed for rain', which had long been due. On August 3rd the diarist repeats the familiar but certainly untrue story of the English conscribing Chinese as soldiers: 'Some roughs from outside the eastern gate were looting outside the western gate when the foreigners lured about three hundred of them on to their ships, cut off their pigtails, gave them a potion that deprived them of the power of speech,[1] put them into uniforms, drilled them in the use of firearms and turned them into black devils. A visitor told me the following story: "A certain high officer fled by water to a certain Prefecture. He had resumed a stiff martial air, his boat was decked out with banners and insignia of State; he looked magnificent as a god. He was surrounded by warriors all armed to the teeth, and everyone gazed awe-struck at the imposing sight. In the evening twenty or thirty stragglers from a defeated unit came along and one of them called out 'The foreign devils are coming!' The warriors instantly stripped off their uniforms, threw away their arms and assumed the role of spectators. The high officer at once ordered the lights on the boat to be put out, took down the banners, scattered the insignia, dis-

[1] Cf. p. 163.

carded his peacock-feather hat and, changing into the blue dress and straw sandals of a peasant, prepared for flight. The Prefect of the place heard of this, hurried to the boat, knocked at the cabin-door and begged for a light. 'They are fugitives from our own army,' he assured the high officer, 'not foreign devils. Please try to calm yourself a little.' The officer was not easily convinced, but after a while the whole alarm subsided".'

August 4th: 'There are now only about twenty foreign ships on the river. Someone came with a letter from my family north of the river. They are getting on fairly well.'

August 5th: 'The foreigners have put up notices everywhere in the city asking for carpenters and plasterers; also for discarded horse-saddles and stirrups.'

August 6th: 'The iron pagoda at the T'ien-lu Monastery [on the heights to the east of the city] was put up by Li Ching [A.D. 571–649]. In Ming times it was blown down by a tornado, and afterwards re-cast; so that it has had an existence of several hundred years. Now the foreign devils have forced the people to try to destroy it. They dug down more than ten feet and still found solid iron. Not being able to get at the foundations, they contented themselves with taking away the ball at the top and destroying the spire.' It was, in fact, intended to bring the iron pagoda to England as Cleopatra's Needle was later brought. It was only thirty feet high and could easily have been transported.

August 10th: 'Up till now the English foreigners have killed every bannerman [Manchu soldier] they met. But at present they let them pass without taking any notice, and one after another the Manchus are coming back into the city. About a hundred Manchu men and women who have lived in the Tartar quarter have come back to their homes, apparently thinking that, once there, they will have the good fortune "to eat the grain from the Great Barn" [i.e. consume their official allowances] in peace.'

August 11th: 'The foreigners, hearing that the Manchus

are again mustering in the Tartar town, sent over a hundred picked troops to drive them out. Several hundred of them, men and women, have straggled out of the city and gone again to draw their rations at Tan-yang [about twenty miles south of Chinkiang]. . . .'

The entries on the 14th and 15th are concerned with the longed-for rain, which did not, however, come to any useful extent till the 17th, when three inches fell, and the harvest was saved.

August 16th: 'The foreigners have put up a proclamation to this effect, "At Nanking peace has not yet been made, but the Commissioner General Ch'i-ying, His Excellency I-li-pu, together with Ch'en Chih-kang and Yen Ch'ung-li, are all to be ordered to go [to Nanking. I-li-pu arrived on August 8th and Ch'i-ying on August 11th]. As regards the question of brigands—whenever captured they are to be brought to the camp to the Commander-in-Chief [Lieut.-Colonel Schoedde] on the Pei-ku-shan, where they will be duly tried and punished. Cattle, sheep, pigs and fowls may be traded in the usual manner. There will be a market for the purpose under the Pei-ku-shan, which will start at dawn, with a second session in the evening. The general population has nothing to fear. Signed, Commander of the garrison Shu-te [Schoedde]."

'Another proclamation says: "Trade on cash terms. Fair prices for all goods supplied".'

August 17th: 'Some foreigners came and bought several pecks of rice. They gave one foreign dollar on the spot and two more when it was delivered at the Pei-ku-shan. The idea was to show that there was to be no more commandeering without payment.'

August 20th: 'I hear that a lot of the foreign ships are returning from Nanking, which must mean that peace has been signed. The foreigners sent an express message to Tan-yang saying: "There is a shortage of sheep, cattle, vegetables and greens at Chinkiang, and supplies must be obtained from Tan-yang. They must arrive within the space of one day; if they fail to do so the Commander [Schoedde] will come himself and take them''.' However, the diarist adds that this alleged note from the English commander turned out to be a forgery. A certain Mr Chang concocted it, hoping to frighten the inhabitants of Tan-yang into parting with their livestock, etc. To his discomfiture they insisted on taking their offering to Chinkiang themselves, and Chang had to go into hiding.

August 25th: 'A rumour is going about everywhere that a great army of twenty or thirty thousand men is coming from the north. The Emperor has reinstated Lin Tse-hsü ['Commissioner Lin'], given him a sword from the Imperial Treasury and put him in command over four provinces. The troops have already crossed the Huai River and will soon be at Yangchow. Another story is that a certain general in command of twenty or thirty thousand men all clad in white has put them into rowing-boats and ensconced them in ambush on the east side of the Sui-shan. As soon as the troops upstream are fully mobilized they will carry out a pincer movement against the English, completely destroying their fleet, so that not a fragment of sail or oar remains. In this way our disgrace will be wiped out and the Middle Kingdom will breathe again. . . . On hearing this I said: ''That is the kind of story that was bound to get about, no matter whether there is a word of truth in it or not''.'

August 26th: 'A Mr P'an of Yangchow has given a sum of money to be spent on presents to the foreigners on their ships, asking them in return for this to allow ships laden with rice, for distribution at reduced prices, to reach Chinkiang from Yangchow. The rice-ships have now arrived and two sheds have been put up to store the rice, one at the west gate and one at the south gate. At the same time a large stock of rough coffins has been brought, that people inside and outside the city may be able to bury the dead. But though the rice-ships have arrived there has been a hold-up of some kind and, after several days, they still have not yet been unloaded.'

August 27th: 'Cattle and sheep are being brought in from the neighbouring villages in vast quantities and are being paid for with foreign dollars. Many of the foreigners have fallen ill. Some people say that it is the plague.'[1]

August 28th: 'The foreigners are selling clothes. These are clothes that they looted. They have put up stalls outside the north gate where they sell them very cheap, but will only take foreign dollars in payment.'

August 29th: 'The foreigners have put up a proclamation. Twenty or more red[2] and black devils, led by white foreigners, are patrolling the town.' The proclamation, issued by Colonel Schoedde, called for 'business as usual' and the restoration of the night-watch. 'If any black soldier comes to this place, he is to be brought to the Pei-ku-shan camp for trial and punishment. There is far too much rubble in the streets. Leading citizens are to come up to the camp and discuss with the Commander what can be done about it.' Schoedde had been an Equerry to the Queen and liked everything to be ship-shape and orderly.

'This afternoon a white foreigner was lying drunk outside the south gate. Someone reported this to the Pei-ku-shan camp, for which he was given a reward in foreign dollars. Seven or eight foreigners were sent to the south gate and ordered the local inhabitants to remove him on a stretcher, for doing which they were given one foreign dollar and four ''small ones'' [shillings?].'

August 30th: 'Today the sale of subsidized rice began, twenty-two copper-cash being charged for a pint of rice. But this only went on for a short time, and large numbers of people came away empty-handed. The market price for rice brought from outside was not more than twenty-seven or

---

[1] Actually, it was chiefly dysentery.

[2] 'Red devils' are often mentioned. The term seems to have been applied to the less dark among the Indian troops.

twenty-eight cash per pint; but some thirty gentlemen sat in the office of their security group eating rice behind closed doors.'

September 1st: 'Peace has been concluded at Nanking. I-li-pu has given a farewell entertainment to the foreigners, who have now duly withdrawn their ships.'

September 3rd: 'The Governor has issued a proclamation saying he has received information from the Governor-General that peace has been concluded with the English foreigners. "The fighting being now over, I call upon all refugees to return to the city. There is to be no more looting".'

September 5th: 'The English have put up a proclamation. After describing the fall of the city and the subsequent peace negotiations with I-li-pu at Nanking, the proclamation continues: "As the people here are still in an uneasy state, we have set aside 1,500,000 dollars, out of the sum to be paid to us in accordance with the treaty, to be used by His Excellency I-li-pu for the relief of distress at Chinkiang and the re-establishment of the people in their peaceful occupations." . . . They are also telling the people to go to Sui-shan, where "opium is on sale very cheap—an opportunity not to be missed".'

That opium ships followed the Royal Navy up the Yangtze is, of course, not mentioned in the English accounts.

September 6th: 'When the foreigners were selling clothes someone tried to pass off on them a copper foreign dollar. They beat him mercilessly. According to one account they cut off his arm before they let him go, saying that he was bereft of all decent feeling. Is it decent feeling, I wonder, that prompts the English to seize other people's clothing and put it up for sale!'

September 7th: 'The foreigners have been making pictures [i.e. maps] at all four gates. Every strategic point along the walls, inside the city and out, and every defence afforded by watercourses or rising ground is marked in their sketches.'

September 8th: 'The foreigners have been at Tan-t'u-chen—to make pictures, of course.'

September 11th: 'A black devil snatched money from a passer-by, and wounded his hand with a knife. A white foreigner saw him do it, and motioned him away. The black devil was then hacked limb from limb; the money was given back to its owner, who was also compensated with three foreign dollars. That gives one some idea of their system of justice!'

September 17th: 'The Prefect has entered the city and made an inspection. Before doing so he ordered the beadle to tell the market people to put out incense-stands, in order to be able to give him a suitable welcome.'

September 21st: '. . . At the Hour of the Monkey [3 p.m.] the child of a white foreigner was robbed, by a man called Ch'ien, of a silver fillet that he was wearing round his head. The foreigners complained to the Prefect, who arrested the man's uncle and sent him to the foreigners' camp. But they sent him back, saying that the culprit himself must be sent. If he was not forthcoming, the north gate would be bombarded. The inhabitants got into a fright, and some of them fled from the city.'

There are several other versions of this story; for example in Yang Ch'i's diary (III. 50): 'The child of Ch'ien Sheng, an employee at the Prefecture, met in the street a small white foreigner and lured him into playing a game with him. While they were at play he snatched away a large gold clasp that the white child was wearing on his arm and a gold chain that he was wearing at his neck and made off with them. The foreign chieftain gave out that unless the culprit were handed over within three days, he would butcher the whole town. The Prefect arrested the child and sent him to the chieftain, who, however, sent him back to the Prefect, to deal with as he thought proper. One sees how easy it is for incidents to occur that lead to open conflict, when Chinese and foreigners live side by side.'

Chinkiang

If there is any truth in the story, the white child must presumably have come from some English merchant-vessel commandeered for service with the expedition. Merchant captains often took their families on board with them.

October 1st: 'Today at noon the foreign ships on the river fired their big guns ten or more times in succession. This gave rise to various rumours, one of which was that two foreign ships had run aground in shallow water, and that they were firing as a signal that they needed help. But next day, I learnt from people living by the river that a large ship had arrived on its way back from Nanking, and that these repeated salvoes were fired as a greeting to it.'

Presumably the guns were saluting the flagship, the *Cornwallis*, with Vice-Admiral Sir William Parker, the Commander-in-Chief, on board her.

October 4th: 'The foreign ships have all gone.'

The Treaty of Nanking, by which England was confirmed in her possession of Hongkong, obtained the right to trade at five other ports and received an indemnity of twenty-one million dollars, has been discussed in so many books and articles that it is not necessary here to say any more about it.[1]

[1] For a contemporary Chinese account of the negotiations see Teng Ssu-yü, *Chang Hsi and the Treaty of Nanking*, Chicago, 1944.

PART FIVE

Gutzlaff and his Traitors. Mamo

OVER and over again in the documents of this period there occurs the term *Han-chien*, meaning literally 'Chinese evil-doers', as opposed to *I-chien*, 'foreign evil-doers'. It was applied, long before the War, to Chinese who entered the service of foreigners, learnt foreign languages, corresponded with foreigners or made friends with them in any way. There were, of course, licensed compradors and interpreters who theoretically were not *Han-chien*; but they were under constant suspicion, as were also the licensed guild-merchants, through whom the foreigners conducted their trade. After the war started, whole new classes of *Han-chien* arose: those who obtained maps and sea-charts for the enemy, who passed on political and military information to them, acted as pilots, worked as craftsmen on board foreign warships and so on. Later the expression became a term of abuse for anyone who favoured appeasement rather than war to the death, it often being assumed that, if he did so, it must be because he was in the foreigners' pay.

There is a natural tendency in times of stress to exaggerate the number of the 'enemy in our midst' and attribute to their machinations everything that goes wrong. In June 1841 Yang Fang and others in a joint report[1] to the Throne speak of 'over ten thousand' traitors at Canton, which if one takes the term in at all a literal sense was certainly a gross exaggera-

[1] IV. 244.

tion. The philosopher Fang Tung-shu (1772–1851), writing[1] in the summer of 1842, even went so far as to say that the strength of the English lay not in their armaments but in the help they got from *Han-chien*. It was, as we have seen, also widely believed that Chinese traitors were used to reinforce the English troops. Ch'i-shan, reporting on the loss of the Bogue ports in January 1841, asserted that several hundred Chinese traitors took part in the storming of both the Taikok and the Shakok forts, and in later legend it is constantly asserted that half the attackers were *Han-chien*.

But 'traitors' were not, of course, altogether a myth. The English naturally had a number of spies and informants in their pay, and in captured towns a certain number of Chinese, usually of a not very reputable kind, 'collaborated' by accepting paid posts.

The individual *Han-chien* about whom we know most are those whom the Prussian missionary, interpreter and information officer Gutzlaff employed as agents. I have no intention of trying to write here this singular man's biography. But as he has been so often mentioned in this book it may not be out of place to give a few facts about him.

Karl Friedrich August Gutzlaff, born in 1803 at Pyritz in Pomerania, was the son of a tailor. His father apprenticed him to a girdler in Stettin. He escaped from this drudgery by an expedient so Chinese as to seem strangely prophetic of his future. He addressed a laudatory poem to the King of Prussia, which had the result of procuring him entry into a school for budding missionaries in Berlin. He continued his studies at Rotterdam and in 1824 was sent by the Netherlands Missionary Society to Siam. Here he learnt the Fuhkien dialect from Chinese settlers. At Malacca in 1829 he married an Englishwoman, Mary Newell, who died shortly afterwards, leaving him a considerable sum of money. His missionary employers having refused to send him to China, he embarked at his own expense on a Chinese junk, and went

[1] V. 594.

up the coast as far as Tientsin, distributing tracts and medicines. Late in 1831 Charles Marjoribanks, President of the Select Committee of the East India Company's branch at Canton, decided to send the ship *Lord Amherst* on an experimental trip[1] up the Chinese coast to see what sale there was for English goods other than opium. The Chinese Government did not, as we have seen, allow English ships to go to any port except Canton, so that in order to avoid friction with the Chinese authorities the *Lord Amherst* sailed under a false name and gave various fictitious accounts of where she came from. 'The expedition', says Sir John Davis (*The Chinese*, Vol. 1, pp. 125-6), 'was upon the whole condemned by the Court [of Directors, in London] and their animadversions were particularly directed against the fictitious characters and false names assumed by those who conducted the voyage. They commented on the inconsistency of the frequent complaints against the duplicity of the Chinese, while the English at the same time were presenting themselves in an assumed shape, and in direct violation of the laws of the country.' The goods that were carried, says Davis, 'amounted to only 200 bales, but comprised every variety of article in demand at Canton. The larger portion were brought back exactly as they went, and of the few things that were not returned a considerable number had been given away. The loss on the expedition amounted to £5,647.'

An interpreter was needed, and Gutzlaff took on the job, armed with medicines and tracts. His standby was *The Dialogue between the Two Friends Chang and Yüan*, which tells how a Chinese convert to Christianity awakened a sense of sin in a pagan friend. But Gutzlaff also mentions the success of a propaganda pamphlet written by Marjoribanks himself and referred[2] to by him as 'A Brief Sketch of British Character and Policy'. 'Scarcely any means adopted to

[1] See above, p. 12.
[2] See *Letter to the Rt. Hon. Charles Grant.* . ., by Charles Marjoribanks, M.P., 1833. Separately catalogued at the British Museum.

promote friendly intercourse proved so effectual', says Gutzlaff (*Three Voyages*, p. 217), 'as the circulation of this paper.'

As the pamphlet is probably the earliest example of English propaganda to the Chinese people in general, I will give some account of it. No English version exists, and I shall translate or rather résumé it from the Chinese text (I.102), which is probably the work of Gutzlaff.

Marjoribanks begins by describing the immense voyage that ships must make in order to get from England to China. But so great, he says, is the skill and courage of her sailors that, despite tempests and all the other hazards of the sea, ships are seldom lost. These ships bring English manufactured goods and return with 'tea and other goods'. This trade, carried on for two hundred years, has always been beneficial to both parties and given employment to an immense number of people. Unfortunately the idea has got about in China that the English are greedy for further territory. Nothing, says Marjoribanks, could be more false. He then gives a catalogue of England's possessions, winding up with Singapore, and asks whether it is thinkable that any nation already possessing such vast territories can want to extend its frontiers.

But though the English Government's great concern is to give happiness, peace and protection to its own people, it is not prepared to put up with insults and injuries. Despite the Chinese Emperor's avowed policy of conciliating foreigners, foreign merchants at Canton have in recent years continually suffered from the extortions imposed upon them by local officials. Moreover Chinese associating with foreigners are accused of being traitors (*Han-chien*) and have frequently been fined, thrashed, imprisoned or even executed. All that the English want is to trade on fair terms, paying, of course, the authorized customs dues. But they find themselves being continually called upon to pay large sums in addition to the proper dues and being secretly approached by officials before any business can be done. All this, of course, happens in absolute secrecy and no echo of it ever reaches the Emperor's ears. In addition to this, notices are put up in the streets abusing foreigners in the filthiest language, and even containing innuendoes suggesting that they are addicted to unnatural vice.[1] This has led certain low characters to think that they can attack foreigners with impunity, and affrays have ensued, sometimes attended with loss of life, followed by suspension of trade and grave detriment to public business. All this has been due to the failure of Chinese officials to carry out their duties in a proper way. 'English sailors may be rough in outward appearance; but they have kind hearts, and it is only when they are provoked by intolerable rudeness and insults that incidents occur, resulting in loss of life.' Our sailors, says Marjoribanks, are subject to stern discipline, but so long as Chinese officials incite low characters to provoke and insult them, no amount of discipline or restraint can prevent incidents occurring. In England anyone who injures either a foreigner or a native is brought to justice, and may either plead his own cause or, even if he is a foreigner, engage a lawyer to assist in his defence. . . . The Sovereign of England commands that all Englishmen, in whatever part of the world they may be, should strive to keep on friendly relations with the people of the country, provided that they can do so without sacrificing England's dignity. Any Chinese who comes to England can live there in peace and quiet, exactly as though he were an Englishman, and no one ventures to insult or injure him. Would it not be better, rather than incite mutual hostilities, to set up a friendly rivalry, each side competing to display a greater love and kindness than the other? Marjoribanks then reminds his readers that English sailors have on countless occasions come to the rescue of Chinese ships that were in trouble; in return for which all the Chinese do is to point out English sailors as suitable objects of insult and injury.

[1] The story that the comprador Pao P'eng was Dent's paramour (VI. 27) is typical of such charges.

Gutzlaff and his Traitors. Mamo

Misguided people have taught the Chinese the absurd and childish idea that nothing good exists outside China, and that all other countries contain nothing that is not completely despicable and valueless. Let them visit the various countries of the world and they would soon see that Heaven has bestowed its favours with no such partiality. In England we can boast that everyone dwells in peace and security, his person or property protected by the law. Again, the religion followed in England, that of our Lord and Saviour Jesus Christ, teaches that God has bestowed 'Peace upon earth and goodwill to all men'. We have made great advances in science, the arts, literature and poetry, thus promoting refinement, civilized manners and virtuous conduct.

England, honoured in peace and feared in war, is the country with which above all others Chinese ought to seek good relations. We are practically neighbours, in that a river (the Salween) which rises in the Chinese province of Yünnan flows into the sea at a point which is English territory (i.e. at Martaban, captured by the English in 1824). Marjoribanks then praises the honesty and industry of Chinese merchants and the kindness and generosity that they have at times shown to the English. He points to the good reputation that the East India Company and its servants have always had during the long period of their activity at Canton, and calls upon the people in general not to overlook the merits of such able and reputable persons, and upon the officials to carry out the Emperor's policy of clemency towards foreigners.

The above, he says in conclusion, was indited with weak and hasty brush by a friend of both countries, whose great desire is that all mankind should enjoy true happiness.

There follows an annex, in which it is explained that the present voyage has no motive but that of trade. The cargo consists of camlet, broadcloth,[1] cotton yarn, calico and

---

1 The text writes *sha-jung*, 'flannel'; we know, however, that the cargo included *ta-jung* (broadcloth), but not *sha-jung*.

other goods. Intending purchasers are invited to come aboard and pay in silver. The ship is in need of provisions, and good prices will be given for chickens, ducks, pigs, sheep and cattle.

The pamphlet is in some parts disingenuous, and in others unconvincing. For example, the statement that English ships brought manufactured goods in return for tea gives an entirely false picture of our trade at Canton, the major import being opium. Again, the argument that we had so much territory that we could not be suspected of wanting any more could hardly, one would have thought, have convinced the Chinese, who knew that they themselves, despite the enormous extent of their empire, had within recent memory mopped up Zungaria and Turkestan. The pamphlet is written in the sort of pidgin-Chinese that is usual in translations of the period, and is not always easy to understand.

The *Lord Amherst* sailed on February 27, 1832, and returned to Macao on September 5th. On October 20th Gutzlaff, who in his writings always expresses great horror at the opium trade, pocketed his scruples and took service as interpreter on the *Sylph*, an opium ship belonging to the firm of Jardine Matheson. This was the third of the Three Voyages described in his book of that name. Needless to say he does not mention in his book that the ship carried opium. He was back in Macao on April 29, 1833. Between then and the outbreak of war he made several other voyages as interpreter on opium ships, of which he himself wrote no account. In 1834 he went to Malacca presumably to visit the Anglo-Chinese college, and met Mary Wanstall, a cousin of Harry Parkes, later to become British Minister at Peking. Miss Wanstall had gone to Malacca in 1832 as a member of the Ladies' Society for Native Female Education to help in missionary work. During the course of 1834 she became the second Mrs Gutzlaff, and lived with him in a large, rambling house in Macao, where she ran a school, and a home for blind Chinese children. Five little girls in her school wrote in 1837 to the Ladies' Society:

'Dear kind Ladies! Please do send us more help; and which of our kind friends will come and teach the little Chinese girls? We are so many, we want many teachers. We are so poor, we cannot pay you. But we are told of the Saviour Jesus, who can.'

The Gutzlaffs also took under their wing seven Japanese, who had landed up in Macao as the result of two shipwrecks. In the summer of 1837 the ship *Morrison*, belonging to the American firm of Olyphant, set out for Japan, carrying Gutzlaff, the American merchant C. W. King and his wife, Dr Peter Parker (whose patient Commissioner Lin became in July 1839), S. Wells Williams, the American missionary, a cargo of legitimate goods and the seven shipwrecked Japanese. It was hoped that by restoring the Japanese to their native land the expedition would win the gratitude of the Japanese authorities and be allowed to trade and missionize. The Japanese, however, refused entry even to their compatriots, and the expedition returned dispirited to Macao. A Japanese, Hayashi Kyūshi,[1] became one of Gutzlaff's most trusted assistants when he was magistrate at Ningpo, and he may perhaps have been one of the seven who had been brought back again to Macao.

When the English expedition sailed north in June 1840 Gutzlaff went with it as interpreter and information officer. When Ting-hai fell in July he became civil magistrate there, and sent for his wife to join him. He caught the prevailing 'China fever', and very nearly died. The Gutzlaffs returned to Macao in February 1841. Then, in the summer of the same year, came the second expedition to the north. Gutzlaff again served with it, and after the fall of Ningpo, in October 1841, he became magistrate there. His unconventional and summary but at the same time efficient methods of justice astonished the Chinese. There is a song[2] about his rule at Ningpo by the local poet Hsü Shih-tung (1814–73):

[1] IV. 275.   [2] *Opium War Literature* (*Ya-pien Chan-cheng Wen-hsüeh Chi*, edited by A-ying, 1955), p. 24.

Up to his high dais
Daddy Kuo[1] comes.
If you are in trouble
He'll get things straight,
If you have been wronged
He'll come to the rescue,
If you have got into difficulties
He'll arrange things for you.
He's a master at speaking the Chinese language,
There is not an ideogram he cannot read.
Daddy Kuo is nothing short of a genius!

Big trouble about a bull,
Small trouble about a chicken—
He'll settle the case with a pen
    that seems to have wings!
And sooner will the Southern Hills move
    than this decision be altered.

On his dais he sits passive and majestic,
While the mob throngs below.
He has no scribes to assist him,
There are no papers on his desk;
Yet never has the business of the court been handled
    so swiftly as by Daddy Kuo.

From down at the side of the dais
Someone cries out that he has been wronged;
A fellow from who knows where came to his house
    and extorted money from him.
Directly he hears it, Daddy Kuo, without another word,
Picks up his stick, climbs down from the dais, and
    waddles off into the town.
A moment later he reappears, dragging the culprit along,
Ties him up, bares his back and gives him
    fifty with the lash.
The man who made the complaint,
Goes home delighted, trusses a pair of fowls
And sacrifices them to Heaven.

[1] Gutzlaff's Chinese name was Kuo Shih-li.

Gutzlaff and his Traitors. *Mamo*

On one occasion Daddy Kuo was sitting alone on the dais
With a great crowd watching him from below.
Suddenly they saw Daddy Kuo tear off a sheet of paper,
Grind ink, lick his brush and start wildly scribbling.
What he wrote was: 'Your great Minister has done
     us a huge wrong.
He burnt hundreds and thousands of boatfuls of
     our choicest product.
He promised us to pay in silver, but did not keep
     his word,
Even when we begged for one-half, we got nothing at all,
Which brought things to the sad pass in which
     we are today!'
He took what he had written and hung it below the dais,
So that it could be seen by all who came with
     their plaints.
Many of those near where it hung read it aloud
     to the rest,
Or else borrowed paper and brush, and copied what
     it said.
Daddy Kuo, seeing this, chuckled to himself with joy.
Out of the folds of his dress he produced a biscuit:
'I should so much like you to try a taste of this!'

Daddy Kuo has come,
He is going up on to his dais.
Trouble or no trouble, day after day the people
     press and throng.
Yesterday an old peasant passed down the street
On which his office stands.
When he got home he heaved a sigh; his heart
     was very sad.
'We once had magistrates of our own; where are they now?'

When the English left Ningpo in May 1842 Gutzlaff went
north with the fleet. He was magistrate at Chinkiang in
July, and then served as one of the three interpreters during
the negotiations at Nanking in August. From November
1842 till the autumn of 1843 he was Superintendent of

Trade at Ting-hai. He then became Chinese Secretary to the Government of Hongkong, but at the same time threw himself heart and soul into a grandiose project for the wholesale conversion of China to Christianity. Native colporteurs were to be sent into every province, distributing tracts. Any Europeans who assisted them were to dress as Chinese and take Chinese nationality. The whole expense was to be borne by Gutzlaff himself. The project was not regarded with favour by other missionaries, and its success did indeed depend on a very uncertain factor—the reliability of the agents whom Gutzlaff employed. The feeling of self-respecting Chinese after the Treaty of Nanking was naturally one of implacable hatred towards the English, and even if Gutzlaff's colporteurs were not drawn from the ranks of the scalliwags he had used for secular purposes during the war, it was inevitable that many of them should be shady characters merely anxious to pocket foreign dollars. It is, indeed, said that some of them were found in opium dens near Canton, fully intending after a decent interval to regale Gutzlaff with stories of their successful missions in the interior of China. It seems certain, at any rate, that the scheme broke down as completely as its numerous critics had predicted.

In 1849 the second Mrs Gutzlaff died and in October her husband went to Europe, lecturing on his scheme for the evangelization of China in England, Holland, Germany, Russia, Sweden, Austria, France and Italy. His hope was that each country would 'adopt' an important province of China and finance its conversion. The tour is described in his *Bericht einer Reise nach England und durch die verschiedenen Länder Europas* (Report of a journey to England and through the various countries of Europe), Cassel, 1851. By looking up contemporary newspapers one could probably find out a good deal about the reaction of his audiences in these eight countries. I can only quote the Edinburgh weekly *Hogg's Instructor*:[1] 'He arrives in a city and hastens to the church

[1] Vol. VII, p. 302, 1851.

which is prepared for his reception. After preaching for an hour with the greatest energy, he takes up his collection, and is gone. He speaks with such rapidity that it is scarcely possible to follow him.'

He returned to China in January 1851. An attack of gout turned to dropsy and he died, aged forty-eight, on August 9th. While in England he had married, on September 17, 1850, his third English wife, Dorothy Gabriel. As we have seen (p. 162), rumour at Ningpo credited him, in addition, with two Chinese concubines, whom he was presumably supposed to have left behind when Ningpo was evacuated.

The three official interpreters, J. R. Morrison, Gutzlaff and Robert Thom were very much overworked and all died prematurely; Morrison in 1843 at the age of twenty-nine, and then Thom in 1846, aged thirty-nine.

'The Rev. Charles Gutzlaff', says Lane Poole,[1] 'has received his full measure of detraction, and undoubtedly he had his faults. His specious manner and intolerable assumption of omniscience procured him the epithet of "humbug". He was always posing as a genius, and those who knew him best put least faith in him. He was not to be unreservedly trusted. Nevertheless his was a strong and original character, interesting as a study for the experienced, and certainly very impressive to his juniors. . . . It often took years to find him out. And he was not all sham. He had a considerable though not very scholarly command of the Chinese language. He was naturally kind-hearted, though irritable, suspicious and thin-skinned.'

As to his personal appearance, 'an eye-witness', quoted by Lane Poole, speaks of the deep impression made upon him by 'the short squat figure, the clothes that for shape might have been cut in a village of his native Pomerania ages ago; the broad-brimmed straw hat; the great face beneath it, with that sinister eye!' In short, a cross between parson and pirate, charlatan and genius, philanthropist and crook.

---

[1] *Life of Sir Harry Parkes*, p. 55.

He wrote or had a hand in about seventy works, chiefly short missionary tracts. Of his longer works the best is probably *China Opened*, consisting largely of facts and figures, probably collected at the library at Macao. But none of his books ever give any sort of references, and it is often impossible to tell whether he is using some relatively good source, repeating gossip or merely inventing. His one autobiographic work, the *Three Voyages*, suffers from the fact that it was written for the eye of the missionary world. It is replete with a rather gushing kind of evangelical sentiment and wholly devoid of frankness about his own situation and personal experiences.

Despite his close relations with Chinese of diverse ranks and callings, up and down the coast from Canton to Tientsin, he remained singularly insular (or I suppose in his case we ought to say Prussian) in his general views about the Chinese, whom he regarded as semi-barbarous idolators, to be rescued from their benighted condition only by the enlightening touch of Christian contacts. 'How much', he exclaims, 'foreign intercourse has improved Chinese manners at Canton!'

I have already said that some of the 'traitors' about whom we know most are the agents used by Gutzlaff. One of the earliest of them wrote[1] to him in May 1832: 'I am writing specially to let you know that I now have the maritime chart of the Inner River [at Foochow]. I was at the provincial capital [Foochow] the day before yesterday and learnt that the Governor gave permission for cannon to be placed at a point near the Lo-hsing Pagoda [on top of a hill near Foochow] and knock holes all over your ship; but the Tartar General would not allow it.' The rest of the letter is so illiterate as to be hardly intelligible, and Gutzlaff (*Three Voyages*, p. 230) only translates the sentence about the threat to bombard the English ship. It is signed 'The Provincial Graduate of San-shan [a place near Foochow]'; but it is inconceivable that

[1] I. 31. MS. now at the Bodleian.

the writer of the letter could ever have passed any examination. In his next letter, however, it becomes apparent why he lays claim to this distinction. He has, he says, passed the Provincial Examination, but cannot afford to go to Peking and compete in the final Literary Examination. England is known to be an immensely rich country and the Captain (i.e. Gutzlaff) is the owner of vast possessions. In short, will Gutzlaff be so kind as to finance his journey to the capital? The same request is repeated in another letter, the writer now promising that if he succeeds in the examination and gets an official post, he will be completely at Gutzlaff's service, working for his interests 'like a horse or dog'.

As the English ship was navigating in forbidden waters, the offer of a sea-chart was clearly illegal and would, if it had become known, have had serious consequences for the anonymous 'Provincial Graduate'.

We know most about the least competent of Gutzlaff's agents, that is to say those who were ultimately caught and brought to trial by the Chinese authorities. We possess a number of the statements that they made in Court. These are unlikely to tell the whole truth, but so far as they go they give the impression of being fairly reliable, and they certainly throw an interesting light on the circumstances and previous careers of the Chinese who entered English service.

Ch'en Ping-chün.[1]
A Chen-hai man, aged forty-seven. Worked with his brother as a doctor; but they were accused of 'seeking to better themselves'[2] and were both conscribed as soldiers and sent to Canton. In 1823 there was a general amnesty; they were released and went back to doctoring. In 1840 the brother, who had got to know some foreigners (presumably

---

[1] IV. 274.
[2] The expression implies that they passed themselves off as belonging to a higher social rank than their own.

at Canton) entered their service and was soon joined at Ting-hai by Ch'en himself. He and a number of other Chinese guided the foreign ships to Chen-hai. Later the brother was sent by the English on a mission to Hangchow and was arrested by the Chinese. Ch'en himself was sent to spy at Yü-yao, about thirty miles north of Ningpo. He, too, was arrested, but during his trial the English arrived (December 27, 1841) and in the ensuing confusion Ch'en escaped. He got into touch with Gutzlaff and was employed by him as a spy, receiving a dollar or two for each item of information. In February 1842 he was sent to Tz'u-ch'i, near Ningpo, where he sat about in tea-houses listening to conversations and picking up military information. He even discovered the date and hour that had been fixed for the great Chinese attempt to recapture Ningpo (March 10th) and duly told Gutzlaff. As we have seen (p. 168 above) Gutzlaff was by no means convinced that the story was true. Ch'en, in his confession, then gives the names of eight other Chinese assistants of Gutzlaff, including the Japanese Hayashi Kyūshi, and some information about the English leaders; for example that Pottinger was killed during the second taking of Ting-hai (October 1, 1841): 'the persons on the foreign ships at present using the surname Po are all impostors'. On March 15th Ch'en was captured by Chinese militia when spying on the movements of Chinese troops to the west of Ningpo.

Liu Fu-kuei.

A Ting-hai fisherman. At first, from November 1840 onwards, did manual work for the English at Ting-hai. But someone introduced him to Hayashi Kyūshi as likely to be useful, owing to the fact that he could speak Fuhkienese dialect; and he worked in Kyūshi's office till the English evacuated Ting-hai (February 1840), after which he again became a fisherman. A few days after the English captured Ting-hai for the second time (October 1, 1841) he went there to work for them again. He happened quite accidentally to meet the Japanese Hayashi Kyūshi, who took him to Chen-hai to act as guide. After the fall of Chen-hai he took Gutzlaff to various pawnshops (which acted as deposit-banks) and assisted him in carrying off their contents. After the English entry into Ningpo (October 14th) he worked there in an office adjoining that of Gutzlaff, presumably translating conversations in Ningpo dialect into the dialect of Fuhkien, Gutzlaff at that time probably knowing very little Ningpo dialect. On November 1, 1841, he got leave to pay a short visit to his home near Ting-hai, Gutzlaff making him a present of two foreign dollars. Having money in his pocket he thought he would renew a previous liaison with a certain Mrs Chiang Lien-yüan. But he found that Mrs Chiang had taken up with a new lover; and the new lover, in order to get Ch'en safely out of the way, denounced him to the Chinese authorities as a traitor, upon which he was seized and put on trial.

Yü Te-ch'ang.

He certainly well qualifies for a place in this picaresque gallery. He said he was a Ningpo man, aged thirty-four. He was the proprietor of a firm that sold singing-girls and was evidently a man of some substance, as he had a concubine as well as a wife. When the English took Ningpo, Gutzlaff made him Chief of Police, with fifty subordinates to work under him, at a salary of twenty foreign dollars a month. In addition to arresting trouble-makers, he collected information about Chinese troop movements and furnished the names of rich people out of whom money could be squeezed by the invaders. He furnished, at his trial, the names of about forty Chinese who worked for the English, pointing out that almost all of them were from Kwangtung or Fuhkien. Very few people of native Ningpo origin had collaborated. When he had worked for the English for six months, the 'Chief of Police' says at the end of his confession, he slipped and hurt his left leg. Loyal Chinese then seized him and handed him over to the authorities.

Fang Hsi-hung.

A man of twenty-four from near Hangchow. Worked in a clothing business, but got into debt through heavy gambling and was turned out of the house by his father. He then went to his mother's brother at Ching-chou in Hupeh province, and asked for help. The uncle gave him forty dollars, and told him to go back home. But he spent it all on the way back, and hearing that he could earn good money from the foreigners at Ningpo, he went there and got into touch with Gutzlaff, who introduced him to two English officers who wanted to learn to write Chinese. He gave them lessons, for which he got from two to three hundred copper-cash a day (about 1s. 6d.). He also wrote out proclamations for Gutzlaff to stick up in the town. In the first month of this year (1842) Wang Kuo-pao (the alias of the 'Chief of Police') arrested a wine-seller. Fang went and pleaded for him with Gutzlaff, and got forty dollars from the man as a reward for his services. Seeing that a lot of people were getting money for furnishing military information, he invented a story that, at many points inside and near the city, Chinese troops were in hiding.

Gutzlaff believed the story and gave him a warrant for the arrest of any such that he could find. On March 7th, a friend told him that the Chinese attack on Ningpo was to be on March 10th and advised him to clear out. Accordingly on March 9th he left the city and spent the night in the Monastery of the Seven Pagodas, on the east side of the Yung River. After the failure of the Chinese attack he ventured back into Ningpo, and was sent by Gutzlaff to spy at Tz'u-ch'i. He had left some luggage at the monastery and went back there first to collect it. He fell into the hands of Chinese troops, and was arrested.

Ku Pao-lin.

From a village near Tz'u-ch'i. Got into touch with Gutzlaff at Ningpo on January 18, 1842, and became one of his 'braves', at 500 cash a day. At the same time he was also receiving 400 cash a day as a member of the Chinese militia. He sent regular reports to the Chinese about the doings of the foreigners and also, when opportunity offered, collected information about Chinese military movements for Gutzlaff, 'getting advantage', as he said, 'out of both sides'. He was in Ningpo at the time of the Chinese attempt to retake the town, but (as he is careful to assure his judges) 'only held up a lantern, and took no part in the fighting'. After the defeat of the Chinese Gutzlaff sent him to Ch'ang-ch'i Ridge[1] to see whether the Chinese were reforming their scattered units. He tried to slip into the Chinese camp after dark, but was caught and put on trial.

Pu Ting-pang.[2]

Unlike the five collaborators mentioned above, he served the English expedition in general, and though highly esteemed by Gutzlaff was never in his special employ. Pu, whose efficiency as a comprador is praised in many Western accounts, was kidnapped by peasants on July 17, 1840, when purchasing bullocks for the English in the neighbourhood of Ting-hai. He had an interesting history.

In May 1839 his father was accused of illicit dealings with the English, and both his father and his brother were imprisoned at Canton. His father was so roughly handled by the gaolers that he died in prison. Another brother fled to Java, and Pu Ting-pang himself took refuge on a foreign ship. When put on trial at Ningpo he appealed for mercy on the ground that his father's concubine (aged forty-six), his own wife (aged twenty-five) and his little girl (aged one) were entirely dependent upon him. What he would like, if his judges were so merciful as to allow it, would be to bring

[1] North-east of Ningpo.   [2] IV. 215.

them to Ningpo, and make a fresh start there. He then gave some information about the English warships and about the English Queen who, he had been told, knew nothing about the English war against China, and would be very cross if she found out about it.

The Director of Affairs Gutzlaff, he informed his judges, is a follower of the Religion of the Lord of Heaven. He is a Russian, but has thrown in his lot with the Red Hairs (i.e. English) and now counts as a Red Hair. His father was in business at Tientsin; Gutzlaff later set up schools in Canton and Macao, where Chinese learnt foreign script. Chinese followers of the Religion of the Lord of Heaven all go there to study, so he had picked up the dialects of Fuhkien, Canton and Ningpo. . . .

'The Capital of the Red Headed People's country is called Principal Port.[1] Its inhabitants are not followers of the Religion of the Lord of Heaven,[2] but there are in the country some small rural localities where this religion is practised. . . . The high officers on their ships all come from the Principal Port, and consequently do not follow this religion. But the rest, who do not come from the Principal Port, are all followers of the religion. The 2,000 black men from Bengal all belong to the Religion of the Lord of Heaven. . . .'

In the prison at Ningpo Pu Ting-pang acted as interpreter to the kidnapped English who were held there and helped them in every way he could. In February 1841, when negotiations were in progress for the return of Ting-hai to the Chinese, it was stipulated that the English imprisoned at Ningpo must first be released. Both Gutzlaff and his fellow interpreter Robert Thom tried hard to secure Pu Ting-pang's release, Gutzlaff even saying[3] roundly that unless Pu were handed over there could be no question of evacuating Ting-

---

[1] Common Chinese name, at the period, for London.
[2] Strictly speaking this term meant Catholicism. But Pu probably regarded it as a name for Christianity in general.　　3 V. 349.

hai. But the Chinese maintained that the English had no right to demand the surrender of a Chinese, and the point was dropped. The situation as regards the English prisoners was urgent. Only two days after their release a new Governor arrived in Chekiang who declared (IV. 224) that he had intended to inflict on Captain Anstruther[1] a lingering death, and then offer up his heart and liver as a sacrifice to propitiate the souls of the officers and men who had fallen in battle against the English. In a proclamation (IV. 235) issued in April 1841 the same Governor announced that the traitor Pu Ting-pang had been decapitated and his head paraded all along the coast, as a warning to other *Han-chien*.

Pao P'eng.

We possess such a wealth of information, both in Western and Chinese sources, about this shady character and his story is so complicated that, in order to reduce my account of him to reasonable proportions, I shall draw in the main only on one document—the evidence[2] given at his trial by his patron Chao Ming-shan, known also as Chao Tzu-yung, a Cantonese painter, poet, musician and official, whose name is well known to English readers owing to his *Cantonese Love Songs* having been translated and commented upon by Cecil Clementi in 1904. Pao P'eng was born at Hsiang-shan, near Macao, in 1793, and began at an early age to study foreign languages. Chao Tzu-yung was tutored at Canton by a relative of Pao P'eng, and as Pao P'eng often visited this relative, Pao the linguist and Chao the young poet got to know one another very well. In 1829 Pao P'eng became comprador to an American merchant, but upon this merchant returning to America Pao found himself without a job. Meanwhile, in 1836, a cousin of Pao's got a licence at Macao to act as comprador to the English opium dealer Lancelot Dent. The cousin became ill, and Pao took over his work without bothering to get a fresh licence. He was paid

[1] See above, p. 161.   [2] III. 255.

about sixty dollars a year as regular wages, but in addition to this could usually earn two or three hundred dollars. In 1837 he began to take commissions for supplying opium to various clients. Early in 1839 one of the official 'linguists' (i.e. Chinese interpreters) attached to the English factory, to whom Pao P'eng had already lent money, demanded a further loan and threatened to denounce Pao P'eng as an opium dealer if the money was not forthcoming. In March 1839 Pao P'eng, 'frightened of complications', fled from Canton and, travelling north, presented himself at the office of the song-writer Chao Tzu-yung, who was now Prefect of Wei hsien in Shantung. He told Chao Tzu-yung of his predicament, and Chao invited him to live with him for a time.

In the spring of 1840 Pao P'eng got a letter from home, telling him that the 'linguist' had not informed against him. Pao's uncle had been arrested by Commissioner Lin, but subsequently released. The Commissioner had then (presumably in consequence of facts that had come out at the interrogation of the uncle) ordered the arrest of Pao P'eng, but as he had never been guilty of any very serious misdemeanour he might now, the letter suggested, safely come home. He was just about to embark (presumably at Tengchou, the nearest port) when a foreign ship appeared off the Shantung coast. Chao Tzu-yung recommended Pao P'eng to the Governor of Shantung as a person who could parley with the foreigners and find out what they wanted. Afterwards Ch'i-shan, now on his way to Canton in order to conduct negotiations there with Captain Elliot, thinking that someone knowing English but unconnected with Canton (as he believed Pao P'eng to be) would be more trustworthy than the interpreters at Canton, who had for so long had dealings with the English, took Pao P'eng south with him. Pao's sudden reappearance, now dressed up in official garb and giving himself very grand airs, immensely tickled the 'old hands' at Canton, and they teased him mercilessly. When Ch'i-shan fell from power and was sent in chains to Peking, Pao P'eng was also put on trial. The charge that he had acted as an agent of the English could not be substantiated. The Court had to fall back on the technicality that he had acted as a comprador without obtaining a licence. This counted as 'illicit intercourse with foreigners', for which the penalty was military service on the frontier. His opium offences occurred before the new regulations of May 1840 came into effect; otherwise he would have incurred the death penalty. But in view of these offences the maximum penalty for 'illicit intercourse' was inflicted, and instead of serving as a free soldier on a near frontier he was condemned to work for Manchu troops as a slave, at I-li, in the far north-west.

Chao Tzu-yung was severely censured for sheltering and recommending someone whom he knew to have had a shady past. He lost his job, and so far as we know never returned to public life.

Mamo.

There were several kidnapped Indians in the gaol at Ningpo; but apparently no effort was made to secure their release. Here is the bewildered voice of the Indian prisoner Mamo: 'I do not know how old I am, nor the names of my father and mother. I have a wife and two sisters. I belong to the Fan-lien district of Bengal. There are three kinds of people in Bengal—upper whites, middle whites and, at the bottom, blacks. All of them follow the religion of the Lord of Heaven [Christianity]. I am a black, and all I can do is to work. Red-haired people came to my country and told the headmen of my country to sell black men to them as servants. For each black man they offered three or four foreign dollars, and if the black men would not go they were to be beaten. I was sold to a ship of the red-haired people, where my work was to wash clothes, sweep and run errands. It was a ship of middling size and carried two hundred soldiers, all of whom were black. There was also an officer called Collinson[?] whose rank was like that of a Chinese lieutenant. The red-haired people call a soldier *su-chih*; but I would be no good as a *su-chih*. All I ask from Your Excellency is to give me food, and I will gladly work for you here. Where I come from they have followed the religion of the Lord of Heaven for a long time. We have a prince who looks after the affairs of the country, and besides that several princes who only look after matters of religion. Those who follow the religion go to Heaven when they die, and those who do not go to Hell. When I have finished eating I lay the palms of my hands together and recite a Scripture [i.e. say grace], as the Lord of Heaven would have me do.'

One is reminded of Blake's 'Little Black Boy'.

Palmerston's letter to the 'Minister of the Chinese Emperor'.

THIS was written in February 1840, at which time Palmerston's latest news from China dated from November 1839. There was no prospect of the letter being seen at Peking till the summer of 1840. It had consequently to be sufficiently general and abstract still to make sense under altered circumstances; for it was obvious that in six months or more the situation might have considerably changed. The main concrete demands are (1) payment for confiscated opium; (2) British officials to be communicated with 'in a manner consistent with the usages of civilized nations'; (3) payment by the Chinese Government of what was owed to the English merchants by the Chinese guild-merchants; (4) one or more sufficiently large and properly situated islands to be permanently given up to the British Government; (5) British war expenses to be indemnified.

The note assumes, quite falsely, that no attempt has been made by the Chinese Government to enforce anti-opium measures in the case of their own subjects. Perhaps the strangest assertion in the letter is (Morse, p. 621) that Elliot was 'in no wise connected with trade'. Why, then, the Chinese must have wondered, was he called 'Superintendent of Trade'? However the denial was, in a way, quite to the point, as Lin had informed the Emperor on November 21 (1839) that Elliot got a rake-off of twenty or thirty dollars on the price of every chest of opium that was sold![1]

The Chinese version, presumably by J. R. Morrison, is so unidiomatic as to be sometimes unintelligible without reference to the English original. It is discussed (in Chinese) by T. F. Tsiang in an article called 'Ch'i-shan and the Opium War', *Ching Hua Hsüeh Pao*, VI. 3 (1931), p. 17.

[1] II. 187.

1839   Arrival of Lin at Canton, March 10th.
      Lin demands surrender of opium, March 18th.
      Elliot agrees to surrender of opium, March 27th.
      Lin becomes titular Governor-General of Kiangnan and Kiangsi, but remains at Canton, April 22nd.
      New opium regulations reach Canton, July 6th.
      Murder of Lin Wei-hsi, July 7th.
      Lin goes to Hsiang-shan Island, August 15th.
      English begin to leave Macao, August 20th.
      Evacuation of Macao complete, August 27th.
      Arrival of H.M.S. *Volage*, August 30th.
      Lin visits Macao, September 2nd.
      Lin leaves Macao, September 3rd.
      Battle of Kowloon, September 4th.
      Arrival of H.M.S. *Hyacinth*, c. September 18th.
      Battle of Chuenpi, November 3rd.
      Sale of the *Cambridge* to Delano, November 30th.

1840   Sale of the *Cambridge* to Lin, January.
      Captain Warner undertakes to bring Lin's letter to Queen Victoria, January 18th.
      Lin hears he is to be Governor-General of Kwangtung and Kwangsi, January 26th.
      Main body of English expeditionary force arrives, June 21st.
      Fall of Ting-hai, July 5th.
      Kidnapping of Vincent Stanton, August 5th.
      Battle of the Barrier, August 19th.
      The Emperor sees Palmerston's letter, August 20th.
      Lin learns that he is no longer Governor-General, October 13th.
      Lin learns that he must go to Peking for trial, October 20th.

Return of Captain Elliot to Macao, November 20th.
Ch'i-shan arrives at Canton, November 29th.
Retirement of Admiral Elliot, November 29th.

1841   Fall of Shakok and Taikok forts, January 7th.
Convention of Chuenpi signed, January 20th.
Ting-hai returned to Chinese, February 25th.
Fall of Middle Bogue forts and death of Admiral Kuan,
    February 26th.
Canton factories reoccupied, March 18th
Yang Fang arranges precarious truce, March 20th.
Lin leaves Canton, May 3rd.
English again quit factories, May 21st.
Chinese agree to pay six million dollars to save Canton
    from attack, May 27th.
Indignant peasants surround sixty British soldiers who
    had been looting, etc., near San-yüan-li, May 29th.
Second expeditionary force sails north, August 21st.
Second fall of Ting-hai, October 1st.
Fall of Chen-hai, October 10th.
Fall of Ningpo, October 13th.

1842   Chinese attempt to recapture Ningpo, March 10th.
Ningpo evacuated by English, May 7th.
Fall of Chapu, May 18th.
Fall of Shanghai, June 19th.
Fall of Chinkiang, July 21st.
Treaty signed at Nanking, August 29th.

Index

Index

Index